Nigel Cawthorne is th[...] *books and is best kno*[...] *prisoners who did not* [...] *World War II and Kore*[...] *...ten extensively on crime for* **Murder Casebook** *and is currently writing a new book, to be published by Boxtree this year, on sex killers.*

Other True Crime titles published by Boxtree:

MICHAEL WINNER'S TRUE CRIMES

MURDER IN MIND

IN SUSPICIOUS CIRCUMSTANCES

DEAD ENDS

SWEENEY TODD

THE MURDER GUIDE TO GREAT BRITAIN

CONTRACT KILLERS

SPREE KILLERS

Nigel Cawthorne

B⊞XTREE

First published in Great Britain in 1993 by Boxtree
Limited, Broadwall House, 21 Broadwall, London SE1 9PL

10 9 8 7 6 5 4 3 2 1

ISBN: 1 85283 4633

Phototypeset by Intype, London

Printed and bound in Great Britain by
Cox & Wyman, Reading, Berkshire

A CIP catalogue entry for this book is available from the
British Library

Cover photograph by Jon Tarrant

CONTENTS

Introduction   vii

Chapter One   1
Sniper in the Tower

Chapter Two   22
Veterans

Chapter Three   43
Existential Heroes

Chapter Four   58
Rebel Without A Cause

Chapter Five   91
Good Boys Turn Bad

Chapter Six   120
Vietnam

Chapter Seven   172
Black Power

Chapter Eight   187
Forty Whacks

Chapter Nine   218
Dying for Sex

Chapter Ten   238
In The Name Of God

Chapter Eleven   270
The Menace Spreads

Chapter Twelve   305
The Body Count Climbs

Introduction

A man who had been kicked out of a nightclub in Fresno returned Sunday 16 May 1993 with two hand-guns and opened fire. He killed seven people and wounded two.

'A lot of shots were fired,' said the homicide officer in charge.

Neighbour Paul Beard said he called police after the security guard jumped over the fence and banged on his door. Then he went to the club.

'There were just dead people all over the place,' he said. 'One was lying right against the door.'

The dead were identified as club owner, Reyes 'Ray' Carrillo; his mother, Rachel Carrillo; his half-brother, Alfredo Carrillo; the club's cook, Mariano Perez; his wife, Alicia Duenas Perez; and employees Mary Ruiz and Rudy Sanchez. One wounded woman was treated for a gunshot to the leg and released. Another underwent surgery and was expected to live.

Neighbours said the club attracted rowdy patrons and prostitutes. Gunfire in the parking lot wasn't uncommon. Beard said the club had been firebombed twice.

Tim Dovali, who lived across the street, said

random gunfire was so common he wasn't alarmed by the commotion early Sunday. Mass murder, it seemed, was just another part of everyday life.

This kind of incident is so commonplace that it hardly rates the news any more. An individual, for the most trivial of reasons – or often for no reason at all, goes berserk and kills five, ten, twenty people they do not even know. These days, to go out on the streets or into any public place means that, at any time, without warning, you could become a casualty in a private war that one alienated individual has declared against the world.

Although spree killing is a thoroughly modern phenomenon, there is an ancient model for these crazed killers – the berserkers, who were Viking shock troops. The word berserk derives from the Old Norse word *bhr-serce* which means 'without mail'. Berserkers did not wear armour. They often went into battle naked. Hurling themselves on the enemy with a deadly fury, they were seemingly oblivious to any risk to their own life. Some authorities believe that they were high on hallucinogenic drugs.

Many modern spree killers use drugs, though few are high when they commit their heinous crimes. Many have military fantasies; a few have actual experience of combat. Almost all have a fetish about guns.

But unlike the ancient berserker, the modern spree killer is not part of any fighting force. The war he is fighting is between himself and the pressures of the modern world. It is a war we are all fighting and, perhaps, spree killers are shock troops in this unequal battle. For spree killers have few distinguishing characteristics. They can be anyone's husband, lover or son – or indeed anyone's wife or daughter too. There have been several cases of female spree killers. The individuals concerned have themselves little warning of the incident that is going to push them over the edge. Some don't realise what they have done. Most have no idea why they did it. It could even be because they are law-abiding citizens, pushed too far. In 1973, James Winfield, a construction worker from Queens, New York, shot and killed a man and wounded three others because he was fed up with crime. He told police that he had just been beaten up and robbed for the sixth time.

However, modern spree killing is not confined to America. The first incident of true spree killings seems to have occurred in Germany in 1913. The first spree killers in America were first or second generation German immigrants. But, by the mid 1960s, spree killing became an all-American institution. Mass murder was as American as mom and apple pie. Much of its macho ethos comes from movies about the Wild West. However, in the history of the Old Frontier I can find no one incident of random mass slaying. In fact, incidents of gunfights and shoot-outs are remarkably rare.

The modern idea of the Wild West is largely a product of Hollywood, created almost exclusively by central European immigrants. These days, with the Americanisation of world culture, spree killing has spread to Australia, England, France, Italy, Belgium, Holland, and Spain. Spree killers have even appeared in Russia and China. Now nobody is safe.

And once they have you in their sights, these killers cannot be deterred. Most actively support the death penalty, even for themselves. Death in the electric chair or gas chamber, by lethal injection or by firing squad, means less to them than the few minutes relief they get gunning down their innocent, nameless, faceless victims.

1

Sniper in the Tower

It was a perfect summer day in Austin. The Texan sun was beating down. By mid-morning, the temperature had already soared to ninety-eight degrees in the shade and the hot air hung heavy over the downtown campus of the University of Texas. The students had taken the opportunity to linger in the sunshine when classes changed at 11.30. But by 11.45, all was quiet again under the University's thirty-storey limestone tower.

At 11.48, on 1 August 1966, seventeen-year-old Alec Hernandez was cycling across the campus, delivering newspapers, when a .35 rifle bullet ripped through his leg. It slammed into his saddle and catapulted him from his bike. Then, out of the clear blue sky, more bullets came raining down. Three students, late for class, fell in quick succession.

At first, no one could figure out what was happening. There was a distant report, then someone would crumple to the ground. On the fourth floor of the tower building twenty-three-year-old postgraduate student Norma Barger heard what she took to be dynamite exploding. In fact, it was the sound of a deer-hunting rifle echoing from the low

1

buildings that nestled around the tower. When she looked out of her classroom window, she saw six bodies sprawled grotesquely on the mall beneath her. At first she thought it was a tasteless joke. She expected them to get up and walk away laughing. Then she saw the pavement stones splashed with blood – and more people falling beneath the sniper's deadly rain of fire.

Eighteen-year-old Mrs Claire Wilson, who was eight months pregnant, was heading across the mall to her anthropology class when a bullet ripped into her belly. She survived, but her unborn child's skull was crushed and the child was later born dead. Nineteen-year-old freshman Thomas Eckman, a classmate and would-be poet, knelt beside the injured mother-to-be when a second bullet shot him dead.

Thirty-three-year-old post-graduate mathematician Robert Boyer was looking forward to his trip to England. He had already secured a teaching post in Liverpool, where his pregnant wife and two children were waiting for him. But when he stepped out on to the mall, heading for an early lunch, he was shot, fatally, in the back. Secretary Charlotte Dareshshori ran to help him and found herself under fire. She spent the next hour-and-a-half crouched behind the concrete base of a flagpole, one of the few people to venture on to the mall and survive uninjured.

The sniper took a shot at a small boy. People began to take cover. A woman on the eighteenth floor of the administration block rang a friend in a nearby university building and said: 'Somebody's up there shooting from the tower. There's blood all over the place.' Soon hundreds were pinned down on the campus.

By 11.52, four minutes after the shooting started, the local police received a hysterical phone call. At first, all they knew was that there had been 'some shooting at the university tower'. In seconds, a 'ten-fifty' went out. All units in the vicinity were to head for the university. Soon the quiet of the Texas high noon was torn by the sound of sirens as more than a hundred city policemen, reinforced by some thirty highway patrolmen, state troopers, Texas Rangers and Secret Service men from President Lyndon Johnson's Austin office, converged on the campus – along with a number of ordinary gun-toting Texan citizens.

One of the first policemen on the scene was rookie patrolman Billy Speed. He quickly figured out what was happening. He spotted the killer on the observation deck of the tower. The young patrolman took cover behind the base of a statue of Jefferson Davis and took careful aim. The sniper shot him dead. Speed was just twenty-three and left a wife and baby daughter.

The shot that brought down Patrolman Speed alerted the other lawmen. Volleys of small-arms fire cracked around the top of the tower. A few rounds smashed into the huge clock-face above the killer. Most pinged ineffectually off the four-foot-high wall around the observation deck, kicking up puffs of white dust.

Ducking down behind the low wall, the sniper was safe. Narrow drainage slits around the bottom of the wall made perfect gun ports. There the unknown gunman proved impossible to hit. And he kept finding new targets.

A hundred yards beyond Patrolman Speed, twenty-nine-year-old electrical repairman Roy Dell Schmidt was getting out of his truck on a call. He looked up at the tower and saw puffs of smoke coming from the observation gallery. The police told him to get back but, nonchalantly, Schmidt told a man standing next to him that they were out of range. They weren't. Seconds later, a rifle bullet smashed into Schmidt's chest, killing him instantly.

To the west of the campus ran a main thoroughfare called Guadalupe Street, known to the students as 'The Drag'. Among the window-shoppers on Guadalupe Street that sunny lunchtime was eighteen-year-old Paul Sonntag. He was a lifeguard at Austin swimming pool and had just picked up his week's pay cheque. With him was eighteen-year-old ballet dancer Claudia Rutt who was on her way to the doctor's for the polio shot she needed before entering Texas Christian University. Suddenly Claudia sank to the ground, clutching her breast. 'Help me! Somebody, help me!' she cried. Bewildered, Sonntag bent over her. The next shot took him out. Both were dead before help could get to them.

Further up Guadalupe Street, visiting professor of government thirty-nine-year-old Harry Walchuk was browsing in the doorway of a newsstand. Father of six and a teacher at Michigan's Alpena Community College, he was hit in the throat and collapsed, dead, among the magazines. In the next block, twenty-four-year-old Thomas Karr, who had ambitions to be a diplomat, was returning to his apartment after staying up all night, revising for a Spanish exam which he had taken at ten o'clock that morning. Before he reached his own front door, he dropped to the sidewalk, dying. In the third block, basketball coach Billy Snowden of the Texas School for the Deaf stepped into the doorway of the barbershop where he was having his haircut and was wounded in the shoulder.

Outside the Rae Ann dress shop on Guadalupe Street, twenty-six-year-old Iraqi chemistry student Abdul Khashab, his fiancée twenty-year-old Janet Paulos – they were to have married the next week – and twenty-one-year-old trainee sales assistant Lana Phillips, fell wounded within seconds of each other. Homer Kelly, manager of Sheftall's jewellery store, saw them fall and ran to help. He was trying to haul them into the cover of his store when the shop window shattered. A bullet gashed the carpeting on the sidewalk outside his shop and two bullet fragments smashed into his leg. Three youths had to wait over an hour, bleeding on Sheftall's orange carpet, before an ambulance could get to them. In all, along picturesque, shop-lined Guadalupe Street, there were four dead and eleven wounded.

To the north, two students were wounded on their way to the biology building. Beyond that, far to the north of the campus, thirty-six-year-old Associate Press reporter Robert Heard was running full tilt from cover to cover when he was hit in the shoulder. 'What a shot,' he marvelled as he winced with pain.

To the east, twenty-two-year-old Iran-bound Peace Corps trainee Thomas Ashton was sunning himself on the roof of the Computation Center. A single round ended his life. A girl sitting at the window of the Business Economics Building was nicked by a bullet. But to the south was the worst killing field. The university's main mall had been turned into a no man's land. It was strewn with bodies that could not be recovered safely.

One man was responsible – one man thirty storeys up the Austin tower had turned the peaceful campus into a freefire zone. The Austin Police Department had never had anything like this to deal with before.

The bullet-scarred clock of the Austin tower was booming out its Big Ben chimes at 12.30 when a local Texan turned up in camouflage fatigues and began chipping large chunks of limestone off the wall of the observation deck with a tripod-mounted high-calibre M-14. Meanwhile a Cessna light aircraft circled the tower with police marksman Lieutenant Marion Lee on board. He tried to get a clear shot at the gunman but the turbulent air currents around the tower made aiming impossible. The plane was eventually driven away when the sniper put a bullet through the fuselage.

Down below an armoured truck laid down smoke cover and a fleet of ambulances, sirens wailing, began loading up the dead and wounded. Students braved the sniper's fire to haul other victims to shelter.

Austin Police Chief Robert Miles decided that he could not risk using any more helicopters against the sniper. His accurate fire could easily bring one down. So Police Chief Miles ordered his men to storm the tower. His directive was curt – 'shoot to kill'.

Patrolmen Houston McCoy and Jerry Day found their way through the underground passageways that connected the university buildings into the foyer of the tower. There they met Patrolman Ramiro Martinez who had been at home cooking steaks when he heard news of the massacre on the radio. A handsome twenty-nine-year-old and veteran of six years with the Austin Police Department, he had driven to within a couple of blocks of the tower, then run, zigzagging across the open plaza with the sniper's bullets kicking up dust around him. None of the three patrolmen had ever been in a gun fight before.

With them was forty-year-old retired Air Force tailgunner Allen Crum, who was a civilian employee of the university. Although he, too, had never fired a shot in combat, Crum insisted on accompanying the officers. He was given a rifle and deputised on the spot. That day, he was to see more action than during his entire twenty-two years in the Air Force. One of the four men punched the lift button. They were about to make the same twenty-seven-floor elevator ride that the crazed gunman had taken less than two hours before.

Dressed in tennis sneakers, blue jeans and a white sports shirt under a pair of workman's overall, the gunman had pulled into a parking space reserved for university officials at around 11 a.m. between the administration building and the library, at the base of the tower. He unloaded a trolley and placed a heavy footlocker on it. Then he wheeled the trolley into the foyer of the building. The ground-floor receptionist thought he was a maintenance man.

He too punched the lift button. When the elevator door opened he wheeled the trolley into the lift and pushed the button for the top floor. During the thirty-second ride, he pulled a rifle from the locker. On the twenty-seventh-floor, he unloaded his heavy cargo, then climbed the four short flights of stairs from the lifts to the observation deck. The observation gallery was open to visitors and the gunman approached the receptionist, forty-seven-year-old Edna Townsley, a spirited divorcee and mother of two young sons who was working on what was normally her day off. He clubbed her with the butt of his rifle with such force that part of her skull was torn away, and dragged her behind the sofa.

At that moment, a young couple came in from the observation gallery. The girl smiled at the gunman, who smiled back. She steered her date around the dark stain that was slowly spreading across the carpet in front of the receptionist's desk. The gunman followed them back down to the lift. As they travelled innocently down in the elevator car, he lugged his heavy locker up the stairs and out on to the observation gallery which ran all the way around the tower 231 feet above ground level. From that height he could see clean across the shimmering terracotta roofs of old Austin's Spanish-style buildings. Below him were the handsome white university buildings with their red-tiled roofs, separated by broad lawns and malls. This gave the gunman a clear field of fire across the campus below and the surrounding streets. He opened his locker and unpacked three rifles, two pistols, three knives, a machete, 700 rounds of ammunition, enough canned food for several days, a five-gallon bottle of distilled water, sunglasses, a compass, an alarm clock and a lantern. Also in the locker was some pink toilet paper, a spray deodorant and a green towel.

As the gunman assembled his equipment for what he plainly imagined would be a long siege, the lift began to climb from the ground floor up to the twenty-seventh storey again. In it were M J Gabour, a gas-station owner from Texarkana, Texas, his wife Mary and his two teenage sons, sixteen-year-old Mark and nineteen-year-old Mike, along with Gabour's sister Marguerite Lamport and her husband, whom the Gabours had come to visit in Austin.

The two boys led the way up the stairs from the lift, followed by the two women. The men dawdled behind. As Mark opened the door on to the observation deck, he was met with three shotgun blasts in quick succession. The gunman slammed the door shut. The two boys and the women spilled back down the stairs. Gabour rushed to his younger son Mark and turned him over. He saw immediately that Mark was dead. He had been shot in the head at point-blank range. Gabour's sister Marguerite was dead too. His wife and his older son were critically injured. They were bleeding profusely from head wounds. Gabour and his brother-in-law dragged their dead and wounded back down in to the lifts.

The gunman quickly barricaded the top of the stairs with furniture and jammed the door shut with the trolley. He went over to the receptionist Mrs Townley and finished her off with a bullet through the head. Then he went out on to the gallery, which was surrounded by a chest-high parapet of limestone eighteen inches thick. He positioned himself under the 'VI' of the gold-edged clock's south face and began shooting the tiny figures in the campus below.

As the elevator reached the twenty-seventh floor again, two hours later, Officer Martinez said a little prayer and offered his life up to God. Immediately the lift doors opened, the officers were faced with a distraught Mr Gabour, whose wife, sister and two sons lay face up on the concrete floor.

'They've killed my family,' he cried.

Mad for revenge, he tried to wrest a gun from the officers.

As officer Day led the weeping man away, Crum, Martinez and McCoy stepped around the bodies and pools of blood on the floor, and began to climb the stairs up to the observation deck. The door at the top of the stairs was all that stood between them and the mad killer they were about to confront.

Although he had already killed fifteen innocent people and injured thirty-one more, the sniper was nothing like the crazed psychopath who rampaged through their adrenaline-charged imaginations. Until the night before, Charles Whitman Jr had seemed the model citizen. Ex-altar boy and US Marine, he was a broad-shouldered, blond-haired, all-American boy who was known to one and all as a loving husband and son.

Born in 1941 at Lake Worth, Florida, Charles Whitman Jr was the eldest of three brothers. He had been an exemplary son. Pitcher on the school's baseball team, manager of the football team and an adept pianist, he brought home good grades and earned his pocket money doing a paper round. At twelve, he became an Eagle Scout, one of the youngest ever.

His father was a fanatic about guns and raised his boys knowing how to handle them. By the time Whitman enlisted in the US Marines in 1959, he was an expert marksman, scoring 215 out of a possible 250, which won him the rating of sharpshooter. He was also a keen sportsman, enjoying hunting, scuba diving and karate.

However, in the Marines, things began to go wrong. Whitman got busted from corporal to private for the illegal possession of a pistol and was reprimanded for threatening to knock a fellow Marine's teeth out. Meanwhile the façade of his perfect, all-American family began to crack.

Charles Whitman Sr was a prominent civic leader in Lake Worth and one-time chairman of the chamber of commerce. But he was an authoritarian, a perfectionist and an unyielding disciplinarian who demanded the highest of standards from his sons. Nothing Charles Jr did was ever good enough for his father. He resigned himself to regular beatings. But what the young Whitman could not resign himself to was that his father was also a wife-beater. Whitman could not stand the sight of his mother's suffering. He withdrew into himself for long periods and bit his nails down to the quick.

In March 1966, just five months before Whitman's murder spree, the long-suffering Margaret Whitman left her violent husband. By that time, Charles Jr had won a Marine Corps scholarship and enrolled at the University of Texas to study architectural engineering. He moved to Austin, Texas, where he met and married his wife, Kathy Leissner, daughter of a rice-grower and Queen of the Fair of her hometown, Needville. They seemed to be the perfect couple – she a teacher, he the local scout-master. But life did not go as smoothly as the young couple had hoped. Whitman began to take his growing hostility out on his wife. He became a compulsive gambler and soon faced court martial for gambling and loan sharking. His academic work suffered and his scholarship was withdrawn. He dropped out of college and went back to finish his tour with the Marines. Then he suddenly quit the Corps in December 1964 and went back to university, determined to be a better student and a better husband. He overloaded himself with courses in an attempt to get his degree more quickly. He tried studying real estate sales part-time in case his degree course did not work out and he took on casual jobs to earn cash. Under pressure of work, he began to lose control of his temper. Fearing that he might lash out at his wife Kathy, he packed, ready to leave her – only to be talked out of it by a friend.

Whitman was summoned home in March to help his mother make the break. While she packed, a Lake Worth patrol car sat outside the house. Charles Jr had called it in case his father resorted to violence. To be near to her devoted son Charles Jr, Mrs Whitman moved to Austin. Her youngest son, seventeen-year-old John, moved out at about the same time. Later, he was arrested for throwing a rock through a shop window. A judge ordered him to pay a twenty-five-dollar fine or move back in with his father. He paid the fine. Only twenty-one-year-old Patrick, who worked in Whitman Sr's lucrative plumbing contractors' firm, stayed on with his father in the family home.

After the separation, Whitman's father kept calling Charles Jr, trying to persuade him to bring his mother home. By the end of March, this constant hassle was troubling Charles so much that he sought help from the university's resident psychiatrist, Dr Maurice Heatly. In a two-hour interview, Whitman told Dr Heatly that, like his father, he had beaten his wife a few times. He felt that something was wrong, that he did not feel himself. He said he was making an intense effort to control his temper but he feared that he might explode. He did not mention the blinding headaches that he was suffering with increasing frequency. In his notes, Dr Heatly characterised the crew-cut Whitman as a 'massive, muscular youth who seemed to be oozing with hostility'. Heatly took down only one direct quote from Whitman. He had kept on saying that he was 'thinking about going up on the tower with a deer rifle and to start shooting people'.

At the time, these ominous words did not cause the psychiatrist any concern. Students often came to his clinic talking of the tower as a site for some desperate action. Usually they threatened to throw themselves off it. Three students had killed themselves by jumping off the tower since its completion in 1937. Two others had died in accidental falls. But others said that they felt the tower loomed over them like a mystical symbol. Psychiatrists say that there is nothing unusual about threats of violence either. Dr Heatly was not unduly concerned, but recommended that the twenty-five-year-old student come back the following week for another session. Whitman never went back. He decided to fight his problems in his own way. The result was that he declared war on the whole world.

Whatever plans Whitman made over the next four months we cannot know. But those who knew him said that in his last days his anxiety seemed to pass and he became strangely serene. On the night before the massacre, Whitman began a long rambling letter which gives us a glimpse of some of the things going through his fast-disintegrating mind. Shortly before sunset on the evening of 31 July 1966, Whitman sat down at his battered portable typewriter in his modest yellow brick cottage at 906 Jewell Street, Austin, Texas.

'I don't quite understand what is compelling me to type this note,' he wrote. 'I have been having fears and violent impulses. I've had some tremendous headaches. I am prepared to die. After my death, I wish an autopsy on me to be performed to see if there's any mental disorders.' Then he launched into a merciless attack on his father whom he hated 'with a mortal passion'. His mother, he regretted, had given 'the best twenty-five years of her life to that man'. Then he wrote: 'I intend to kill my wife after I pick her up from work. I don't want her to have to face the embarrassment that my actions will surely cause her.'

At around 7.30, he had to break off because a friend, fellow engineering student Larry Fuess, and his wife dropped round unexpectedly. They talked for a couple of hours. Fuess said later that Whitman seemed relaxed and perfectly at ease. He exhibited few of his usual signs of nervousness. 'It was almost as if he had been relieved of a tremendous problem,' Fuess said.

After they left, Whitman went back to the typewriter, noted the interruption and wrote simply: 'Life is not worth living.'

It was time to go and pick up his wife. Whitman fed the dog then climbed into his new black '66 Chevrolet Impala and drove over to the Southwestern Bell Telephone Company where Kathy had taken a job as a telephonist during her summer vacation from teaching, to augment the family income. After driving his wife back to the house, he apparently decided not to kill her immediately. Instead, he picked up a pistol and sped across the Colorado River to his mother's fifth-floor flat at Austin's Penthouse Apartments at 1515 Guadalupe Street. There was a brief struggle. Mrs Whitman's fingers were broken when they were slammed in a door with such force that the band of her engagement ring was driven into the flesh of her finger and the diamond was broken from its setting. Then Whitman stabbed his mother in the chest and shot her in the back of the head, killing her.

He picked up her body, put it on the bed and pulled the covers up so it looked like she was sleeping. He left a handwritten note by the body addressed 'To whom it may concern'. It read: 'I have just killed my mother. If there's a heaven she is going there. If there is not a heaven, she is out of her pain and misery. I love my mother with all my heart. The intense hatred I feel for my father is beyond all description.'

Before leaving, Whitman rearranged the rugs in his mother's apartment to cover the bloodstains on the carpet. And he pinned a note on the front door saying that his mother was ill and would not be going to work that day.

Back at Jewell Street, he typed another line to his letter: '12.30 a.m. Mother already dead.' Some time after that he walked through into the room where his wife was sleeping. He stabbed her three times in the chest with a hunting knife, then pulled the bed sheet up to cover her naked body. He added to his letter, this time in longhand: '3.00 a.m. Wife and mother both dead.' Then he began making preparations for the day ahead.

He got out his old green Marine Corps kit-bag which had his name, 'Lance Cpl. C. J. Whitman', stencilled on the side. Into it he stuffed enough provisions to sustain him during a long siege – twelve tins of spam, Planter's peanuts, fruit cocktail, sandwiches, six boxes of raisins and a vacuum flask of coffee, along with jerrycans containing water and petrol, lighter fuel, matches, earplugs, a compass, rope, binoculars, a hammer, a spanner, a screwdriver, canteens, a snake-bite kit, a transistor radio, toilet paper and, in a bizarre allegiance to the cult of cleanliness, a plastic bottle of Mennen spray deodorant. He also stowed a private armoury that was enough to hold off a small army – a machete, a Bowie knife, a hatchet, a 9-mm Luger pistol, a Galesi-Brescia pistol, a .357-calibre Smith and Wesson revolver, a 35-mm Remington rifle and a 6-mm Remington bolt-action rifle with a four-power Leupold telescopic sight. With this, experts say, a halfway decent shot can consistently hit a six-and-a-half inch circle at 300 yards. He left three more rifles and two derringers at home.

It is not known whether Whitman slept that night. But at 7.15 a.m. he turned up at the Austin Rental Equipment Service and rented a three-wheeled trolley. At 9 o'clock he called his wife's supervisor at the telephone company and said that she was too ill to work that day. Then he drove to a Davis hardware store where he bought a second-hand .30 M1 carbine, which was standard issue in the US Army at that time. At Chuck's Gun Shop he bought some thirty-shot magazines for his new carbine and several hundred rounds of ammunition. And at 9.30 a.m. he walked into Sears Roebuck's department store in Austin and bought a twelve-bore shotgun, on credit.

Back at Jewell Street, he took the shotgun into the garage and began cutting down the barrel and stock. The postman, Chester Arrington, stopped by and chatted to Whitman for about twenty-five minutes. He was probably the last person to speak to Whitman before the massacre. Years later he recalled: 'I saw him sawing off the shotgun. I knew it was illegal. All I had to do was pick up the telephone and report him. It could have stopped him. I've always blamed myself.'

At last everything was ready. Whitman loaded his kit-bag and the last of his guns into a metal trunk and loaded the locker into the boot of his car. He covered it with a blanket, then zipped a pair of grey nylon overalls over his blue jeans and white shirt and, around 10.30 a.m., set off for the university.

Nearly three hours later, Whitman was still

fulfilling his deadly mission. Dead bodies were strewn across the streets and plazas below him and hundreds cowered from his bullets. But it could not last for ever. Outside the door to the observation deck, just a few feet away, were two policeman and a veteran Air Force tailgunner determined to put an end to his psychopathic spree.

Crum, the civilian, took charge.

'Let's do this service style,' he whispered. 'I'll cover you and you cover me.'

They cleared away the barricade at the top of the stairs and, while the cops on the ground intensified their fire to distract the killer, Martinez slowly pushed away the trolley that was propped against the door. Using an overturned desk as a shield, they crawled towards the observation gallery. Crum, carrying a rifle, headed west, while Martinez, with a .38 service revolver, headed eastwards around the gallery, followed by McCoy who was carrying a shotgun.

Martinez rounded one corner then, more slowly, turned on to the north side of the walkway. About fifty feet away, he saw Whitman crouched down and edging towards the corner Crum was about to come round.

But Crum heard Whitman coming and loosed off a shot. It tore a great chunk out of the parapet. Whitman turned and ran back, into the sights of Officer Martinez. Martinez, who had never fired a gun in anger before, shot – and missed. Whitman raised his carbine and fired, but he was trembling and could not keep the gun level. As he squeezed the trigger the gun jerked and the bullet screamed harmlessly over the officer's head. Martinez then emptied his remaining five rounds into the gunman. But still he would not go down. McCoy stepped forward and blasted him twice with the shotgun. Whitman hit the concrete still holding his weapon. Martinez saw that he was still moving. Grabbing the shotgun from McCoy, he ran forward, blasting Whitman at point-blank range in the head. Crum then took Whitman's green towel from his footlocker and waved it above the parapet. At last the gunman was dead.

At 1.40 p.m. two ambulance men carried Whitman's blanket-shrouded body from the tower on a canvas stretcher. The police quickly established his identity and his name was broadcast on the radio. His father rang the police department in Austin and asked them to check his son's and estranged wife's apartments. Along with the bodies of the two women and the notes he had written, Whitman left two rolls of film with the instruction to have them developed. The photographs had been taken over the previous few weeks, but only showed the killer in various ordinary domestic poses, such as snoozing on the sofa with his dog, Smokie, at his feet.

Interviewed later by the press, Whitman's father announced proudly that his son 'always was a crack shot'. In fact, he said, all of his sons were good with guns.

'I am a fanatic about guns,' he admitted. 'My boys knew all about them. I believe in that.'

Whitman had learned the lesson well. In his house, guns had hung in every room.

An autopsy later revealed that there was, as Whitman himself had suspected, something wrong with his brain. He had a tumour the size of a pecan nut in the hypothalamus, but the pathologist, Dr Coleman de Chenar, said that it was certainly not the cause of Whitman's headaches and could not have had any influence on his behaviour. The state pathologist agreed that it was benign and could not have caused Whitman any pain, but a report by the Governor of Texas said that it was malignant and would have killed Whitman within a year. The report also concluded that the tumour could have contributed to Whitman's loss of control.

A number of Dexedrine tablets – known at the time as goofballs – were also found in Whitman's possession, but physicians were not able to detect that he taken any before he died. He may simply have laid in the stimulants to keep him alert during a long siege.

As it is, he had claimed the lives of fifteen people during his murderous rampage, not including his own. Thirty-one others had been injured. One would die later in hospital. Others were permanently scarred or disabled.

The bodies of Charles Whitman and his mother were returned together to Florida, his in a grey metal casket, hers in a green-and-white one. With hundreds of curiosity seekers gawking and jostling in the rolling, palm-fringed cemetery in West Palm Beach, mother and son were interred with full Catholic rites. The priest said that Whitman had obviously been deranged which meant he was not responsible for the sin of murder and was therefore eligible for burial in hallowed ground. The grand jury also found that Whitman was insane.

Flags were flown at half-mast on the Austin

campus of the University of Texas for a week. The tower was closed to the public for a year, but reopened in July 1967. Following a number of suicide attempts, it was closed for good in 1975.

The material Whitman had assembled for his murder spree remained in police custody until 1972. Then it was auctioned off to augment the fund set up to help the victims of his crimes. Whitman's guns fetched $1,500 from a dealer in Kansas.

2

Veterans

Charles Whitman's tower-top massacre threw America into a fit of self-examination. What disturbed America so much was that the lives of so many innocent passers-by had been snuffed out randomly, for no reason. In almost every case they were unnamed and unknown to their killer, the incidental and impersonal casualties of the uncharted battlefields that existed only in his demented mind. The massacre coming just two-and-a-half years after the assassination of President Kennedy, which had also taken place in Texas, Americans were concerned that something was going badly wrong in the land of the free. The Governor of Texas, John Connally, who had been riding with John F. Kennedy when he had been shot, broke off a Latin American trip, hurried home and demanded legislation requiring any individual freed on the grounds of insanity in murder and kidnapping cases be institutionalised for life.

The murdered president's brother, Robert Kennedy, at that time a senator for New York, also spoke out on the issue. He proposed that people acquitted of all federal crimes on the grounds of insanity should be committed for psychiatric treatment. Had Whitman lived to face trial, Kennedy argued, he would undoubtedly have been acquitted because he was so clearly insane.

Austin's police chief said that 'this kind of thing could have happened anywhere'. But that was no comfort. Psychiatrists began to speculate that there was something intrinsic to modern American society that created crazed killers like Whitman. *Time* magazine reported that nearly 2,500,000 Americans had been treated for mental illness in hospitals and clinics that year. Almost a third of them were classified as psychotic – people who, by the minimum definition, had lost touch with reality. They lived in a world of fantasy, haunted by fears and delusions of persecution. An accidental bump on a crowded sidewalk or a passing criticism from an employer or relative could set any of these psychotics off like a time-bomb.

Emanuel Tanay, professor of psychiatry at Wayne State University, pointed out that murder is not the crime of criminals, but that of ordinary citizens. The great majority of murders are family affairs, committed by outwardly ordinary people who never murder or commit any other crime – except on the one fateful occasion. And when the psychotic does strike, the result is often wholesale slaughter.

The menace of the psychotic killer was all the more frightening because they may seem like the model citizen – until they go berserk. Many of these people have a feeling that there is a demon within themselves, said Los Angeles clinical psychiatrist Martin Grotjahn. They try to kill the demon by model behaviour. They live the opposite of what they feel. Like Whitman, they become gentle, very mild, extremely nice people who often show the need to be perfectionists.

Some psychiatrists estimated that the percentage of potential mass killers in the US ranged as high as one in every thousand, or at that time 200,000. Most of these, of course, would never carry out their murderous desires. But Houston psychiatrist C.A. Dwyer warned the American public: 'Potential killers are everywhere these days. They are driving cars, going to church with you, working with you. And you never know it until they snap.'

Perhaps he was over-reacting, but the history of the last thirty years has shown that there is some truth in what he said.

Americans were warned to stay alert. They were to watch for sudden personality changes in friends and loved ones. Special attention should be paid to habitually shy and quiet people who suddenly become aggressive and talkative – or the reverse. Other danger signs were depression and seclusion, hypersensitivity to tiny slights and insults, changes in normal patterns of eating or sleeping, uncontrolled outbursts of temper, disorganised thinking and a morbid interest in guns, knives or other instruments of destruction.

Psychiatrists were quick to point out that the appearance of any of these symptoms does not necessarily mean that someone is about to turn killer. However, those exhibiting them were in need of psychiatric help. Unfortunately, even if a dangerous psychotic – like Charles Whitman – did reach the examining room, it was by no means certain that they could be headed off. Most doctors agreed that the University of Texas psychiatrist who took no action, even after Whitman confessed his urge to climb the Austin tower and kill people several months before the actual incident took place, was not at fault. University of Chicago psychiatrist Robert S. Daniels said that 'thousands – and I mean literally thousands – talk to doctors about having such feelings. Nearly all of them are just talking.'

Deciding who was, and who wasn't, going to follow their murderous impulses was more of an art than a science. It was also a matter of practicality. The practice of psychiatry depended on trust between patient and doctor. Psychiatrists could hardly be expected to report every threatening remark. Besides, as the New York deputy police commissioner pointed out, 'We can't arrest people because they are ill'. New Jersey psychiatrist Henry A. Davidson added: 'We are in a situation now where there is the enormous pressure of civil rights. The idea of locking someone up on the basis of a psychiatrist's opinion that he might in future be violent could be repugnant. It would be a very poor way to help the vast majority of disturbed people who make threats that they will never carry out.'

However, some American states had already empowered doctors to forcibly commit any patient they thought dangerous – at least for long enough for a thorough psychiatric examination. But most states insisted that the individual commit themselves voluntarily or that their family or the courts place them in hospital care. Usually the doctor could only try and persuade the patient that voluntary commitment was in their own best interest.

Unfortunately, most psychotics were not amenable to having themselves locked up and, in the 1960s, most families regarded mental illness as a shameful thing and resisted formal commitment to a mental institution until it was too late.

Medical opinion, at the time, believed that the best way of catching psychotics before they began shooting was a long-term programme of mental hygiene. They favoured more psychological testing in schools and colleges, and the spread of community clinics to give instant help to all who needed it. What was needed was a massive investment of money and manpower. Far too little was known about the psychology of the spree killer, psychiatrists conceded. The problem was they erupted infrequently – and few survived to tell the tale. Those who did, the medics said, were a vital research resource. Pilot studies of juvenile offenders in Massachusetts and Illinois at that time indicated that many potential psychotics may be identifiable, and even curable, if caught in their teens. And the medical profession had still not given up on the idea that they could find the cure to all mental illness in the chemistry of the brain. Generally, though, it was considered that there was little hope of some sort of psychiatric Geiger counter or cerebral pap smear test to spot psychotics in advance. Instead, Americans should put their faith in President Johnson's Great Society and those massive welfare resources that were set to pare down the danger of sudden, irrational murder.

While some searched for clues to Charles Whitman's crime in the dark tides of blood and destruction that haunt the deepest layers of men's psyches, others looked to Americans' abiding love affair with the hand-gun. Charles Whitman may have been unusual in having a dozen guns at his disposal, but he was by no means unique. Americans – especially Texans – have always been gun-toting people. Guns had been used by the first settlers to protect and feed themselves and to subdue the hostile land. Later the colonists became a nation of riflemen who used the gun to win their freedom from the British in the American Revolution. Guns tamed the West and became synonymous with frontier justice. In the lawless 1920s, the gun had become a means of self-protection. And by the 1960s, there was a massive market for guns among collectors and sportsmen. America had the largest cache of civilian hand-guns in the world – with over 100 million in private hands. Sales were running at over a million a year by mail order alone. Another million or so were imported. But, following the assassination of President Kennedy, Americans became very conscious that there were very few legal controls over the possession of firearms. Federal law curbed the inter-state traffic in machine guns, sawn-off shotguns and silencers, but the regulation of firearms had been left largely to the cities and individual states. Until Charles Whitman's senseless slaughter, only Philadelphia required police permits for buying, keeping or even roaming Main Street with a shotgun or rifle. The week after Whitman's murder spree, that statute was extended to New Jersey – one of the few states that had experienced a spree killing before. Only seven states and a handful of municipalities required permits for hand-guns. This leniency showed up in the crime statistics. The FBI reported that fifty-seven per cent of the 9,850 homicides in the US in 1965 were committed with firearms. And all but one of the fifty-three policemen killed on duty were the victims of gunshots.

In Texas, gun laws were practically non-existent, and in Dallas – the scene of Kennedy's murder in 1963 – some seventy-two per cent of all murders in 1965 were committed with guns. This compared with but twenty-five per cent in New York City, where New York State's fifty-five-year-old Sullivan Law required police permits for the possession of hand-guns. Veteran FBI chief J. Edgar Hoover said: 'Those who claim that the availability of firearms is not a factor in the murders in this country are not facing reality.'

American legislators were very conscious that most other countries had much stricter gun-control laws. But given America's passion for firearms, trying to ban them would be unthinkable – especially as it would curb such legitimate activities as hunting, target shooting and, in some cases, possessing a gun for self-defence. Nevertheless, in the wake of the Austin slaughter, the US Justice Department, the bar association and most American police forces felt that much tighter gun controls were called for. This prompted Connecticut Senator Thomas Dodd to propose a federal bill limiting the inter-state shipment of mail-order hand-guns, curbing the importing of military-surplus firearms, banning over-the-counter hand-gun sales to out-of-state buyers and anyone under twenty-one, and prohibiting long-arm sales to anyone under eighteen.

Reacting to what he called the 'shocking tragedy' in Austin, President Johnson urged the speedy passage of the bill 'to help prevent the wrong persons from obtaining firearms'. However, no one was sure how you could recognise the 'wrong persons'. Besides, even under Dodd's bill, Charles Whitman would still have been able to amass his sizeable arsenal, as none of the bill's provisions applied to him.

Several individual states backed the Dodd Bill, as they felt it would help them enforce their own gun laws. Some proposed statutory cooling-off periods, so that buyers would have to wait a few days before they could obtain guns, and prohibiting sales to known criminals and psychotics. Yet opposing even these trivial proposals was the influential National Rifle Association, whose 750,000 members vigorously lobbied against any gun-control legislation. Some right-wingers even claimed that gun control was a Communist plot to disarm Americans. Even ordinary citizens claimed the constitutional right to bear arms – even though, at that time, the Supreme Court denied that there was such a right. True, the Second Amendment to the American constitution mentioned the 'right of the people to keep and bear arms' but it actually read, in full: 'A well-regulated Militia being necessary to the security of a free state, the right of the people to keep and bear arms shall not be infringed.' What the Founding Fathers had in mind, the Supreme Court argued, was the collective right to bear arms, not the individual right. Since Americans already needed licences to marry, drive, run a shop or, in some states, own a dog, it was difficult to see why making them take out a licence to own a lethal weapon was any particular infringement of their liberty.

Despite Americans' refusal to introduce gun controls that might prevent any future spree killer, the image of Charles Whitman found a place deep in the American psyche. Two films were made about him. In *Targets*, made in 1968, director Peter Bogdanovich switched the action to a drive-in movie theatre, where a psychotic sniper picks off the innocent viewers of a horror movie. *The Deadly Tower*, in 1975, gave a literal version of events, though policeman Ramiro Martinez sued the network NBC for $1 million over his portrayal. However, these movies were not entirely without precedent in America. In 1952, a film called *The Sniper* had been released. It was about a youth who shot blondes. And in 1962, Ford Clark published a novel called *The Open Space*. In it, the protagonist climbs a tower in a Midwestern university and begins picking off people. As far as the police could ascertain, Whitman had neither seen the film nor read the book.

Whitman's murderous spree had also been seen to be associated with the Vietnam War, which was bringing true-life violence directly into America's living-rooms every night at the time. The first televised war, network coverage of Vietnam became the backdrop to the late 1960s and early 1970s. It brought with it an unprecedented tide of assassinations, urban violence and spree killings. By the end of the war, the American Army or Marine veteran had turned in the public perception from an upstanding citizen who had served his country to a degenerate butcher who might explode at any moment and kill again at the slightest excuse. This attitude was made explicit in the 1976 movie *Taxi Driver*. Made just one year after the end of the war, it showed Robert De Niro as a brooding ex-Marine, Vietnam veteran Travis Bickle. The film follows the insomniac psychopath as he meticulously prepares himself to declare war on the world. It ends, predictably, in a violent bloodbath.

However, although Charles Whitman was a Marine, he was honourably discharged in 1964, a year before President Johnson committed ground troops to Vietnam. Whitman experienced none of the alienation that the veterans of that unpopular war suffered. Although many spree killers have been in the armed forces – or have had delusions about being in them – few of them are actually combat veterans. One who was, was Howard Unruh. But he had not been in Vietnam. His murderous spree had taken place sixteen years before the Vietnam War had begun.

A German-American, Howard Unruh was born in 1921 in East Camden, on the Delaware River in New Jersey. The only child of hard-working, religious parents, he shunned the noisy games of his boisterous schoolmates, preferring to sit quietly reading the Bible on his own. He was deeply attached to his mother, Freda, who worked in a local soap factory.

Unruh graduated from high school and planned to go on to college to study pharmacy. But World War II intervened. He was called up and enlisted, not unwillingly, in the army. Surprisingly he fitted in well, though he wrote long letters home to his mother every day. When he was given a gun, it became his obsession. Early in training he became a sharpshooter.

While other GIs were out drinking, Unruh would stay in the barracks and sit quietly on his bunk reading the Bible or stripping down his rifle, lovingly cleaning it, greasing it and reassembling it. He would even offer to clean other men's rifles for them.

During the Italian campaign, Unruh distinguished himself as a tank gunner. He moved on into France and fought in the Battle of the Bulge. Throughout the war Unruh kept a diary. One day a fellow soldier took a sly look at it. He was horrified. The diary listed every German Unruh had killed, giving date, time, place and how the body looked in death.

At the end of the war Unruh was honourably discharged with several citations for bravery under fire. He resumed his plan to become a pharmacist, took a high-school refresher course and enrolled at Temple University in Philadelphia.

He also enrolled in a Bible class, where he met a girl and began dating her. The relationship led nowhere though. His feelings for his fellow student could not rival his love of guns.

He bought a number of weapons – a 9-mm German Luger pistol with several clips, several other pistols with thousands of rounds of ammunition, a hunting knife with a nine-inch blade and a machete honed to a razor-sharp edge. These were kept locked in his bedroom. Not even his parents were allowed to enter. In the basement he set up a firing range, where he practised daily.

After ditching his girlfriend so he could spend more time practising, he became withdrawn, then increasingly paranoid. He began to keep a diary, detailing the slights and imagined slights he had suffered at the hands of others. His nextdoor neighbours, the Cohen family, were his chief target. When they chided him for taking a short cut through their back garden or their twelve-year-old son made too much noise, Unruh's diary spoke of 'retaliation' against them. His diary used the word 'retaliation' 180 times.

Unruh erected a high wooden fence around the rear of the house to block out the world he hated. His father helped him, thinking it might calm his increasingly disturbed son. When it was finished, Unruh was triumphant. But on the afternoon of 5 September 1949 he returned home to find the gate missing, leaving a gaping hole in the fence. Unruh concluded that it had been taken by one of his neighbours. He lay on his bed fully clothed, staring at the ceiling and plotting his revenge.

At 8 a.m. Unruh went downstairs for breakfast. His mother had prepared cereal and eggs for him. He sat at the breakfast table but would not eat. He would not speak and there was a wild look in his eyes. Suddenly he shot back his chair and ran from the room. His mother followed him to his room, where he threatened her with a heavy wrench. Terrified, she ran to a neighbour's house.

Unruh loaded his Luger and stuffed another pistol into his pocket. He loaded himself up with ammunition and grabbed his hunting knife. At 9.20 a.m., wearing his best tropical worsted suit, the twenty-eight-year-old veteran went out through the gap in the back fence, on to the street.

He walked deliberately to a delivery truck parked two blocks away, thrust his gun through the window and pulled the trigger. The driver, thirty-three-year-old Roxy DiMarco, hurled himself backwards from his seat as the bullet whizzed past the steering wheel. Unruh shrugged and moved on.

A little way down the street was a shoe repair shop run by John Pilarchik, who had known Unruh since he was a boy. Pilarchik was on his knees, nailing the heel on a shoe, when Unruh came in. Unruh walked to within three feet of him. When Pilarchik looked up, Unruh shot him in the chest. Without a word he turned and strode on to the Clark Hoover barber's shop next door. Orris 'Brux' Smith, a six-year-old boy, was perched on a white, painted, carousel horse with a barber's bib around his neck. Clark Hoover was cutting his blond hair, while Brux's mother, forty-two-year-old Mrs Edwina Smith, and his eleven-year-old sister, Norma, sat watching.

Another patron witnessed the hollow-cheeked Unruh, with his brown crew-cut hair, walk into the barber's. 'I've got something for you, Clarkie,' Unruh said to Clark Hoover, who had known him since he was a child. Unruh walked up to the boy, put the Luger to his chest and fired. Then he gunned down the thirty-three-year-old barber with a second shot. Ignoring the screams of the child's mother and sister, Unruh then stepped quietly back out on to the sunlit street.

Local restaurant owner Dominick Latela ran to the barber's shop, picked up the bleeding boy and

raced to the Cooper Hospital in a futile rescue dash.
The child was dead.

In annoyance, Unruh sent a volley of bullets
through the door of Dominick Latela's restaurant,
just missing Latela's wife Dora and six-year-old
daughter who were taking cover behind the
counter.

Unruh headed on to the drugstore owned by his
hated neighbour Abe Cohen. On the way he
bumped into the family insurance agent, forty-five-
year-old James Hutton. Hutton said hello. Unruh's
savage reply was two 9mm slugs from his Luger –
one in the head, one in the body – killing the
insurance agent instantly. Unruh later told the
police that he had politely asked Hutton to get out
of his way, but Hutton had not moved fast enough.

The shots alerted Abe Cohen who ran up the
stairs into the stock-room above his store to warn
his wife Rose, his mother Winnie and his son
Charles. Sliding a fresh clip into his Luger, Unruh
bounded up the stairs after him. The stock-room
was open and Unruh saw thirty-eight-year-old
Rose Cohen as she took cover in a cupboard. Unruh
put a bullet through the cupboard door. The weight
of her body pushed the door open and she fell
sprawling across the floor. She was still moaning
when Unruh put another shot through her head.

Hiding in another cupboard in the stock-room
was the Cohens' son, but Unruh was distracted by
a noise from the adjoining office. In it he found
sixty-two-year-old Winnie Cohen, phone in hand,
dialling the police. Two shots ended the call, and
her life.

As she fell, the receiver dropped from Winnie

Cohen's hand with a loud thud. Then there was silence, broken only by a soft scraping sound. It came from above. In an effort to escape, Abe Cohen was crawling across the pitched porch roof. Unruh climbed out of the window and fired twice, hitting Cohen in the back. Cohen lost his grip and rolled off the roof, crashing to the sidewalk below. Unruh put another bullet through his head, just to make sure. By the time Unruh walked back out on to the pavement, twelve-year-old Charles Cohen was up on the roof, screaming hysterically. Unruh turned and walked away. He had no quarrel with the boy.

He had no quarrel either with TV repairman Alvin Day from nearby Mantua who was driving up the street. Unruh walked to the car window and shot once with deadly accuracy. Another passing motorist, Charles Petersen, the eighteen-year-old son of a local fireman, also stopped. He and two teenage friends got out of the car to tend the dying James Hutton. Unruh fired several times, wounding Petersen in the legs. The other two ran off unharmed.

Unruh reloaded again and started hunting more strangers. At the end of the street a coupé was waiting at a stop light. Unruh walked over to it and leaned in the open window. The driver, a forty-three-year-old Mrs Helen Wilson, found herself staring down the barrel of a loaded pistol. Unruh pulled the trigger. Mrs Wilson died instantly. Unruh went on to pick off the passengers one by one. In the back of the car were Mrs Wilson's elderly mother, sixty-six-year-old Mrs Emma Matlock of Pennsauken, who was killed outright, and her twelve-year-old grandson John Wilson, who was fatally wounded.

A long shot wounded a truck driver climbing from his cab in the next block. Unruh then headed for a tavern owned by Frank Engel. The customers made a concerted rush for the rear as a rain of bullets tore through the panelling of the front door. Engel went upstairs to get his .38 revolver. From a second-storey window he took a pot-shot at Unruh, wounding him in the leg. But Unruh took no notice and continued about his murderous business.

By now the local residents were alerted. Shopkeepers and restaurant owners started barricading their doors. Unruh tried firing a few shots through the door of a supermarket, but the lock held. Next door, though, the tailor's shop was open. The tailor, Thomas Zegrino, was away, but in the kitchen at the back, Unruh found the owner's wife, Mrs Helga Zegrino. The twenty-eight-year-old woman fell to her knees and begged for her life. Unruh shot her twice.

Back on the street Unruh spotted a two-year-old boy, Tommy Hamilton, watching his murderous progress from a window. A single shot smashed the window and hit the child between the eyes, killing him instantly.

Then Unruh saw a small yellow house with its door slightly ajar. Inside he found a woman, Mrs Madeline Harrie, and her two sons cowering in a kitchen at the back. The older boy flung himself at the gunman. Unruh loosed off two shots, one hitting the boy in the arm, the other wounding Mrs Harris in the shoulder. The younger child escaped unscathed.

Unruh was now out of ammunition. As he turned to walk back home, he could hear police sirens wailing in the distance. Soon the house was surrounded. Machine-gun rounds came pouring through the window. In the middle of the mayhem the telephone rang. Unruh picked it up. It was local newspaper reporter Philip Buxton.

'I'm a friend,' said Buxton. 'How many have you killed?'

'I don't know yet,' said Unruh in a matter-of-fact voice, 'but it looks like a pretty good score.'

Buxton asked him why he was killing people.

'I don't know,' Unruh replied. 'I can't answer that yet – I'm too busy. I'll have to talk to you later.' He put the phone down and went back to the fray.

Tear-gas canisters were then being lobbed through the windows. The choking fumes drove Unruh downstairs. A few minutes later he laid down his weapons, opened the back door and came out with his hands up. The guns of fifty police marksmen were trained on him.

Police officers scrambled forward and handcuffed him. As he was hurried off, one cop asked him: 'What's the matter with you? Are you a psycho?'

'I'm no psycho,' said Unruh, apparently unconcerned. 'I have a good mind.'

Unruh never stood trial. He was declared incurably insane and committed to New Jersey State Mental Hospital. He never expressed the slightest remorse for the victims of his murderous spree. He had only one regret – that there were so few. 'I'd have killed a thousand if I'd had enough bullets,' he said years later. However, his conscience was troubled by the fact that he had threatened his mother with a wrench. He also admitted that, while he had never had sex with a woman, he had indulged in furtive homosexual activities.

There was another spree killer who was also a veteran – a veteran of World War II, like Unruh. Frank Kulak was a big man and a good soldier. He was five foot eleven and weighed fifteen stone. At sixteen he lied about his age to enlist in the Marines. He saw action against the Japanese in the bitter fighting on Okinawa, one the bloodiest battles of the Pacific war. Later he re-enlisted to fight the Communists in Korea. When he returned to his home in Chicago's South Side in 1952, he had a Purple Heart and a right hand with only two fingers on it. The other three had been lost to enemy artillery. But he was, perhaps, more seriously scarred internally by the violence he had seen.

Kulak's missing fingers made it impossible for him to hold down a regular job. Over the years he soured into the neighbourhood crank who yelled at children and made them cry. Unmarried, he lived with his sister in a seven-room flat on the third floor of a large house. Brooding in the apartment, he constantly relived the nightmares of combat. 'He was always talking about the war,' recalled Susan Kulak, a niece who was nineteen when Frank Kulak finally exploded. 'He was always talking about the Japs.' But Kulak's problem went a lot further than talking.

The beginning of the Vietnam War disturbed Kulak deeply. His ugly memories of war were being made terribly real again. And he could not get away from it. News of the war filled the newspapers and the TV news. In 1967, seeking in his own warped way to bring the reality of war home to the American public, Kulak began making bombs and setting them off around the neighbourhood. The campaign gathered momentum and culminated with a blast at a local department store.

The Chicago bomb-squad's investigation led them to Kulak. Two officers – Sergeant James Schaffer, forty-eight, and Detective Jerome A. Stubig, forty – arrived at Kulak's apartment. Kulak reacted like he was back in a foxhole. Inside the apartment he had a massive arsenal – two carbines, an M-1 rifle, two automatic pistols, two twelve-bore shotguns, 2,000 rounds of ammunition, hand grenades and a launcher, 25 lbs of gun powder, chemical explosives and an assortment of home-made bombs.

In Kulak's eyes the knock on the door meant the enemy was now massing for attack. The ex-Marine knew how to deal with this situation. He tossed a grenade out of the window at the two officers standing on the wooden stairs that led up to the third floor. The stairs splintered and the two men fell over twenty feet to the ground. Then Kulak emptied his carbine into their twisted bodies. Satisfied they were dead, he quickly prepared for a fresh assault. He set up weapons at each of the apartment windows and began heaving bombs at the street below. Then he started firing randomly at pedestrians who scrambled for cover.

The five other tenants in the building cowered in the basement and the school children huddled under their desks at the Sacred Heart Parochial

School across the road. Meanwhile, Kulak traded fire with a force of over one hundred policemen outside. Special sharpshooters were brought in, but ex-Marine Kulak was too good for them. They could not pin him down.

The police used bullhorns to plead with Kulak to come down. Relatives were brought in. Kulak's fifty-one-year-old brother Harold shouted: 'Frank, Frank, this isn't a war zone. The war is over. We have a Marine ambulance here for you.'

Kulak's sister, Mrs Katherine Potts, made the same appeal. But for Frank Kulak the war was still on. His sister's plea was answered with another rifle shot.

The siege continued for another three hours until the cops stopped firing and sent a squad of men creeping into the building. From a sheltered position on the second floor Police Deputy Superintendent James Rochford managed to talk to the gunman. Three hours later, at 8.45 p.m., Kulak appeared at the back window. Instantly a hundred guns were trained on his head and chest. He stood in the window for a while, then sat down on the windowsill. Slowly running his disfigured hand through his Marine-style crew-cut, he began to cry. Twenty minutes later he surrendered. Four were dead; twenty wounded.

The next day, his forty-second birthday, Frank Kulak was arraigned on two murder charges. He confessed to the bombings, claiming that his self-appointed mission was to show people 'what the Vietnam War was like'. He had attacked the department store to blow up war toys in the toy department. Kulak also explained that he was trying to alert the American people to the threat of Chinese Communism.

Kulak was found unfit to stand trial. He was remanded to the custody of doctors at the psychiatry facility in the state prison at Chester, Illinois. But Illinois law makes prisoners incarcerated in mental institutions eligible for release after the same period that would make them eligible for parole, if they were serving a regular sentence. In January 1981, after he had served eleven years at Chester, Kulak was brought back to Chicago where he appeared in the criminal court before Judge Frank B. Machala. Machala refused to dismiss the charges against Kulak – and Kulak was returned to the jail at Chester, where he remains to this day.

3

Existential Heroes

Spree killing seems to be a curiously twentieth-century phenomenon – restricted almost exclusively to the late twentieth century, post-World War II – unless you throw your net a little wider. It could be argued that the great Mongol ruler, Genghis Khan, was a life-long spree killer. Between 1206 and 1227 he killed an estimated twenty million people – that is nearly a million people a year and around one-tenth of the world's population at the time.

Born in 1162, he was the son of Yesukai, the chief of a small, impoverished Mongol clan. Orphaned at thirteen, the young Genghis Khan – his name meant 'universal ruler' – began his career in casual butchery by murdering his brother over a fish. In the spring of 1206, at the age of thirty-three, Khan established his rule over all the Mongol tribes and, in 1211, he began his legendary conquest of imperial China, burning and pillaging every city and village that stood in his way. Three years after his invasion, the Mongol hordes controlled the entire country north of the Yellow River and Khan forced the Kin Tartars to deliver to him 500 young men and women, plus 3,000 livestock, as the price of peace.

To the west lay the kingdom of Khwarizms, the vast territory between the Ganges and the Tigris rivers, covering what today is India and Iran. Khan promised the ruler of Khwarizm, Shah Mohammed, peace and favourable trade agreements. But the Shah's answer was to murder a caravan of one hundred Mongol traders near the border town of Otrar. Khan sent more envoys, but they too were murdered. Khan did not try and make peace again. Between 1218 and 1222 Khan's armies swept through Khwarizm, killing 400,000 enemy troops who stood in their way. The governor of Otrar was executed by having molten metal poured in his eyes and ears. In Bukhara the defeated inhabitants were ordered outside the city walls and forced to watch their women being raped.

In May 1220 the Mongol armies reached as far west as Samarkind, where they defeated a garrison of 50,000 men. Most of the defenders were murdered for refusing to surrender their city. And at Termez every dead body was torn open by Khan's men after one old woman had swallowed her pearls to prevent them falling into the hands of the marauders. Genghis Khan took no prisoners. He would stack the severed heads of his victims in bloody pyramids.

Shah Mohammed retreated farther and farther west. Khan followed. He began killing all the men and taking all the women and children into slavery. While the carnage grew, Shah Mohammed died of pleurisy in a village on the Caspian Sea. But this was not the end of it. Khan continued to pursue the Shah's heir, Jelaleddin, cutting a wide swathe of death through Afghanistan, killing thousands of innocent people along the way. His bloody empire stretched from the China Sea to the Persian Gulf at the time of his death, of natural causes, at the age of sixty, in August 1227. But even death did not stop his killing. He ordered that if anyone gazed on his coffin, the next coffin would be theirs.

Throughout history there have been many other mass murderers. Many, like Khan, have their murderous desires cloaked in political ambitions. Vlad the Impaler – the historical Dracula – was a minor Romanian king who was hardened by the war fighting the Turks. He took tremendous pleasure from the senseless killing of large numbers of people. Woodcuts show the massed ranks of his victims impaled with spears through their stomachs. In fact he had his victims impaled with blunt wooden stakes stuck up their anus or vagina, so that their own weight made them sink slowly down on to it. Impalements were regular entertainment at meals. One Russian boyar who held his nose because the smell of blood put him off his food found himself impaled on a particularly long pole. After a quarrel with a Saxon merchant in 1460, Vlad held another mass impaling and burnt 400 apprentices alive. When Vlad discovered that there were a large number of beggars and sick people in his kingdom, he invited them to a banquet, locked them in and set fire to the building. Imprisoned in Hungary for twelve years and unable to satisfy his lust for killing, Vlad would torture animals to death. He was killed in battle against the Turks, in 1476, probably by his own men.

Gilles de Rais – the legendary Bluebeard – was a contemporary of Vlad the Impaler's. He was also a distinguished soldier who saw battle against the English at the side of Joan of Arc. After she was captured and killed, he returned to his estate, where he kidnapped, tortured and killed perhaps as many as 140 children. He would lure his victims to his castle and sodomise them – both male and female – while strangling them or cutting off their heads. He also enjoyed disembowelling his victims and masturbating over their entrails. Some fifty dismembered bodies were found in a disused tower in his castle when he was arrested.

Other hardened soldiers in history have committed huge and senseless atrocities. Russia's warrior-tsar Ivan the Terrible had 64,000 people tortured and killed when he suspected, probably wrongly, that the citizens of Novgorod were planning to rebel. However, it was not until the twentieth century that individuals took up arms in their own war on the world.

German-American Carl Panzram dedicated himself to a thirty-year campaign of motiveless mayhem and slaughter in the early years of this century. Born in 1891 to a family of immigrant Prussian farmers in Warren, Minnesota, Panzram became a criminal as a young boy. His father deserted the family soon after his birth and his mother could not control him. When he was just eight years old, in 1899, Panzram was brought before a juvenile court for being drunk and disorderly. Then, after burgling the house of a well-to-do neighbour, he was sent to Minnesota State Training School in Red Wing. The discipline was rigid, if not sadistic. Panzram burned the place down.

Released in 1906, he began his war against the world in earnest. He started in the West, committing a series of robberies and assaults. Travelling the country, he was raped by four hoboes. This gave him a new mode of revenge. 'Whenever I met a hobo who wasn't too rusty looking,' he wrote later in his autobiography, 'I would make him raise his hands and drop his pants. I wasn't very particular either. I rode them old and young, tall and short, white and black.' Ending up in Montana State Reformatory, he quickly escaped. Over the next couple of months he robbed and burnt down several churches. Then he joined the army, only to be court-martialled on 20 April 1907 for insubordination and pilfering US government property. Three years at Fort Leavenworth, busting rocks under the blistering Kansas sun, honed his meanness to a razor edge.

Released in 1910, Panzram headed down to Mexico where he joined the rebel leader Pascaul Orozco, who fought alongside Pancho Villa and Emiliano Zapata in the Mexican Revolution. Later he returned to the States, moving up through California and the Pacific Northwest. He left a trail of murder, robbery, assault and rape. Totting up his score, he claimed to have killed twenty-one people, committed thousands of burglaries, robberies, larcenies and arson, and sodomised more than a thousand men.

Arrested in Chinook, Montana, for burglary, he was sentenced to a year in prison. He escaped after eight months. A year later, Panzram was arrested again, this time under the alias 'Jeff Rhoades'. He was given a two-year sentence. Paroled in 1914, he went straight back to crime. In Astoria, Oregon, he was arrested again for burglary and offered a minimal sentence if he would reveal the whereabouts of the goods he had stolen. He kept his side of the bargain but, in exchange, he was sentenced to seven years. Outraged at this injustice, Panzram escaped from his cell and wrecked the jail. The guards beat him up and sent him to Salem correctional facility, the toughest prison in the state. Almost as soon as he arrived there he threw the contents of a chamber-pot in a guard's face. He was beaten unconscious and chained to the floor of a darkened cell for thirty days. This did not break his spirit. He spent his time screaming defiance. When he was let out into the body of the prison again, he helped another prisoner escape. In the hunt, the warden was shot dead. The new warden was even tougher, but Panzram burned down the prison workshop and a flax mill. He went berserk with an axe and incited a prison revolt – for which he was given another seven years. But by now the atmosphere in the prison was so tense that the guards would not venture into the yard and the new warden was dismissed.

The next warden was an idealist who believed that Panzram might respond to kindness. When Panzram was caught trying to escape, the warden told him that, according to reports, he was the 'meanest and most cowardly degenerate' the prison authorities had ever seen. Panzram agreed. But instead of punishing him, the warden let him out of the prison, provided he returned that evening. Panzram left with no intention of going back, but that evening he did return. The liberal regime continued and Panzram responded – until one night he got drunk with a pretty nurse. He absconded, only to be recaptured after a gun-battle. He was returned to a punishment cell, where he was fed on a diet of bread and water, beaten and sprayed with a fire-hose. But, ever resourceful, Panzram constructed his own tools and hacked his way out of the prison in May 1918.

He headed east, stealing $1,200 from a hotel in Maryland, and signed on a merchant ship bound for South America. He jumped ship in Peru, where he worked in a copper mine. In Chile, he became a foreman for an oil company but, for no apparent reason, set fire to an oil rig. Back in the US, he stole $7,000 from a jewellery shop and $40,000 in jewels and liberty bonds from the home of the former president William Howard Taft in New Haven. With the money he bought a yacht and hired sailors to help him refit it. He raped them, shot them and dropped their bodies in the sea, killing ten in all.

Panzram served a six-month jail sentence in Bridgeport for petty theft before being arrested again for inciting a riot during a labour dispute. Jumping bail, he headed for West Africa, where he continued his murder sprees. He was approached by a twelve-year-old boy, begging. 'He was looking for something. He found it too,' wrote Panzram. 'First I committed sodomy on him and then killed him.' He smashed the boy's head in with a rock.

'His brains were coming out of his ears when I left him and he will never be deader.'

Panzram decided to go crocodile hunting. He hired six black porters to guide him through the backwaters. He shot them in the back and fed them to the crocodiles. Back in America, he raped and killed three more boys. In June 1923, while working as night watchman for the New Haven Yacht Club, he stole a boat. He killed a man who clambered aboard and tossed the body into Kingston Bay in New York. Eventually he was caught attempting to rob an express office in Larchmont, New York, and sentenced to five years in Sing Sing. But the guards there were unable to handle him and he was sent to Clinton Prison in Dannemora, considered to be the end of the line for hard cases. There he received savage beatings and smashed his leg after falling from a high gallery. He spent his days plotting revenge against the whole human race. He planned to blow up a railway tunnel with a train in it, poison a whole city by putting arsenic in the water supply and start a war between Britain and America by blowing up a British battleship in American waters.

When he tried to escape he was tortured by having his hands tied behind his back then being suspended from a beam with the rope. He could endure this for twelve hours on end, screaming and cursing his mother for bringing him into the world. Despite his horrendous treatment, one of the guards, Henry Lesser, was sympathetic and persuaded Panzram to write his autobiography. In it Panzram makes no excuses for himself. He says that he had broken every law of God and man –

and if there had been more laws he would have broken them also.

Released yet again in 1928, Panzram hit the Washington–Baltimore area like a one-man crime wave, committing eleven robberies and one murder, and was soon arrested again. At his trial, he told the jury: 'While you were trying me here, I was trying all of you. I have found you guilty. Some of you I have already executed. If I live, I'll execute some more of you. I hate the whole human race.' The judge sentenced him to twenty-five years in jail. 'Visit me,' Panzram snapped back.

At Leavenworth Panzram told his guards: 'I'll kill the first man that bothers me.' True to his word, he killed mild-mannered civilian prison laundry supervisor Robert G. Warnke with an iron bar. After a hasty trial Panzram was sentenced to hang. Meanwhile Lesser had been showing Panzram's autobiography around the literary establishment, including legendary newspaperman H.L. Menken. People were impressed. But when Panzram heard that they might start a movement to get him reprieved, he protested: 'I would not reform if the front gate was opened right now and I was given a million dollars when I stepped out. I have no desire to do good or become good.'

The Society for the Abolition of Capital Punishment also stepped in. He told them to forget it. Hanging would be a 'real pleasure and a big relief,' he said. 'The only thanks you or your kind will ever get from me for your efforts is that I wish you all had one neck and I had my hands on it. I believe that the only way to reform people is to kill them.

My motto is: "Rob 'em all, rape 'em all and kill 'em all."'

He even turned on Henry Lesser in the end. In his last letter Panzram wrote: 'What gets me is how in the heck any man of your intelligence and ability, knowing as much about me as you do, can still be friendly towards a thing like me when I even despise and detest my own self.'

The end could not come soon enough for Carl Panzram. He raced towards the gallows on 11 September 1930. When the hangman asked him if he had any last words, Panzram said: 'Yes, hurry it up, you Hoosier bastard. I could hang a dozen men while you're fooling around.'

While Panzram was on his lifelong crusade of robbing, raping and murdering, back in Germany a mild-mannered school teacher named Wagner von Degerloch killed fourteen and severely injured twelve more in a single night. Born in 1874, in the village of Eglosheim near Ludwigsburg, Wagner was the son of a peasant – a drunkard and a braggart – who died when Wagner was two. His mother, allegedly a promiscuous woman, married again, but divorced her new husband when Wagner was seven. In the village Wagner, a sensitive boy, was taunted as the 'widow's boy' and began to suffer from nightmares and bouts of suicidal depression.

An intelligent boy, he did well at school. He became a schoolmaster himself, but nursed ambitions to become a playwright. While living and working in a village called Muehlhausen, Wagner found lodgings in an inn. After a brief affair with him, the landlord's daughter fell pregnant. Wagner was horrified. He felt that the girl was socially beneath him, little more than a servant. But when the affair became public, he married her, out of honour.

Following the scandal, Wagner was transferred from prosperous middle-class Muehlhausen to a more lowly post in the impoverished district of Radelstetten. There his wife gave birth to four more children, though the last died while still a baby.

Wagner continued to write, but none of his work was ever performed. He had it published at his own expense. No one took any notice. Feeling himself a failure, he toyed with the idea of suicide, but did not have the courage to go through with it. Then in 1906 he began to plot his revenge. In the woods around Radelstetten he practised marksmanship and began drafting a detailed plan of action.

Throughout, he maintained the façade of the model citizen, although in Radelstetten he was considered rather eccentric. He always dressed extremely formally and insisted on speaking High German while those around him, whatever their social background, spoke the local dialect. But his record as a schoolmaster was excellent and in 1912 he was promoted to a position in Stuttgart. There, after a glass or two of beer, he would still boast of his literary prowess. But nothing ever came of it.

On the night of 4 September 1913, the citizens of Muehlhausen were awoken by several large fires. As they ran into the street, they were shot at by a masked man armed with two pistols. He killed eight men and a girl, wounding twelve more, before he was beaten unconscious by a mob. The inn-keeper identified him as his brother-in-law, the mild-mannered school teacher Wagner. Earlier he had killed his wife and their four children – out of pity, he said.

When he was overpowered Wagner still had 198 bullets in his possession. His plan was to murder the entire population of Muehlhausen, then go back to Eglosheim, kill his brother and his family, burn down his brother's house and the house he himself had been born in, then go to the royal castle in Ludwigsburg, overpower the guard, set the castle on fire and die by flinging himself from the battlements into the flames below.

Wagner was declared insane and confined to a lunatic asylum. He continued to insist that he was sane and demanded to be executed. In the asylum he admitted to homosexual activities shortly before he was married. He also exhibited feelings of guilt over what he considered excessive masturbation. People, he felt sure, gossiped about his sexual practices. To protect himself from their slander, he had always carried a loaded pistol.

Wagner eventually settled into asylum life and used his time to forward his literary career. However, his plays were never performed and his only readers were psychiatrists who studied them as symptoms rather than as works of art. Wagner was proud of the fact that he was the first inmate of his asylum to join the Nazi Party and he turned his literary talents to producing propaganda. He died of pneumonia in 1938.

Although in his later years Wagner stopped writing plays he did accuse others of stealing his ideas. He even believed that the plot for the 1907 version of *Ben Hur* was stolen from one of his dramas. But his idea for randomly murdering innocent people was certainly pinched, and, in the cafés and salons of Paris, intellectuals began giving such murderous actions a spurious pretext. Disillusioned by the mass slaughter of World War I, the Dadaists, Surrealists and other artistic movements found themselves cut off from the individual 'bourgeois' morality. Surrealist poet André Breton speculated on the philosophical significance of taking a machine-gun and mowing down innocent people. Breton was, perhaps, the intellectual precursor of the modern spree killer.

While Breton was philosophising, Hungarian businessman Sylvestre Matuschka was putting the theory of mass murder into practice. After World War I his company prospered, but Matuschka was accused of fraud. Although he was acquitted, he sold his businesses in Budapest and started afresh in Vienna. It was there that he began to experiment with causing train crashes. His first attempt was on 1 January 1931, when he tried unsuccessfully to derail the Vienna to Passat express near Asbach. Then on 8 August he managed to overturn several coaches at Juelerboy in Hungary. They rolled down an embankment, injuring seventy-five people. But his greatest success came on 12 September 1932. The crowded Budapest to Vienna express was crossing a viaduct at Bia-Torbagy when Matuschka set off an explosion which blew out part of the track. The train plunged from the elevated track, killing twenty-two people – some literally blown to pieces. As the dust settled, Matuschka smeared blood on his face and lay down among the victims.

A journalist covering the train crash grew suspicious, though, when he noticed that Matuschka's clothes seemed well-kempt compared to those of the other victims. None of the other passengers could remember seeing him on the train and his ticket had not been punched. Nevertheless, Matuschka tried to sue Hungarian Railways over his feigned injuries. They grew suspicious and when the police were sent to search his house, they found plans for similar train disasters in France, Italy and Holland. Matuschka was arrested and soon confessed. At his trial it was claimed that train crashes sexually excited Matuschka and that witnessing them was the only way he could achieve orgasm. Matuschka himself blamed a hypnotist whom he had met at a country fair and an invisible spirit named Leo. After a second trail Matuschka was found guilty and sentenced to life imprisonment. During World War II, though, he was released by the Soviets who used him as a demolition expert. He reappeared in 1953 in the Korean War as head of a unit that specialised in blowing up trains.

While World War II was still raging, another French intellectual lent new insight into the philosophical stance of the spree killer. Albert Camus, a leading figure in the French resistance, wrote in 1942 a novel called *L'Étranger*. Published in America as *The Stranger* and in Britain in 1946 as *The Outsider*, it was hailed as a brilliant depiction of twentieth century alienation and as one of the first expositions of the post-war philosophy of existentialism. In the novel the protagonist – this was the age of the anti-hero – kills an Arab for no discernible reason, but is condemned to death more because he refuses to say what he genuinely feels and refuses to conform to society's demands. Existentialism rejected objective reality and the conformity of society, and held that each person must discover values for themselves through action and living each moment to the full.

Camus's ideas spread far beyond France. They were taken up by the poets and writers of America's 'beat generation' and were soon translated into the wholesale rebellion of youth. Marlon Brando and James Dean would certainly have come in contact with them at The Actors' Studio in New York, before they began their film careers. Dean – who, like Camus, died in a senseless automobile accident – became a symbol of teenage restlessness and rebellion. So it may not be surprising that, in 1958, three years after Dean's death, a nineteen-year-old James Dean lookalike took to the highway in a three-day motiveless killing spree that left eleven dead.

4

Rebel Without A Cause

Born on 24 November 1938 in a poor quarter of Lincoln, Nebraska, Charles Starkweather was the third of eight children – seven boys and a girl. His father, Guy Starkweather, was a convivial man who liked a drink. A handyman and a carpenter, he suffered from a weak back and arthritis, and could not always work. His wife, Helen, a slight, stoical woman, worked as a waitress and, after 1946, became practically the sole provider for her large family.

Although the Starkweathers knew little of their roots, the first Starkweather had left the old world in the seventeenth century, sailing from the Isle of Man in 1640. The name was well known across the mid-West. There was even a small town called Starkweather in North Dakota. Somehow the name Starkweather seemed eerily redolent of the wind sweeping the Great Plains.

Charles Starkweather had only happy memories of his first six years, which he spent playing with his two elder brothers, Rodney and Leonard, helping around the house with his mother and going fishing with his dad. But all that changed in 1944 on his first day at school. When they enrolled at

Saratoga Elementary School, all the children were supposed to stand up and make a speech. When it came to Charlie's turn, his classmates spotted his slight speech impediment and began to laugh. Starkweather broke down in confusion. He never forgot that humiliation.

Starkweather soon gained the impression that the teacher was picking on him, and he believed that the other children were ridiculing him because of his short bow-legs and distinctive red hair. Later, from his condemned cell, he wrote: 'It seems as though I could see my heart before my eyes, turning dark black with hate of rages.' On his second day at school he got into a fight, which he found relieved his aggression. He claimed to have been in a fight almost every day during his school life, though his teachers remembered little of this.

Despite his high IQ, Starkweather was treated throughout his school career as a slow learner. It was only when his eyes were tested at age fifteen that it was discovered he could barely see the blackboard from his place at the back of the class. He was practically blind beyond twenty feet.

Starkweather felt that life had short-changed him. He was short, short-tempered, short-sighted and short on education. He was forced, by poverty, to wear second-hand clothes. Classmates called him 'Little Red' and he remembered every perceived slight. It made him as hard as nails.

Starkweather's reputation as a fighter spread throughout Lincoln and toughs from all over the city came to take him on. He said later that it was the beginning of his rebellion against the whole world, his only response to being made fun of. At the age of fifteen, he was challenged by Bob von Busch. They fought each other to a standstill. Afterwards they became firm friends. Von Busch was one of the few people who saw the amusing and generous side to Starkweather's nature. The rest of the world saw barely repressed hostility.

Starkweather dropped out of Irving Junior High School in 1954, when he was just sixteen years old. He took a menial job in a newspaper warehouse. His boss treated him as if he was mentally retarded and he hated it.

Although Starkweather continued to love and respect his mother, his relationship with his father sometimes degenerated into open hostility. In 1955 they had a fight and Starkweather moved in with Bob von Busch and his father. The two teenagers were car fanatics. They spent a lot of their spare time at Capital Beach, the local race-car track. Starkweather raced hot rods there and participated in demolition derbies. The two boys also took to joyriding in stolen cars, occasionally stripping them down for spare parts.

When von Busch started dating Barbara Fugate, Starkweather began to see less of him. Then, in the early summer of 1956, Bob took Charlie to a drive-in movie on a double date with Barbara and her younger sister Caril. Caril Fugate was just thirteen years old, though she could easily pass for eighteen. She and Barbara were the daughters of Velda and William Fugate, a drunkard and a convicted peeping Tom. The couple divorced in 1951 and Fugate later died in jail. Barbara and Caril's mother married again and the family lived at 924 Belmont

Avenue, an unpaved road in the poor quarter of Lincoln.

Caril Fugate seemed the perfect mate for the moody Charlie Starkweather. Although she was short – five foot one – she was self-confident and most people found her opinionated and rebellious. She often wore a man's shirt with the sleeves rolled up, blue jeans and boots. Like Starkweather, she did badly at school. Considered slow, she had little experience of life. She had left Lincoln only once, for a holiday in Nebraska's Sand Hill.

To the girls of Lincoln, Charles Starkweather did not seem like much of a catch. He had never had a proper girlfriend before. He was just five foot five, with bow legs, a pug face and the reputation of a hoodlum. But Caril liked him. His tough, rebel image appealed to her. She did not care about his working class origins or his dead-end job. Far more fascinating were the stories he told, his fantasies about being a cowboy or the fastest hot-rod driver in town. What's more, with his slicked back hair and cigarette dangling from his lips, he looked the spitting image of the latest teenage idol, James Dean, whom Starkweather consciously modelled himself on.

Starkweather liked Caril too. He liked the way she wore make up and swore. After their first date, Caril went out with another local boy. Starkweather tracked him down and threatened to kill him if he saw Caril again.

Caril Fugate and Charles Starkweather started going steady. It made Starkweather feel good to be wanted. With Caril, he forgot about his problems. They lived in a world of their own. He quit his job at the warehouse. He had been working part-time as a garbage collector with his brother Rodney since he was thirteen. Now he worked the garbage trucks full-time. He earned a pittance – just forty-two dollars a week – but he got off work early enough to meet Caril from school.

Caril's mother and stepfather were against the match. They thought that seventeen-year-old Starkweather was too old for Caril – and they thought that he was leading their daughter astray. Starkweather's parents were no more favourable. Starkweather's father, who co-owned Starkweather's pale blue '49 Ford sedan, banned Caril – whom Starkweather had taught to drive – from taking the wheel. In the late summer of 1957, however, Caril was involved in a minor accident with the car. Starkweather's father hit his son so hard that he knocked him through a window.

Starkweather left home for good. He moved in with Bob von Busch, who had just married Barbara. Soon he was persuaded to move out of their cramped apartment and took a room of his own in the same apartment block, one of the very few in town at the time.

Starkweather and Caril went on dates to the movies, sometimes alone, sometimes with Bob and Barbara. Or they would just drive around, listening to distant rock 'n' roll stations on the radio. Starkweather also liked to get out of the small city of Lincoln, which had a population of just 100,000 in 1958. He found Nebraska's capital city claustrophobic and felt contempt for the local people's law-abiding, Christian ways. Lincoln had just three murders a year before Starkweather went on his spree, and boasted more churches per head than any other city in the world. Out in the huge, flat countryside around Lincoln, Starkweather felt at home. He had craved the solitary life of a back-woodsman since he was a child. 'When the sun was setting in its tender glory,' he later wrote of an early experience of the wilderness, 'it was as though time itself was standing still. The flames still burn deep down inside of me for the love of that enchanted forest.'

Out in the woods he would experience that feeling again. 'I would set down against a large tree. I gazed above and between the lagged limbs into the sky of miles and miles, of undiscover.' Caril shared that romantic view of the natural world. She would accompany him on hunting trips and, in the evening, they would lie back, holding hands, and stare up into the clear, starry, black Nebraskan sky. There he told her of the deal he had done with death. Death, he said, had come to him in a vision. Half-man, half-bear, it had taken him down to hell, but hell was not as he had always imagined, 'it was more like beautiful flames of gold'. The few other people he had trusted enough to tell his vision to had thought him crazy and had changed the subject. But Caril said she loved him and that she wanted to go there, to hell, with him. And in his love for her, Starkweather thought, at last he had found 'something worth killing for'. His one great aim in life now was for Caril to see him 'go down shooting, knowing it was for her'.

Starkweather liked to buy presents for Caril – soft toys, a record player and a radio, so she could enjoy music at home. He also bought her jewellery, including a locket with 'Caril' and 'Chuck' – her nickname for him – engraved on it. But buying presents on the forty-two dollars a week he earned as a dustman did not come easy – especially when there was rent to pay and a car to keep on the road. Starkweather soon began looking around for an easier way of making money.

Nebraska was on the eastern edge of the old Wild West. Cattle ranchers had wrested it from the Sioux and it had been cowboy country until the cereal farmers fenced it in and forced the cattlemen to move on. Starkweather felt himself very much part of that old tradition. He loved guns and spent hours stripping them down and oiling them. And he loved to shoot. Although he was short-sighted, he was a good shot and practised shooting from the hip like an old time gunfighter. He also loved detective movies and true crime comics, and he began to fantasise about being a criminal. But he was not interested in being a burglar or a sneak thief. To Starkweather, crime meant armed robbery.

Although he had had a few adolescent scrapes, he had never been in any real trouble with the law. Now, to keep Caril, he started planning a criminal career. Bank robbery was plainly the pinnacle of the profession, but he thought he had better start small – by knocking over a gas station. He chose the Crest Service Station on Cornhusker Highway that ran out of Lincoln to the north. He used to hang out there tinkering with his car and knew the gas station pretty well. A couple of times, when he had been locked out of his room for not paying the rent, he had slept there in his car, surviving on chocolate bars and Pepsi from the vending machines. The gas station attendant would wake him at 4.15 a.m. so that he would be on time for work.

On 1 December 1957 a new attendant had just taken over. Robert Colvert was twenty-one and just out of the Navy, where he had been known as 'Little Bob'. He was nine stone, and around five foot five. Earlier that year he had got married. His wife Charlotte was expecting and he had taken the night job at the gas station to support his growing family. He was new to the job and barely knew Starkweather, though they had had a row the day before when he refused to give Starkweather credit on a toy dog he wanted to buy Caril.

It was a freezing night and a bitter Nebraskan wind was blowing in from the plains. Starkweather pulled into the service station around 3 a.m. Colvert was alone. Starkweather was nervous. At first he bought a pack of cigarettes and drove off. A few minutes later he came back. This time he bought some chewing gum and drove off again. The coast was clear. It was now or never.

Starkweather loaded the shotgun he had stolen from Bob von Busch's cousin, Sonny. He pulled a hunting cap down over his red hair and tied a bandanna around his face.

Back at the gas station, Starkweather pointed the shotgun at Colvert and handed him a canvas money bag. Colvert filled the bag with the notes and loose change from the till. But then Starkweather's plan went badly wrong. Although he knew the station's routine and how much money was kept there overnight, the new man did not know the combination of the safe and could not open it.

Starkweather forced him into the car at gunpoint. Colvert drove. Starkweather sat in the passenger seat, the shotgun trained on Colvert. They headed for Superior Street, a dirt road a little way north, used by teenagers and a lovers' lane.

The only witness to what happened next was Starkweather. He claimed that, as they got out of the car, Colvert made a grab for the gun. 'I got into a helluva fight and shooting gallery,' he said. 'He shot himself the first time. He had ahold of the gun from the front, and I cocked it and he was messing around and he jerked it and the thing went off.' Colvert was hit and fell, but he was not dead. He tried to stand up. Starkweather reloaded the shotgun. He pressed the barrel to Colvert's head and pulled the trigger. 'He didn't get up any more.'

Although Starkweather had been nervous before, the killing filled him with a feeling of serenity he had not experienced since childhood. He felt free, above the law. The robbery had culled him just $108. Five months later, on 24 April 1958, Robert Colvert's widow Charlotte gave birth to a daughter.

When Starkweather picked up Caril later that day, he told her about the robbery, but claimed that an unnamed accomplice had done the shooting. That evening he threw the shotgun in a creek. A few days later he fished it out, cleaned it and put the gun back in Sonny's garage. It had not even been missed.

During the police investigation, several of the other service station attendants mentioned Starkweather's name, but no one came to visit him. He paid off his back rent, had his car resprayed black and spent ten dollars on second-hand clothes, paying in loose change. The owner of the store was suspicious and reported the matter to the police. But no effort was made to question him.

The fact that no one seemed even to suspect him of the robbery and murder gave Starkweather a great deal of satisfaction. It was his first taste of success. Until then he had always been the under-dog, picked on at school, hauling other people's garbage. Now he had showed that he could outwit authority. 'I learned something, something I already knowed. A man could make money without haul-ing other people's garbage.'

He stopped turning up for work and was fired. He spent his time going to the movies, reading comics, playing records, working on his car and practising shooting and knife-throwing. The money from the robbery did not last long. He got behind with the rent again and ended up sleeping in his car in a garage he rented. But it did not bother him. He knew he could get cash again as soon as he wanted. And the idea of killing again did not bother him one little bit.

On Sunday 19 January 1958 there was a terrible row. Caril was putting on weight and her family feared she was pregnant. When Starkweather turned up, Caril told him that she was sick of his wild ways and that she never wanted to see him again. He did not take her seriously. He had already arranged to go hunting jack-rabbits with Caril's stepfather, Marion Bartlett, two days later, and he figured that he would see her then.

On the morning of 21 January 1958 Starkweather helped his brother Rodney out on the garbage round, then went to check that his room was still padlocked. It was. His hunting rifle was inside and he had to borrow Rodney's, a cheap, single-shot, .22 bolt action rifle. He took some rugs he had scavanged from his garbage round with him to Belmont Avenue and gave them to Caril's mother, Velda, as a peace offering. Velda was not appeased. As Starkweather sat cleaning his brother's rifle in the living-room, she told him that her husband Marion was not going hunting with him and that he should leave and never come back. When he did not respond, according to Starkweather: 'She didn't say nothing. She just got up and slammed the shit out of me . . . in the face.' As Starkweather ran from the house, he left the rifle. A few minutes later, he returned to collect it. Caril's father was waiting. 'The old man started chewing me out. I said to hell with him and was going to walk out through the front room, and he helped me out. Kicked me right in the ass. My tail hurt for three days.'

But that was not the end of it. Starkweather walked down to the local grocery store and phoned the transport company where Marion Bartlett worked. He told them that Mr Bartlett was sick and would not be in for a few days. Then he drove his car over to a friend's house nearby, left it there and walked back to Belmont Avenue. Caril and her mother were still yelling their heads off when Starkweather turned up. Then Velda accused him of making her daughter pregnant. She began slapping him around the face again. This time he hit back, knocking her back a couple of steps. She let out a strange cry – 'a war cry,' Starkweather thought. Marion Bartlett came flying to the rescue. He picked

Starkweather up by the neck and dragged him towards the front door. But Starkweather was younger and stronger. He kicked the old man in the groin and wrestled him to the ground. Bartlett managed to slip from Starkweather's grasp and went to look for a weapon. Starkweather thought he had better do the same.

As Starkweather hurriedly slipped a .22 cartridge into his brother's hunting rifle, Marion Bartlett ran at him with a claw hammer. Starkweather fired, shooting the old man in the head. Velda Bartlett grabbed a kitchen knife and threatened to cut Starkweather's head off. Starkweather reloaded the rifle, but Caril grabbed it from him. She threatened her mother, saying she would blow her to hell. The old woman did not take her daughter's threat seriously and knocked her down. Starkweather grabbed the rifle back and shot the old woman in the face. He hit her with the butt of the gun as she fell, then hit her twice more.

Caril's two-and-a-half-year-old sister Betty Jean was screaming. Starkweather hit her with the rifle butt too. She screamed all the louder, so Starkweather picked up the kitchen knife and threw it at her. He said he aimed for the chest, but the knife pierced her neck, killing her. Caril then pointed out that her stepfather was still alive in the bedroom. Starkweather went through and finished Marion Bartlett off, stabbing him repeatedly in the throat.

The house fell quiet. Starkweather reloaded his gun and sat down to watch television. 'I don't even remember what was on,' he later told police. 'I just wanted some noise.' That evening he and Caril wrapped the bodies of her murdered family in rugs and bedclothes and dragged them out into the frozen backyard. They stuffed Velda's body into an outside toilet. Betty Jean's body was placed in a box on top of it. Marion Bartlett's corpse was hidden in a disused chicken coop.

Back in the house the two teenagers tidied up as best they could. They mopped up some of the blood and mess with rags and splashed perfume around to hide the smell. Then they went into the living-room to watch television together.

Caril later claimed that she had not been present during the slaughter of her family. She had come home to find Starkweather there with a gun and her family gone. She said that he had told her that he was planning a big bank robbery. Her parents had found out and the family had been taken hostage by the rest of the gang. He had only to make one phone call and they would be killed, unless she co-operated. Starkweather said that Caril had participated in the slaughter of her family, egging him on.

The young couple settled down together for what Starkweather would later describe as the best week of his life. They were alone together, with no one to push them around. Certainly he had no conscience troubling him. Later he confessed: 'Shooting people was, I guess, a kind of thrill.'

In Starkweather's eyes they were now living like kings. With money taken from Marion Bartlett's pockets he made the occasional run to the local grocery store to stock up on chewing gum, ice cream, potato chips and Pepsi Cola. Caril claimed that he tied her up when he went out. Starkweather denied it.

They lived, for the first time, as man and wife. The two of them played cards, watched television a lot and tended the family pets – two parakeets, a dog called Nig and a puppy called Kim which Starkweather had bought for Caril. Everything would have been idyllic except for the bodies in the backyard.

Visitors were warned off by a sign on the kitchen door saying: 'Stay away Every Body is sick with the Flue'. Brave souls who knocked were told by Caril that the family was sick and they were in quarantine, while Starkweather hid in a room off the hall with his rifle cocked.

Then on Saturday, 25 January Caril's sister Barbara came to visit with Bob von Busch and their new-born baby. Caril spotted her sister before she was halfway up the pathway. She called out that the whole family had the flu and that the doctor had said no one should come near the house. But Barbara, who was concerned that her mother had not been in touch, kept on coming. Fearing the game was up, Caril screamed: 'Go away! If you know what's best you'll go away so mother won't get hurt.'

Barbara stopped, turned around and went back to Bob's car. Something in her sister's voice scared her. Once the baby was safely home, Bob von Busch and Rodney Starkweather returned to the house to find out what was going on. Again, Caril sent them away. Her mother's life would be in danger if they did not go, she said.

They reported the matter to the police and a patrol car was sent out to Belmont Avenue that evening. Caril gave the officers the regular story about the family having the flu. She also mentioned that her family did not get on with Bob von Busch – that was why he had called the police. Noting that Caril was calm and controlled, the policemen left their inquiries at that.

After the police had left, Starkweather took his brother's rifle to the house of a mutual friend. He called Barbara von Busch to reassure her. He had bought some groceries for Caril's family, he said, and he left a message for Rodney, saying that he should go and pick up his gun at the friend's house. When Rodney went to collect his rifle, he noticed it was damaged. The butt plate had been knocked off.

The next day, Sunday, Starkweather's sister Laveta arrived at Belmont Avenue. She was not put off by the story of the flu. She was one of Caril's few friends and, when she would not go away, Caril pulled her close. Her brother was inside planning a bank robbery, Caril confided, and that was why she could not come in. Laveta went home and told her father what had happened. He did not believe a word of it. But next day he began to get concerned.

On Monday morning Velda's mother Pansy Street was also getting worried. She turned up at Belmont Avenue and shouted until Caril showed herself. When Mrs Street refused to believe the flu story, Caril reverted to the story about her mother being in danger. Mrs Street went straight to the police precinct. While she was there, Guy Starkweather phoned, relating the story Laveta had told him. The police sent a second squad car out to Belmont Avenue. When they knocked on the door, they got no answer. So they broke in. Charles Starkweather and Caril Fugate had already figured that the game was up. Caril had packed a bag with some clothes and a few family snapshots. Starkweather had wrapped his hunting knife, Marion Bartlett's shotgun, the barrel of which he had sawn down, and a .32 pistol he had found in the house in a blue blanket. And they slipped out of the house the back way. By the time the police turned up, everything was neat and tidy. With nothing to excite their suspicions, they took Pansy Street home and let the matter rest.

Bob von Busch and Rodney Starkweather were not so easily satisfied. At 4.30 p.m. they went over to Belmont Avenue to check the place out for themselves. Almost immediately they found the Bartletts' bodies. The hunt was now on, but the young lovers had several hours' start.

After picking up two spare tyres from the lock-up garage Starkweather rented in the wealthy part of town, the couple stopped at the Crest Service Station to fill up with petrol and buy maps. Then they turned south, out of Lincoln, on to the open highway. They headed out across the frozen farmlands of the Great Plains. They stopped at the small town of Bennet, where Starkweather bought some ammunition at a service station and they ate a couple of hamburgers. Starkweather often came to Bennet to spend time in the surrounding countryside. An old family friend, seventy-year-old August Meyer, would let him hunt on his land in return for half the kill.

Meyer lived two miles east of Bennet, down a dirt track. Starkweather thought they might be safe

there, for the night at least. But there had been a
six-inch fall of snow and the track was muddy.
Their car got stuck. Nearby was a derelict school-
house with a cyclone cellar, where the children
would have taken shelter from the tornadoes that
tore across the Great Plains every spring. Starkweather and Caril went down into the cellar to warm
up before traipsing up to Meyer's farm on foot,
ostensibly to ask the old man's assistance in shifting
the car. At the farmhouse Starkweather shot Meyer
and his dog. 'Caril got pissed off because we got
stuck,' he said. 'She said that we ought to go up
and blast the shit out of him because he did not
shovel the lane.' He also claimed that he had shot
Meyer in self-defence. After a heated argument the
old man, Starkweather said, went into the house to
get a coat, but came out on the porch firing a rifle.
'I felt a bullet go by my head,' he said. But Meyer's
gun had jammed after the first shot. 'Meyer started
running back in the house, and I shot him at almost
point-blank range with the sawn-off.' Caril said
that Starkweather had simply asked Meyer if he
could borrow some horses to drag the car out of
the mud, then shot the old man as he went into the
barn.

Starkweather dragged Meyer's body into the
wash-house and covered it with a blanket. The two
of them ransacked his house for money, food and
guns. Their total haul was less than a hundred
dollars. It included a pump-action .22 repeating
rifle, some socks, gloves, a shirt, a straw hat and
some jelly and biscuits. They took a brief nap before
trudging back to the car. After an hour or two of
digging they managed to shift it. But it slid off

the track into a ditch and Starkweather stripped the
reverse gear trying to back it out. Eventually they
were rescued by a farmer, a neighbour of Meyer's,
who towed the car out with his truck. Starkweather
insisted on giving the farmer two dollars for his
trouble.

They drove up towards Meyer's farmhouse,
where Starkweather planned to stay the night. But
fearing that the body had been found Caril insisted
they turn back. When they did, the car got stuck in
the mud again. It was already dark so they abandoned the car and headed back to the derelict
school to spend the night in the cyclone cellar. On
the way they were offered a lift by seventeen-year-
old Robert Jensen, the son of a local store-owner,
and his fiancée, sixteen-year-old Carol King. When
Starkweather explained his car trouble, Jensen
offered to take them to the nearest service station
where they could telephone for help. As they got in
the back seat, Jensen asked why they were carrying
guns. Starkweather had the .22 and Caril the sawn-
off shotgun. Starkweather insisted they were not
loaded.

Starkweather later claimed that, at this point, he
toyed with the idea of ringing the police and turning himself in. But when they reached the service
station, it was closed. On their brief acquaintance-
ship, Starkweather had already decided that these
two high-school kids were exactly the sort of people
he hated – clever, popular at school, conservative,
middle-class. Jensen was a football player. King
was a cheerleader, drum majorette and a member
of the school choir. They planned to get married
once they had graduated. It struck Starkweather

that if he turned himself in, Jensen would get the credit. He could not bear the thought of this chubby, all-American boy being fêted as a hero.

He put his gun to the back of Jensen's head and told him to hand over his wallet. Caril emptied it and handed the money to Starkweather, who then ordered Jensen to drive them back to Lincoln. After a couple of miles, he changed his mind and told him to drive back to the derelict school where they had been stuck earlier that day. He said he was going to leave Jensen and King there and take their car – a dark blue, souped-up 1950 Ford with white-wall tyres.

When they got there, Starkweather left Caril in the car, listening to the radio, while he marched his prisoners off at gunpoint. As they walked down the steps into the cellar, Starkweather shot Jensen from behind. Later he claimed that Jensen had tried to grab the gun but, when the body was found, there were six shots in the left ear. Starkweather made several conflicting statements about how King died. He was alone with her for fifteen minutes and claimed to have shot her when she started screaming. Later he claimed that Caril had killed her.

Carol King was killed with a single shot from behind. When their bodies were found the next day, Jensen was found lying on his stomach in a pool of blood at the bottom of the stairs. King was partly nude and lying on top of him. Her coat had been pulled over her head, her jeans and panties were round her ankles. And her back was scratched and streaked with mud as if she had been dragged across the floor. She had been stabbed viciously, several times, in the groin, The autopsy found internal damage to the vagina, cervix and rectum. It had been caused by a rigid, double-edged blade that could not have been Starkweather's hunting knife. But doctors found no semen and no indication of sexual assault. Starkweather at first said that he had raped King, but later admitted only to having been tempted to rape her and having pulled down her jeans. Caril, he insisted, had then murdered and mutilated King in a fit of jealousy.

Starkweather closed the heavy storm doors on the cellar and went back to Jensen's car. But it, too, was stuck in the mud. He and Caril managed to dig it out by about 10.30 p.m. Starkweather claimed that he was now determined to abandon the spree and give himself up to the police, but Caril talked him out of it. They headed back to Lincoln to see if the Bartletts' bodies had been discovered yet.

Squad cars lined Belmont Avenue and number 924 was crawling with policemen. Starkweather slowly drove by. He headed west out of Lincoln with the vague idea of finding refuge with his brother Leonard who lived in Washington State, over a thousand miles away. But after about three hours driving, before they had even crossed the state line out of Nebraska, they turned back and headed for Lincoln once more. Starkweather was tired, had a streaming cold and the car was not running too well. The idea was to rest up in one of the wealthy mansions in the country club area of town, steal a new car and make a run for it again the following night. Starkweather knew the area well. He had collected garbage there and deeply resented its affluent residents. It was 3.30 a.m. when they arrived back in Lincoln. They parked up in the secluded street and took a nap. When they awoke in the early morning they began cruising the streets, househunting for a suitable property. Starkweather pointed out several possibilities before they settled on the five-bedroomed mansion belonging to millionaire industrialist C. Lauer Ward. It was just down the street from the garage Starkweather rented.

Mr Ward was the forty-seven-year-old president of Lincoln's Capital Bridge Company and Capital Steel Company, and had gone to work before Starkweather rang the doorbell. The fifty-one-year-old maid, Lillian Fencl, answered the door. She had been with the Wards for twenty-six years and may have known Starkweather from this time as a garbage man in the area. Starkweather and Caril brandished their guns and forced their way into the house.

Mrs Ward, a forty-six-year-old graduate of the University of Nebraska who was active in community affairs, was the only other person at home. The Wards' fourteen-year-old son, Michael, was at boarding school in Connecticut. When Mrs Ward came downstairs, Starkweather ordered her to sit down at the table. Mrs Ward readily agreed to co-operate – the Bartlett murders were front-page news.

While Mrs Ward and Lillian Fencl got on with their household chores, Starkweather went wandering about the mansion's elegant rooms, amazed by their opulence. Before noon, he ordered Mrs Ward – not the maid – to serve him pancakes in the library, then petulantly changed his order to waffles.

While Starkweather was enjoying his late breakfast, twenty-five armed policemen were surrounding August Meyer's farm. Starkweather's abandoned car had been found nearby and the police were convinced the two fugitives were holed up there. A bulletin on the radio news said that they would be taken just as soon as the tear gas arrived. But when the gas cleared and the state troopers went in all they found was August Meyer's dead body. The bodies of Robert Jensen and Carol King were found soon after. Within the hour a hundred policemen were combing the frozen countryside.

Around 1 p.m. Starkweather allowed Mrs Ward to go upstairs to change. When he went to check on her, he claimed, she came out of her son's room with a .22-calibre pistol and took a shot at him. She missed and turned to run. Starkweather threw his hunting knife at her. It stuck in her back. He dragged the groaning woman into her bedroom and put her on the bed. The Wards' dog then began to worry him. He broke its neck with a blow from his rifle butt. Later, suspecting that Mrs Ward might try and make a phone call, he bound and gagged her and covered her with a sheet.

Later in the afternoon Starkweather called his father and asked him to tell Bob von Busch that he was going to kill him for coming between him and Caril. He also wrote a note, addressed to 'the law only', saying that he and Caril had intended to commit suicide after he had killed the Bartletts but

Bob von Busch and others prevented them by coming round to the house.

Around 6 p.m. Mr Ward's Chevrolet came up the drive. That afternoon he had been visiting the state governor, who was a personal friend. When Mr Ward came in through the kitchen door he was confronted by Starkweather brandishing a rifle. Ward made a grab for the gun. In the ensuing fight, the rifle fell down the stairs into the basement. Ward tumbled down after it, and Starkweather followed. Starkweather got to the gun first, and Ward turned and ran back up the stairs. Starkweather shot him in the back. Despite his wounds, Ward kept going. He ran through the kitchen and the living-room and was opening the front door when Starkweather caught up with him. He shot Ward again, this time in the side of the head. 'I asked him if he was all right,' Starkweather said later, 'but he did not answer.' Ward was dead.

Starkweather took the maid upstairs, took ten dollars from her and tied her up. He left Caril to watch her, while he took seven dollars from Mrs Ward and tried to dye his hair black with shoe polish. Caril packed some clothes while Starkweather loaded up Mrs Ward's blue Packard with tins of food he found in the kitchen. As evening fell they drove down Belmont Avenue one last time, then headed west out of Lincoln on Highway 34.

Next morning a relative of Lauer Ward went to his house to find out why he had not shown up at work. He found Ward shot and stabbed just inside the front door. The two women were dead too. Both had been stabbed repeatedly, with the same double-edged blade that had been used to mutilate Carol

King. The knife was never found. Starkweather maintained that the two women had been alive when he left them. But Caril said later that Starkweather had admitted to her that he had killed Mrs Ward with a kitchen knife and that, after he had tied Lillian Fencl up and stabbed her, she screamed. So he put a pillow over her face and kept on stabbing her every time she hollered.

News of the killings spread quickly. A grinning picture of Starkweather and Caril was on the front page of the evening paper. Now nine were dead and Starkweather was still in the area. People in Bennet and Lincoln barricaded themselves in their houses. Gun stores were packed. People were buying anything that would shoot. One shop reported selling over forty guns in two hours as parents armed themselves to escort their children to school. Lincoln's mayor posted a $1,000 reward for Starkweather's capture. Soon a hundred-strong posse gathered outside the sheriff's department – though some of its members were not entirely sober. The governor called out the National Guard. Soldiers cruised in jeeps with machine guns mounted on them. The city was sealed off and searched block by block. And an aircraft circled the city, looking for the blue Packard Starkweather had stolen. A car answering the description was found and searched. It belonged to a prominent local lawyer.

Mrs Ward's Packard was long gone. The fugitives pressed on westwards throughout the night. They claimed that, as they went, they wrote notes, boasting of what they had done, and tossed them out of the window. None was ever found.

In the small hours of morning Starkweather fell asleep at the wheel and only just managed to keep the car out of a drainage ditch at the side of the road. He persuaded Caril that having sex was the only thing that would wake him up enough to keep driving. It did not work. Ten minutes later he pulled off the road again to sleep.

At first light they set off again. At around 9 a.m. they crossed the state line into Wyoming and found themselves in the Badlands – an area scarred by ravines that provided a safe haven for the outlaws of the Wild West. At midday they stopped in the small town of Douglas where they filled the car with petrol and bought Pepsi and candy bars to keep themselves going. It was there that they heard on the radio that the Wards' bodies had been found and police were looking for Mrs Ward's Packard. Starkweather decided to look for another car.

About twelve miles beyond Douglas, Starkweather saw a Buick parked off the highway. In it, Merle Collison, a thirty-seven-year-old shoe salesman, was asleep. Married with two children, he was on his way home from a sales trip to Grand Falls, Montana. Starkweather woke Collison and told him they were going to swap cars. Collison left the door locked and ignored him. Starkweather got the .22 pump-action rifle from the Packard and shot at Collison twice through the window of the car. Collison agreed to the trade and opened the door. But Starkweather coldbloodedly blasted him seven times – in the nose, cheek, neck, chest, left arm, right wrist and left leg. The fugitives transferred their belongings – and their booty – into Collison's Buick. With Collison still jammed in the front seat and Caril in the back, Starkweather tried to drive off. But the handbrake was stuck fast. Caril said Starkweather turned to Collison's corpse for help. 'Man, are you dead?' Starkweather asked when there was no reply. While Starkweather struggled with the handbrake, Joe Sprinkle, a twenty-nine-year-old geologist, drove by. Seeing Collison slumped in the front seat of the Buick, he thought there had been some sort of accident. He stopped and walked back to the Buick. 'Can I help?' he asked. Starkweather stuck the rifle in his face and explained that he could. 'Raise your hands. Help me release the emergency brake or I'll kill you,' Starkweather snarled. It was then that Sprinkle noticed the bullet wounds in Collison's dead body. Instinctively he grabbed for the gun. Sprinkle knew that if he did not get the gun away from Starkweather he was a dead man. As the two men grappled in a life-or-death struggle in the middle of the highway, Wyoming Deputy Sheriff William Romer drove by. He pulled up about twenty-five yards down the road. Caril got out of the Buick and ran down to the patrol car. 'Take me to the police,' she said, pointing at Starkweather. 'He just killed a man.'

Sensing the danger, Starkweather spun round, letting go of the gun. Sprinkle lost his balance and fell back into a shallow ditch. Abandoning the Buick, Starkweather ran back to the Packard and roared off back towards Douglas. The deputy put out an all points bulletin and, with Caril on board, gave chase. A few miles down the road he was joined by another police car. In it were County Sheriff Earl Heflin and Douglas Chief of Police

Robert Ainslie. With the two police cars in hot pursuit Starkweather pushed his speed up to a hundred mph. When he hit Douglas, the traffic slowed him and Heflin got off a couple of pot shots at his tyres with his hand-gun. For a moment, Ainslie got close enough to lock bumpers, but the bumper tore loose as Starkweather jumped a red light and overtook a lorry on the inside. As he cleared the town, Starkweather put his foot down on the gas pedal again and his speed climbed towards 120 mph. Heflin got out his rifle and started shooting at the Packard. One shot smashed the back window. Then Starkweather screeched to a halt. Bleeding copiously, he thought he had been shot. In fact, a piece of flying glass had nicked his ear.

The police pulled up behind him. Starkweather got out of the car and started to walk towards them. The police shouted for him to put his hands up. As the police shot at the road in front of him, Starkweather put his hands behind him and coolly tucked in his flapping shirt tail. Then he lay face down on the road and surrendered.

The police blustered about his arrest. 'He thought he was bleeding to death. That's why he stopped. That's the kind of yellow son of a bitch he is,' the arresting officer told reporters. However, in the public's mind, Starkweather was already a new kind of brooding anti-hero. When the prisoners were taken to the state penitentiary they were met by a crowd of newsmen, photographers and newsreel cameramen. Caril, with her head covered by a scarf, played up to the cameras. But it was Starkweather, ignoring the media, who got all the attention. Wearing tight jeans, a black motorcycle jacket, cowboy boots with a butterfly design on the toe, handcuffed, with a cigarette dangling from his lips, he was the perfect young rebel killer. America had already been rocked by the image of the wayward teenager. They had seen a brooding James Dean in *Rebel Without a Cause* and a cocky and threatening Marlon Brando as the motorcycle gang leader in *The Wild One*. Elvis Presley had just burst on the scene with wild pelvic gyrations that scared the pants off conservative middle America. But here, in the person of Charles Starkweather, was the embodiment of their fears. Here was the ultimate juvenile delinquent. Local Nebraskan newspaper the *Omaha World Herald* captured the mood. In a vitriolic leader it declared: 'The Starkweather story brought back to mind a thousand others. The sideburns, the tight blue jeans, the black leather jacket have become almost the uniform for juvenile hoodlums. And the snarling contempt for discipline, the blazing hate for restraint, have become a familiar refrain in police stations and juvenile courts.' FBI chief J. Edgar Hoover promised a nationwide crackdown on juvenile crime.

At first Caril told police that she had been Starkweather's captive and had had no part in the murders. She had only gone along with him because her family were held hostage. But later she undermined her story by saying that she had witnessed their murders. Then she became incoherent and had to be sedated.

Starkweather remained unrepentant. In a note to his parents, ostensibly apologising for the trouble he had caused them, he wrote: 'I'm not real sorry for what I did cause for the first time me and Caril have more fun, she helped me a lot, but if she comes back don't hate her she had not a thing to do with the killing all we wanted to do was get out of town.' He later compared himself to a soldier, killing only when he had to, to achieve an objective.

He quickly confessed to all the murders – except those of Clara Ward and her maid Lillian Fencl. As far as he knew, he maintained, they were alive when he left the house. Despite being charged with the murder of Merle Collison in Wyoming, Starkweather was quickly extradited back to Nebraska. He was ridiculed for being afraid of flying when he refused to go back to Lincoln by plane. In fact he thought that travelling by car he would stand a better chance of escaping.

Caril Fugate and Charles Starkweather were both charged with murder. They pleaded not guilty and were to be tried separately. Starkweather's lawyer tried to get him to enter an insanity plea. Starkweather refused. 'Nobody remembers a crazy man,' he said, insisting that all the killings had been in self-defence.

Starkweather's trial for the murder of seventeen-year-old high-school student Robert Jensen began on 5 May 1958. The prosecution quickly established that the six bullets in Jensen's head had all be shot from behind, demolishing Starkweather's self-defence argument. Throughout the prosecution case Starkweather acted cool, chewing gum and rocking back on his chair. The only time he showed any emotion was when an ex-employer said that Starkweather was the dumbest man who ever worked for him. Starkweather went crazy and had to be restrained.

The ex-employer's testimony was part of the defence lawyer's strategy to show his client was mentally incompetent. In fact, Starkweather had an above-average IQ. The defence attorney also read out some of Starkweather's confessions, hoping to show that his state of mind was abnormal and confused.

When Starkweather took the stand, he was asked why he was mad at Caril when they were at the derelict school. He replied that it was because of what she had done.

'What did she do?' he was asked.

'Shot Carol King,' said Starkweather.

This was not the first time that Starkweather accused Caril of killing Carol King. During his time on remand he had begun to fall out of love with her. He had also accused her of finishing off Merle Collison when his gun jammed.

Three psychiatrists appeared for the defence. They claimed that Starkweather had a diseased mind. But, under cross examination, they admitted that this did not amount to a recognised mental illness and none of them would be prepared to have Starkweather certified insane. Prosecution psychiatrists agreed that Starkweather had an anti-social personality disorder, but was legally sane. The jury also agreed. They returned a guilty verdict and recommended the electric chair.

During his court appearance, Starkweather become a TV celebrity, appearing on the news each night. Many teenagers identified with the cool and unrepentant Starkweather. Fan mail flooded in, though some urged him to turn to God. Admirers overlooked the fact that one of his first victims was Caril's stepsister, a two-and-a-half-year-old child.

Five months later Caril Fugate became the youngest woman ever to be tried for first-degree murder in the US. She was tried for being an accomplice in Jensen's murder. Although there was no suggestion that she had actually pulled the trigger, her admission that she had taken Jensen's wallet meant that this case would be easier to prove than one where it was simply her word against Starkweather's.

Starkweather himself was the prosecution's star witness. Taking the stand, he told the jury that he no longer loved Caril and did not care if she lived or died. At one time he was even reported as having said: 'If I fry in the electric chair, then Caril should be sitting on my lap.'

He said that she had known he was involved in the murder of the filling-station attendant Robert Colvert and that she had been present when he had killed her family. She had gone with him willingly and had even expressed a desire to be shot down with him when the denouement came.

Caril's attorney believed that she was innocent, but could not shake Starkweather's story, which was partially corroborated by witnesses to their spree and early statements to the police. She was found guilty and sentenced to life imprisonment.

She continued to protest her innocence, but settled in to become a model prisoner at the state women's reformatory at York, Nebraska. In 1972 she was the subject of a documentary called *Growing up in Prison* and in 1976 was released on parole. In 1983 she appeared on TV to protest her innocence once more and took a lie detector test on camera. It indicated that she was telling the truth. However, a public opinion poll in Nebraska showed that most people did not believe her.

On death row Starkweather spent his time writing. He also talked for more than eighty hours to James Melvin Reinhardt, professor of criminology at the University of Nebraska, explaining why he had taken to crime. His main motive was to take 'general revenge upon the world and its human race'.

'The people I murdered had murdered me,' he said. 'They murdered me slow, like. I was better to them. I killed them in a hurry.'

Poverty was another reason. 'They had me numbered for the bottom,' he said. He blamed the world and was sure that other people hated him 'because I was poor and had to live in a goddamned shack'. But there was a way out of this class trap – 'all dead people are on the same level,' he said.

He saw his murderous spree as the only way out of a life of drudgery. 'Better to be left to rot on some high hill, and be remembered,' he wrote, 'than to be buried alive in some stinking place.'

Now Starkweather had everything he wanted. He was going to die – but he was famous. Nothing gave him more pleasure than to see his name in the papers.

Professor Reinhardt published *The Murderous Trail of Charles Starkweather*, which alleged that Starkweather was paranoid and that this problem was self-inflicted. Starkweather's own account was published in *Parade* magazine under the title 'Rebellion'. The piece was heavily cut and ended up as a homily to wayward youth, advising commitment to God, regular church-going, and respect for authority. 'If I had followed these simple rules, as I was advised to many times, I would not be where I am today,' it concluded.

In fact, Starkweather did have something of a change of heart in prison. His murderous rampage seemed to have quenched his hatred. A gentler side took over. One of his prison guards said: 'If somebody had just paid attention to Charlie, bragged on his drawing and writing, all of this might not have happened.'

At the parole board Starkweather spoke of his remorse and his new-found Christian faith. It did no good. The execution was scheduled for 22 May 1959. He wrote to his father, talking of repentance and his hopes of staying alive. The execution was delayed by a federal judge, then rescheduled for 25 June.

When the prison guards came for him, he asked: 'What's your hurry?' Then, in a new shirt and jeans, he swaggered ahead of them to the electric chair with his hands in his pockets. Outside, gangs of teenagers cruised the streets, playing rock 'n' roll on their car radios. Fifteen years later the Starkweather story was retold in the 1974 cult movie *Badlands*, starring Martin Sheen and Cissy Spacek.

5

Good Boys Turn Bad

Starkweather became a powerful symbol of youth rebellion. An ill-educated midwest teenager had taken the absence of meaning in post-war life, identified by the French existentialists, and mixed it with the ethos of Jack Kerouac, whose seminal novel about drifting across America, *On the Road*, was a bestseller in the 1950s. He had added the well-honed rebel pose of Dean and Brando, the gun-laden outlaw myths of the Old West and given the whole thing a rock'n'roll soundtrack.

Eight years after Starkweather was executed, two other teenagers went on a eerily similar rampage. On 17 August 1967 stocky six-footer Thomas Eugene Braun and his smaller, leaner best friend Leonard Maine, both eighteen, began a murder spree that spread across three states. Tom Braun left his job as a gas-station attendant in the service depot at Ritzville, Washington that evening and went to pick up Maine. Braun was driving a battered old black German-made Borgward open-top sedan.

'Are you still driving that old boneshaker?' said Maine.

'Take your last look,' Braun said. 'We are going to have ourselves a new car.'

'How come?' Maine asked.

'You'll see,' said Braun. He had stashed in the car a Frontier Colt single-action .22 pistol, an automatic .22 Luger and several hundred rounds of ammunition.

The two youths headed for Seattle, Washington's state capital, where they decided to stay for the night. But the landlady of the rooming-house they stopped at took fright when one of them pointed a gun at her. She screamed and fled into an adjoining room. The two teenagers took off at speed. They headed back out of the city and drove aimlessly around the local countryside.

By morning they were driving down Route 202 outside Redmond, Washington, when they saw an attractive twenty-two-year-old woman driving a maroon Skylark up ahead. Braun stepped on the gas. Pulling alongside, the two boys signalled frantically, indicating that something was wrong with one of her wheels. The driver was newlywed Mrs Deanna Buse. She was returning from her job to her mother's house. When she saw the youths' frantic gestures, she pulled to a halt on the grassy verge. The two boys pulled their car up in front of her. Mrs Buse got out of her car and examined each of the wheels in turn. There was nothing wrong with them. She turned to the boys to ask for an explanation and found a gun pointing at her head.

Braun ordered her back into her Skylark. He got in with her, keeping the gun trained on her. Maine took the wheel of Braun's Borgward and the two cars drove off slowly down the highway. At the next junction they turned off and wound through a series of side roads until they reached a dirt track which came to a dead end in the woods near Echo Lake.

The two cars stopped and Braun forced Mrs Buse at gunpoint into the woods. Maine waited by the cars. A little later he heard five shots. A few days later Mrs Buse's naked body was discovered, her clothes piled neatly beside her. She had been forced to strip at gunpoint, but she had not been raped and no semen was found near the corpse.

Braun and Maine drove the two cars back to Seattle, where they abandoned Braun's Borgward in a sidestreet. In Mrs Buse's Skylark they drove down to Fife, Washington, twenty-two miles south of Seattle, to visit Maine's uncle who lived there. He put them up for the night. During their stay, they asked the quickest way to Portland Oregon.

Next morning the two teenagers crossed the state line into Oregon. Again they tried to rent a room, but the motel manager, alerted by their dishevelled appearance, demanded identification and quizzed the boys about their car registration. They sped off.

Sports fisherman Samuel Ledgerwood was returning home in his green late-model Buick with an impressive day's catch when he spotted two youths changing a tyre on their car. He stopped to give them a hand. Braun shot him through the head, twice, killing him instantly.

The two youths bundled their gear into Ledgerman's Buick and put a couple of slugs through the petrol tank of Mrs Buse's Skylark, setting it on fire. They headed south, following the Pacific coast highway until they reached northern California. On deserted, mountainous Route 120 they spotted two young hitchhikers, Timothy Luce and his girlfriend, student Susan Bartolomei. Both were seventeen. They were both at the same teacher training college and were on a hitchhiking vacation together.

Braun shot Luce out of hand and ran over his chest with the car to make sure he was dead. Bartolomei was then raped repeatedly before she, too, was shot. But she did not die immediately. At six o'clock the next morning she was found lying on the road, still alive. Fatally injured, she was still able to give a description of her assailants. They were two eighteen-year-olds who had said they were from Oklahoma. They called each other 'John' and 'Mike'. Before Bartolomei died from her injuries about a week later, she gave the police a detailed description of their appearance and of their car. She said it was a Buick, which tied the attack to the murder of Ledgerwood, and the burnt-out Skylark by Ledgerwood's body tied that murder to the slaying of Mrs Buse.

Police throughout Oregon, California and Washington started to be on the lookout for Ledgerwood's Buick. It was spotted outside a small hotel in Jamestown, California by a local patrolman. He called in back-up.

Braun and Maine were registered in the hotel under the names John and Mike Ford. Maine was surprised in his room and gave up without a fight. As the police broke down the door of Braun's room, Braun grabbed for a gun. But a policeman leapt on him and pinned him to the floor before he could let off a shot.

Braun and Maine protested their innocence. Even

in the face of all the evidence they pleaded not guilty. In court they sat emotionless while still photographs and even a movie film of their victims were shown. Only when the case was proved did they admit their guilt. Braun was sentenced to death, Maine to life imprisonment. Neither had given police investigators, psychologists or researchers any clue to the motive behind their senseless crimes.

Sixteen-year-old Michael Clark did not tell why he suddenly went on a killing spree in 1965 either – because, by the end of it, he was dead. Until the moment he first squeezed the trigger, Michael Clark had been the perfect son. On the morning of 8 May 1965, for example, he put on his starched, neatly pressed whites and went to a Sea Scout inspection. In the afternoon the gangling, soft-spoken youth went shopping with his mother and scrubbed the bathroom floors in the house. That evening he tended the pigeon with a broken wing that he was nursing back to health. Then suddenly, without warning or permission, he took the family's Cadillac and drove off to a rendezvous with mass murder.

Concerned that Michael had taken the car, Michael's mother called her husband, Forrest Clark, who was working late at the Clark Tank and Manufacturing Company, in Long Beach, California. Mr Clark sped home to find that his gas-station credit card was also missing. Michael had only a provisional driving licence and, after an hour, when he had not come home, the Clarks called the police. Then, with their younger son Ronnie, they sat down in the spotless living-room of their colonial house and waited.

Michael was driving north on the freeway. Bypassing downtown Los Angeles, he continued driving up the coast all night. In the car beside him was his father's Swedish Mauser deer rifle with a four-power telescopic sight and several dozen armour-piercing bullets.

Sometime before dawn he was on Route 101 near Santa Maria when he collided with the crash barrier. He abandoned the car, crawled through a gap in the barbed wire fence that bordered the highway and climbed the hill at the side of the road. At the top he lay prone in the dewy, three-foot-high wild oat grass. From there he had a commanding view over the four-lane highway below. The place where he had decided to play 'king of the hill' was the exact spot where Mexican bandito Solomon Pico had fired on passing stage-coaches a century before.

At around 6 a.m. Michael Clark fired his first shot at a driver of one of the cars below – and missed. When the driver stopped to see what was happening a second bullet hit his front fender. He sped off to alert the police.

Shortly after, William Reida was driving down that section of Route 101. His wife and four small children were in the car. They were on their way back from a funeral in Portland. At a few minutes past six Reida drove into Clark's sights. Two bullets were fired in rapid succession, hitting both Reida and his five-year-old son Kevin in the neck. Their car veered off the road and pulled to a halt on the hard shoulder. Mrs Reida leapt from the car and waved down passing motorists. Two stopped, but both drivers were shot dead before they could get out. Mrs Reida stumbled back to her car and, though a non-driver, managed the next five miles to a highway patrol station. Her husband survived. Her son did not.

Back at the hill, Michael Clark's sniper spree was in full swing. He shot at anything that passed. Two more passing motorists were hit, though not fatally, and six more were wounded by flying glass. The police arrived and tried to encircle the hill. But they could not locate the sniper properly as he slithered around the hill in the long grass. Keeping up a constant stream of fire, he hit one officer in the arm.

For over two hours the sniper managed to hold them off. Then around 8.30 a.m., as police and armed civilians closed in, he stood up, waved, and shouted: 'Come and get me.' Then he turned the muzzle of his rifle to his own forehead and blew his brains out.

The Clarks had sat up all night waiting for news of Michael. It came an hour later – at exactly the time Michael Clark would normally have been going into his Sunday school class at the Fifth Christian Science Church a few blocks from home. At 9.30 a.m. that Sunday morning Long Beach Police Department called to say that their model son had killed three people, injured ten and, finally, taken his own young life. The Clarks were aghast. 'He was always full of love,' Michael's mother said. 'We always tried to protect him.'

No one could make out why a young boy, who had never been in trouble in his life, should suddenly turn into a spree killer. Only local psychiatrist Edward Stainbrook, of the University of Southern

California School of Medicine, would hazard a guess. 'If feelings dammed up in the heart don't come out the mouth,' he said, 'they will be acted out in some way.'

1965 was still an age of innocence and people believed that motiveless multiple murders like Unruh's, Starkweather's and Clark's were isolated incidents. But a year later, just a month before Charles Whitman climbed Austin Tower, a mass murder in Chicago started an epidemic. Eight student nurses in Chicago were brutally slain in a single night. The senseless spree shocked America. It even sickened the man who had done it. The morning after the hideous crime the killer woke up to hear a radio report of the multiple slaying. He had no idea that he had committed it.

In 1966 there was a long hot summer in Chicago, and the city exploded in a full-scale race riot. On 12 July 1966 the police had arrested a black youth who had turned on a fire hydrant so the local children could play in its cool spray. Soon the West Side of Chicago was up in arms. Hundreds of stores were looted. The National Guard was called in. Two blacks were killed by stray sniper fire. The police arrested over 200 people. But the violence only subsided after Martin Luther King had stepped in and the authorities conceded that sprinklers would be fitted to some hydrants.

But on the evening of 13 July the disturbances were still at their height. The authorities were praying for a break in the weather to cool things off. Thunder clouds began rolling in off Lake Michigan, and the temperature dropped a few degrees. But the humidity climbed. In the peaceful suburb of Jeffery Manor the houses had their windows thrown open to catch any breeze in the sultry night air.

On East 100th Street, in the block between Crandon Avenue and Luella, there were six identical two-storey town houses. Three of them belonged to the local hospital. They were used as hostels for student nurses. In the house at 2319 East 100th Street, three of the eight occupants were qualified nurses from the Philippines who had come to Chicago for post-graduate studies. One of them, Corazon Amurao, had just settled down to sleep in the upstairs front room she shared with Merlita Gargullo when she heard four soft knocks on the bedroom door. It was 11 p.m.

Thinking it was one of the other nurses, Corazon unlocked the door. A young man pushed his way into the room. He smelt strongly of alcohol and swayed slightly. His eyes were soft and gentle, but in his hand there was a gun.

'I am not going to hurt you,' he assured her. 'I need your money to go to New Orleans.'

The six nurses who were in the house at the time were ushered into the master bedroom at the back at gunpoint. The gunman made them sit on the floor in the darkened room and asked them for their money. One by one they were sent to get it. The haul came to less than a hundred dollars. At 11.30 p.m. Gloria Davy, another of the nurses resident in the house, returned from a date. Unsuspecting, she walked into the back bedroom to be confronted by the gunman. He took two dollars from her and she was made to join the others. The gunman then cut a bed-sheet into strips with a small pocket knife and, again insisting that he had no intention of harming anyone, tied all the women up.

Instead of leaving, the gunman sat down on the floor with the nurses. For a while he chatted to them amiably, though he tapped the barrel of his gun nervously on the floor and frequently peered anxiously out of the window. Then he untied the ankles of one of the girls, twenty-year-old Pam Wilkening from Lansing, Illinois and led her out of the room. The six girls left behind let out a sigh of relief. They quickly discussed what to do. The American nurses counselled caution. The man was probably just a burglar. It was best to go along with him and not to antagonise him. From outside the room there was silence.

The last of the eight nurses who lived in the house, twenty-one-year-old Suzanne Farris, got home about midnight. With her was the sister of her fiancé, another student nurse, Mary Ann Jordan. When the two nurses came into the master bedroom, the gunman appeared behind them. He ordered them out at gunpoint. There was a commotion outside and the women in the bedroom heard muffled shouts. Silence followed, then they heard water running in the bathroom.

About twenty minutes later the gunman came back. This time he picked twenty-four-year-old former Sunday-school teacher Nina Schmale. By now the young women were terrified. The intruder, they figured, was a rapist. They tried to hide. Corazon Amurao rolled across the floor and managed to wriggle under a bed.

When the gunman came back again he took Merlita Gargullo – a twenty-two-year-old Filipina from Santa Cruz who had been in Chicago less than a month – and twenty-three-year-old Valentina Pasion from Jones City in the Philippines who was a devoted Catholic. From her hiding place under the bed, Corazon Amurao heard both girls sigh or grunt and Merlita Gargullo call out 'It hurts' in her native tongue.

After a long period of silence the man returned to the master bedroom once more. He bent down and picked up twenty-year-old Patricia Matusek, the daughter of a liquor salesman. 'Will you please untie my ankles first?' she asked as he carried her away. By this time only Corazon Amurao and twenty-two-year-old Gloria Davy, daughter of a steel mill worker from Dyer, Indiana were left.

After another twenty-five minutes the gunman came back once again. From her vantage point under the bed Corazon Amurao saw him remove Gloria Davy's jeans. He then unzipped his own black trousers and climbed on top of her. Corazon looked away, but the creaking of the bedsprings left her in no doubt about what was going on. At one point she heard the intruder ask, in his disconcertingly gentle voice: 'Will you please put your legs around my back?'

When the bed springs eventually fell silent, Corazon Amurao found a safer hiding place under the other bed, where she was hidden by the bedclothes. Some forty-five minutes later she heard footsteps. They were coming towards the bedroom. She lay absolutely still and held her breath. The man came in and switched on the light and looked around.

There were eight beds in the house, and eight girls had been taken from the master bedroom. He did not know that one of the student nurses, Mary Ann Jordan, did not live there. Apparently satisfied, he switched off the light and went out.

Corazon Amurao lay still in her cramped hiding place, afraid to move or make a sound. There was complete silence in the house until 5 a.m., when an alarm clock went off in one of the other bedrooms. Normally the girls left the house at 6.30 a.m. to start their hospital shifts.

At around 6 a.m. Corazon Amurao plucked up the courage to squeeze out from under the bed. She managed to wriggle out of the strips of sheet that bound her hands and feet. Fearfully she crept out of the master bedroom and down the landing to her own bedroom. There she found the bodies of Pamela Wilkening, Mary Ann Jordan and Suzanne Farris. Blood was everywhere.

Still too frightened to go downstairs in case the killer was still there, she smashed the screen on the bedroom window and crawled out on to the two-foot-wide ledge outside. She crouched there, ten foot about the ground, and started screaming uncontrollably and shouting: 'Help me, help me. Everybody is dead. I am the only one alive.'

Robert Hill, who was out walking his dog, heard her cries. So did Betty Windmiller, a neighbour, who had come out to see what all the noise was. They called the police.

Patrolman Daniel Kelly was the first policeman on the scene. He found the rear door swinging open. One panel had been shoved in. Inside, in the living-room, he found the body of a young woman, naked, with a piece of cloth tied tightly around her neck. He turned her over. It was Gloria Davy. He recognised her immediately. Gloria's sister, Charlene Davy, had once been his girlfriend.

He found seven more dead bodies upstairs. In the bathroom was Patricia Matusek. After being kicked in the stomach she had been strangled. Nina Schmale was found on one of the beds in the westernmost of the two front bedrooms. Valentina Pasion and Merlita Gargullo were found in a heap on the floor. They had been stabbed. Schmale and Gargullo had been strangled.

Suzanne Farris and Mary Ann Jordan had also been stabbed several times, then strangled. They were lying on the floor of the other front bedroom. Suzanne Farris must have put up some sort of a fight. She had been stabbed eighteen times. Pamela Wilkening had been stabbed just once, in the breast, then strangled with a piece of sheet wound around her neck.

Even the Cook County coroner Andrew Toman was shocked by what he saw. 'There has never been anything like it that I have heard of,' he told the reporters who flocked to the house. 'It is the crime of the century. It is the worst crime I have ever seen.' And this was in Chicago, the home of Al Capone and organised crime. But even the infamous St Valentine's Day Massacre in 1929 had only claimed the lives of six people. In East Street, eight young nurses lay dead. That year there were only seventy-two murders, all told, in Chicago.

At 11 a.m. a drifter named Richard Speck woke up in his room at the Shipyard Inn, a sleazy hotel on Chicago's South Side. He was fully clothed, still in the dark shirt and trousers he had worn the day before. When he got up to splash his face with water, he noticed a blood stain on his right hand, though his clothes were clean. He did not know how it had got there. He assumed he had cut himself. He also found that he had a gun. He had no idea how he had come by it.

Richard Franklin Speck had been born on 6 December 1947 in Kirkwood, Illinois. He was the seventh of eight children, three boys and five girls. His father, Benjamin Speck, a potter, died in 1947. But in 1950 his mother Mary married again. The two youngest children took the name of their stepfather, an insurance salesman called Lindberg, and the four of them moved to Dallas, Texas.

Lindberg was a heavy drinker. Domestic rows often ended up in fist fights and Richard hated him. To everyone's relief, Lindberg walked out on his wife and stepchildren while Richard was still a teenager. But already the problems with his home life were putting him behind at school. 'He seemed sort of lost,' one of his junior high-school teachers reported. 'It didn't seem like he knew what was going on. I wasn't able to teach him anything. I don't think I ever saw him smile. No one could get through to him. He was a loner. He seemed to be in a fog, sort of sulky. He did not have any friends in class.'

He had been drinking from the age of twelve and began to take drugs. 'When I got to seventeen,' he later confessed, 'I just went wild.' Soon he was getting in trouble with the police. His early arrests were mainly for drunkenness and brawling.

Leaving school with no diploma and a developing police record, he seemed set for a lifetime of dead-end jobs. He worked as a truck driver, a carpenter, a labourer and a dustman. He also graduated into trespass and petty burglary. In 1962 he reverted to the name Speck and married fifteen-year-old Shirley Malone. On 2 July 1962 Shirley had a daughter named Robbie. Speck was fond of Robbie and treated her well, although he claimed that the child was not his.

The following year Speck was sentenced to three years in prison for forgery after signing another man's name to cash a stolen pay cheque. He was sent to Huntsville Penitentiary where the discipline was tough. The able-bodied prisoners spent all summer picking cotton on the prison farm. Speck ended up in hospital, suffering from sunstroke.

In 1965 he was released from prison and returned to his wife. Soon they were fighting all the time and in January 1966 Shirley divorced him. Speck hit the bottle hard and became involved in a series of drunken brawls. He was arrested but skipped bail. He found work on a boat on Lake Superior, but after a week he had appendicitis. While convalescing, he dated a nurse, Judy Laakaniemi, who was impressed by his gentle manner. When he was better, Speck drifted on to Chicago to stay with his married sister, Martha Thornton, and her husband.

Arriving in late June, Speck set about searching for a job. But it was not to be easy. The city was sweltering, with temperatures soaring to over ninety degrees. Like many Chicagoans, Speck found a haven from the baking streets in the city's air-conditioned bars. Soon his pale, pock-marked face became a familiar sight in Chicago's shadier haunts. He started taking barbiturates too, but he would take any drug that was handed to him.

He moved out of his sister's and checked in to a series of seedy skid-row doss-houses. Every day, though, he would go to the seamen's union on East Street to see if there were any jobs going. Speck's plan was to work his passage to New Orleans. On Tuesday 12 July 1966 he was told that there was a job on an ore ship in Indiana. He quit his rented room and headed off, but when he arrived at the dock he was told that there had been a mix up. Someone else had got the job. Dejected, he returned to Chicago. He arrived penniless, left his bags at a petrol station across the road from 2319 East Street, just a few yards from the National Maritime Union at 2335, and took shelter in a half-finished house for the night.

The next day, though, his luck changed. He found a job on an ocean-going ship that was sailing the following Monday. Speck phoned his brother-in-law, borrowed twenty-five dollars and checked in to the Shipyard Inn, a sleazy hotel on Chicago's South Side. Later he went to play pool. A good player, he won some money. Things were looking up. He took six 'redbirds' – barbiturate tablets – and went for a walk by Lake Michigan.

At 3 p.m., still stoned, Speck returned to the local bars to continue his day-long drinking spree. He fell into conversation with three men who said they were sailors. Around 6 p.m. he left with them. In a discreet spot, the men produced a bottle of clear liquid and began injecting themselves. Speck neither knew nor cared what the clear liquid was. When it came to his turn, he tied off his arm and stuck the syringe into one of his bulging veins. He remembered nothing from that moment until the next morning.

Speck was a hardened drinker. There were plenty of black holes in his life, nights that were surrounded by an alcoholic haze and nights when he could remember nothing at all. So when he woke up on the morning of 14 July 1966 with no recollection of what had happened the night before, it did not worry him. He left his room and went downstairs to buy a bottle of cheap liquor. On the radio in the bar he heard a report about the murder of the eight nurses.

'I hope they catch the son of a bitch,' Speck said to the bartender. What the radio did not say was that the police were already closing in.

Once Corazon Amurao had been coaxed from the ledge, she had been taken to South Chicago Community Hospital, where she was sedated. However, she was still able to give a detailed account of what had happened the night before. By 8.30 a.m. the police had a full description of the suspect. Police artist Otis Rathel drew this up and a picture was circulated to the newspapers.

Forensic experts scouting the house found an abundance of clues. Fingerprints were lifted from the furniture, walls and doors. A sweat-soaked man's T-shirt was found in the living-room. Another was wrapped up in Gloria Davy's jeans.

A man answering the suspect's description had left his bags in the gas station across the road the night before the murders. He had told the attendant that he was looking for a job on a ship. The police checked with the seamen's union down the block.

They said that someone had called by looking to work his passage to New Orleans. His name was Speck.

The police then set a trap. They asked the branch office of the National Maritime Union to offer Speck a job on a ship bound for Louisiana. Speck phoned in around 3.10 that afternoon and was told that there was a job waiting for him. He said he would come down to the seamen's union. The call was traced to the Shipyard Inn, which was about a mile away. Police raced there, but when they arrived they were told Speck had left a few minutes after making the call.

The US Coast Guard found that they had a record of Speck. They sent a photograph of him to the police, who took it to the hospital. But Corazon Amurao had lapsed into a state of shock and her doctors refused to let the police show it to her.

Speck did not turn up at the Maritime Union. Instead he went bar-hopping with his friend Robert 'Red' Gerrald. In a bar called the Ebb Tide, the murder of the nurses came up in conversation. 'Whoever did it must have been a maniac,' said Speck.

Speck saw his own picture in the newspaper, but did not recognise it. Rathel, the police artist, had made the skin too smooth. Speck's face was pock-marked.

That evening Speck said he was heading off to check out some action. He wanted to get out of the area. All police leave had been cancelled and the South Side was swarming with cops. Speck still had an outstanding warrant in Texas. He jumped into a cab and headed for the North Side. There he hustled some bar-room pool, found himself a hooker and went with her to a cheap hotel.

The next morning, around 8.15 a.m., the hotel manager phoned the local precinct. The hooker told him that the man she had been with had a gun. The police arrived to find Speck still in bed. He insisted that the gun belonged to the prostitute. The cops confiscated it, and left it at that. The name Speck had still not been circulated as that of the murder suspect. As soon as the patrolman's report was filed, the police realised their mistake. They went rushing back, only to find that Speck had checked out fifteen minutes earlier.

After she had had a good night's sleep, the doctors decided that Corazon Amurao was well enough to be interviewed again. She picked Speck's picture out from a hundred photographs of convicted rapists. The police checked with the FBI. He had a rap sheet as long as your arm in Texas. By 7.30 p.m. the Chicago murder squad had a new description of Speck from the Texas police. It detailed Speck's tattoos. These included a snake coiled round a dagger on his right forearm, a skull in a pilot's helmet above his left elbow, a crude jailyard drawing of a penis on his left shin, and the words 'BORN TO RAISE HELL' emblazoned across his left arm. In jail in Texas he had tried to burn it off with a cigarette butt. That earned him thirty days solitary confinement for destroying state property. He had also tried to destroy tattoos that said 'R.L.' (Richard Lindberg) and 'Richard and Shirley'.

The FBI also supplied Speck's fingerprint card. By 4.30 a.m. the next morning the Chicago police labs were certain that they had found a match for three of the prints lifted from the house on East Street. Speck was definitely their man. That afternoon, at 2.40 p.m., Superintendent Orlando Wilson announced: 'The killer of the eight nurses from South Chicago Community Hospital on Thursday, July 14, 1966, has been named as Richard Speck, white male, twenty-four, a seaman. Latent fingerprints taken at the scene of the mass killings identified Speck as the killer.'

Speck was sitting in a bar when he heard his name on the radio. He was stunned. The police must have made some mistake. He thought of making a run for it, but could think of nowhere to go. Perhaps he should give himself up – but, even if he proved himself innocent, there was still the outstanding warrant from Texas. So, instead, he bought a bottle of cheap wine.

He realised that there was only one way out of his present predicament. He took a room in sleazy doss-house called the Starr Hotel, lay on the bed and drank the wine. And with the broken bottle he hacked open his wrists.

Around midnight Speck's courage failed him. Weakly he called out to anyone who might hear: 'Come and see me. You got to come and see me. I done something bad.'

The man in the next room, George Gregorich, a drifter, heard him, but did not care. 'Leave me alone,' he yelled back.

Speck shouted out again. But Gregorich would take no notice. He yelled back: 'You're a hillbilly, you just want to get at me. I don't trust no hillbilly.'

Speck dragged himself to his feet, staggered to

Gregorich's door and started pounding and kicking it. Another resident spotted Speck standing there with blood streaming from his wrists. He told the desk clerk, who called the police.

Suicides are ten-a-penny in skid-row flop-houses like the Starr Hotel, where Speck was registered as B. Brian. That was the name the cops gave at the Cook County Hospital, little realising that the man they had just delivered to the emergency room was the subject of a citywide manhunt.

Dr LeRoy Smith, the duty intern, thought he recognised the attempted suicide he examined at 12.30 a.m. And when he cleaned up the man's wounds, he spotted the word 'BORN' tattooed on his left arm. Dr Smith bent over the patient and asked him his name.

'Richard,' the man whispered. 'Richard Speck.'

Dr Smith called the police, then stitched Speck's wrists and gave him a blood transfusion. When Speck came out of surgery, the police were there to arrest him. They clamped him to his bed with leg-irons and took him, bed and all, by ambulance to Bridewell prison hospital.

When the police told him of his horrific crimes, Speck lay on his bed in apathetic resignation. His answer to all their questions was the same: 'I don't know any more about it than you do.'

He did not deny that he had killed the eight nurses. He simply said that he could not remember doing it. He could not remember anything at all between injecting himself with an unknown drug on the evening of 13 July and waking up in his room in the Shipyard Inn on the morning of the fourteenth.

'I woke up with a pistol and with blood on my hands,' he told a doctor. 'Where did I get the gun, doc?'

His amnesia, feigned or real, was of no consequence. Corazon Amurao picked him out of a line-up and there was more than enough evidence against him. On 26 July 1966 he was indicted on eight counts of first-degree murder. And on 1 August he was formally arraigned. Feelings in the city were still running high and security in the courtroom was tight. Speck was pale and haggard. His suicide attempt had brought on inflammation of the heart, and he was suffering withdrawal from alcohol and barbiturates.

Speck had no money, so the public defender Gerald Getty was appointed to represent him. Getty entered a formal plea of not guilty. Prison psychiatrist Marvin Ziporyn was also assigned to the case, to check Speck's suicidal intentions. Ziporyn found Speck depressed and resigned to his fate.

'If they say I did it, I did it,' Speck told Ziporyn. And he fully realised the consequences. 'If I burn, I burn,' he said.

When Speck's physical health improved, he was transferred to a maximum security prison. Ziporyn continued to examine him and came up with the theory that Speck was suffering from brain damage, caused by drug abuse and head injuries he had sustained as a youth. For years he had been suffering from excruciating headaches and a white haze would form in front of his eyes, as if he had been staring too long at the sun. Drugs and alcohol aggravated the condition. Ziporyn came to believe that Speck was insane at the time of the crime.

A panel of eight psychiatrists declared Speck fit to stand trial. But Speck did not tell them about his use of drugs, or the head injuries he had sustained. When Ziporyn asked why not, Speck simply replied: 'They didn't ask me.'

Speck was equally unhelpful with his defence attorney, Gerald Getty. When it was suggested that he may have gone on a date with one of the girls – which would explain fingerprints in the house – Speck vehemently denied it. Getty had to build a defence without his client's help and entered no less than thirty-five pre-trial motions which made evidence like the pocket knife the police had found in the Calumet River and the gun confiscated from Speck by North Side police inadmissible.

The police radio announcement that Speck had killed the nurses made any trial in Chicago impossible. So on the night of 14 February 1967 Speck was transferred to the small town of Peoria, 150 miles south-west of Chicago, in a convoy of three unmarked cars full of armed deputies.

The trial started on 20 February. It took more than a month to pick a jury. More than 610 people were cross-examined before twelve jurors were picked. Getty was keen to find people who knew nothing of the case. The prosecutor, thirty-year-old Assistant State Attorney William Martin, was determined that no one on the jury would shrink from recommending the death penalty.

Speck watched the whole proceedings with studied indifference. He wore a blue suit, chewed gum nervously and stared blindly into the distance.

The prosecution case was rock solid. The gas-station attendant and two sailors established that

Speck was in the neighbourhood. Patrons of the Shipyard Inn testified that they had seen Speck with a gun and a knife two hours before the first murder. And fingerprints put Speck at the scene of the crime. Then came the testimony of the eye-witness, twenty-three-year-old Corazon Amurao. Just four feet ten, she was a formidable witness. When Martin asked her whether she could point out the man she had seen in the house on East Street that night, she stepped out of the witness box and, without a word, walked across to Speck. Slowly she raised her right hand until it was within inches of Speck's cheek.

'This is the man,' she said without flinching. Speck's eyes momentarily flickered up at her, then he resumed his distant pose.

Martin then unveiled his star witness – a doll's house. It was an exact model of the two-storey house at 2319 East Street. It was five feet wide, three feet high and three feet deep, and it took four bailiffs to carry it into the courtroom. Getty objected strenuously. The wooden figures with the victims' names printed on them resembled tiny coffins, he maintained. When Speck heard that the State of Illinois had spent $5,609 to have it built, he said: 'Boy, they sure love me.'

As Martin took Corazon Amurao through her story, he moved the wooden figures from room to room in the doll's house. She broke down three times during her testimony. The effect on the jury was devastating.

The defence's only quibble was with her identi-fication. Based on her description, police artist Otis Rathel had drawn the suspect with smooth skin and short hair. Speck had unmistakably pock-marked skin and wore his hair long. But Miss Amurao insisted that she had told the police about the pock marks and had never mentioned a crew cut. She had been in shock at the time she had given the description and her command of English was poor. No matter how Getty pressed, she never wavered in her identification of Speck.

Speck did not take the stand in his own defence. He had a phobia about being the centre of attention and talking in front of strangers. Besides, he would have had little to say.

His mother, brother and five sisters loyally spoke up for him as character witnesses. But the main thrust of the defence was an alibi that Getty had established. Gerdena Farmer, a short-order cook at Kay's Pilot House on Chicago's South Side, and her husband, Murrill Farmer, the bartender there, claimed that Speck had come into the bar around 11.30 p.m. on 13 July. He had been wearing a short-sleeved black shirt that showed his tattoos. He drank bourbon and Coke and ate a hamburger and left around 12.30. They remembered the time because a crowd of night-shift workers turned up at midnight. At 11.30, according to Corazon Amurao, Speck had already begun his butchery.

Although the Farmers' story remained unshaken by Martin's savage cross-examination, the jury were not impressed. They found Speck guilty in less than fifty minutes and recommended the electric chair.

Even though an insanity plea had not been entered by Getty, as Speck had not admitted the murders, Getty had a second chance to raise the psychiatric evidence in a plea for mitigation. Psychiatrist Marvin Ziporyn testified that he firmly believed Speck was not faking his amnesia. Nor was he a psychopath as the psychiatric board had contended. Psychopaths would lie and cheat to any extent to their own advantage. Speck refused to help himself. Psychopaths felt no guilt. Speck had tried to kill himself when he heard what he was accused of. And psychopaths severed all emotional bonds with their family. Speck felt the same loyalty towards his family that they exhibited towards him.

Ziporyn's alternative theory was that Speck was suffering from brain damage. At the age of three he had contracted pneumonia which had restricted the blood-flow to his brain. At five, playing in a sandbox, he had hit himself on the head with a claw hammer. At ten he had fallen from a tree and landed on his head, remaining unconscious for an hour and a half. Aged eleven he ran into the steel support of a shop awning. And at fourteen he had been knocked out again by a bicycle accident and by another fall from a tree. He had sustained more injuries in numerous drunken fist-fights. His headaches had begun a year after he was clubbed by a Dallas policeman and he had been hit over the head seven or eight times with a tyre lever during a bungled burglary. The sunstroke he had suffered picking cotton on the prison farm at Huntsville had not helped, nor had years of alcohol and drug abuse.

Speck exhibited all the classic symptoms of brain damage – impulsiveness, irritability, poor memory, headaches and a reduced tolerance for drink and drugs. Added to that he had a deep-seated hostility towards women. This derived both from the fact that his mother had replaced his beloved father with a man he hated and from his feelings about his ex-wife Shirley.

'She used to say she wanted me to love her more than I did my mom,' Speck told Ziporyn. He told her that that would never be and he would get angry.

Speck told Ziporyn: 'I like girls – I wouldn't hurt women.' But he had attacked his mother when he was eighteen. He had beaten his wife Shirley in a jealous rage. Early in 1966 he hit a Dallas prostitute. And a month or so before the killings he had shown a drinking buddy a picture of his wife and vowed to kill her 'if it was the last thing he ever did'.

There was one single clue as to how this hostility towards his wife could have turned into murder. When Speck was shown a picture of murder-victim Gloria Davy he said: 'You know what? This is a dead ringer for Shirley.'

Gloria Davy was the last of Speck's victims. She was the only one who had been stripped and sexually assaulted. After she had left the room where Corazon Amurao had been hiding, she had been taken downstairs where she was sodomised and murdered. Speck claimed he was revolted by anal sex. Perhaps in anally assaulting Gloria Davy he was showing the disgust he felt for his ex-wife.

When Speck was sober, Dr Ziporyn found him witty and charming. But when he was drunk, the demons took over. 'Speck's motor is like everyone else's,' Dr Ziporyn said. 'It is his brakes that fail him.'

On 13 July, Ziporyn concluded, a day-long binge

of drink and drugs had turned a simple, befuddled burglary into an orgy of murder.

Judge Paschen was not impressed by these arguments and sentenced Speck to death. The execution was scheduled for September. Getty blitzed the courts with new petitions, which delayed the execution long enough for the United States Supreme Court to declare a moritorium. Speck was then sentenced to eight consecutive terms of fifty to 150 years – giving him a total term of imprisonment of between 400 and 1,200 years. This was the longest sentence ever given in United States legal history.

That, sadly, was not the end of it. An intelligent, handsome, shy, eighteen-year-old high-school senior called Robert Benjamin Smith followed the Speck case with obsessive interest. The son of a retired US Air Force major in Mesa, Arizona, he had idolised the gunfighter Jesse James and the Emperor Napoleon. But when he read about Speck's horrendous crimes, he found a new hero. Smith's dreams were of full of sadistic torture and mass murder.

On 12 November 1966 Smith walked the two miles from his home in Mesa to the Rose-Mar College of Beauty. He was armed with a revolver his father had thoughtfully given him for his birthday, a knife, lengths of nylon cord and 200 plastic bags. He fired one shot into a mirror and ordered the five women and two children who were in the salon to lie on the floor. He tried to put the plastic bags over the heads of the women, but the bags were too small. So instead he began shooting the women, at point-blank range. He killed eighteen-year-old

Glenda Carter, nineteen-year-old Carol Farmer, twenty-seven-year-old Joyce Sellers, her three-year-old daughter Debbie, and one other woman. Three-month-old Tamara Sellers was saved when her mother cradled the baby as she, herself, was being shot. One other woman survived the attack. When the police turned up, they found a smiling Smith about to leave. He offered no resistance. 'I've just killed all the women in there,' he said, as he was taken away in handcuffs.

6

Vietnam

At 7.30 a.m. on 16 March 1968 American helicopters landed to the west of the village of My Lai in South Vietnam. Vietnam was at war and the helicopter-borne assault was part of a search-and-destroy mission launched by three companies of the 11th Light Infantry Brigade in the Son May area of Quang Ngai province about sixty miles south-east of Da Nang. They were known as 'Barker's Bastards' after their commanding officer, Lieutenant-Colonel Frank Barker.

According to military intelligence one of the six hamlets that made up the fishing village of My Lai was a stronghold of the Viet Cong, the Communist resistance dedicated to driving the Americans out. Vietnam was their country and My Lai was their village. As far as the Americans and their maps were concerned, the communist stronghold where they believed the Viet Cong's 48th Battalion was stationed, My Lai-1, was called Pinkville. For convenience, on American maps it was coloured pink.

Company C was nervous. They had never been in a full-scale fire-fight before. In the past months they had patrolled near My Lai and been under sniper fire. Snipers and ambushes had cost them over a third of their men – four killed and thirty-eight injured. Their 'kill ratio' was poor.

While they had been slaughtered they had never even seen the Viet Cong soldiers who had fired on them, let alone killed any of them. They had called down millions of dollars of artillery shells in barrages, blowing up water buffalo and empty houses as the inexperienced troops tried to locate the enemy.

Only once had they had claimed any kills – six to nine VC, bodies they had seen in a tapioca patch. This had been reported up the chain of command not as six to nine, but as sixty-nine. Still, MACV – Military Assistance Command Vietnam, the American headquarters in Saigon – was demanding a higher 'body count'. And today they were going to get one.

Only six weeks earlier the Viet Cong had practically overrun South Vietnam during the so-called Tet offensive. They had even stormed the compound of the American embassy in South Vietnam's capital Saigon and held it for several hours. For the world's greatest superpower, this humiliation had to be redressed. The newly arrived commander of the 11th Light Infantry Brigade, Colonel Oran K. Henderson, made it clear he expected just one thing – aggression.

Barker told his senior officers as they pored over maps of My Lai in their heavily fortified bunker: 'We're going in and if we get just one round out of there we're gonna level it.'

There is some dispute over the orders Captain Ernest Medina conveyed to the men of Charlie Company. Most agreed that he had said that this was a chance to get back at the enemy for the losses they had suffered. Livestock was to be killed, crops burnt, houses destroyed. One man said that Medina told them to 'waste anyone who ran from us or fired on us'. Others, who had already seen buddies beating children and kicking a woman to death, thought that they were being hyped up. The impression was given that it was market day and that anyone who was not in the Viet Cong would be out of the village by 7.30 a.m. and My Lai would be, in the savage jargon of the Vietnam War, a 'free-fire zone'. In fact, the women and children who saw the GIs coming that morning had not even had breakfast.

Charlie Company had 20,000 rounds for their M-16s – 400 rounds for each rifle. They had four hundred grenades, grenade launchers and a dozen 81-mm mortars. Charlie Company was also supported by helicopter gunships carrying rocket launchers, grenade launchers and heavy machine guns. C Company's own artillery battery at their local headquarters, Uptight, was ready with supporting fire, and two heavy batteries at nearby firebases also had their sights trained on My Lai.

The US Navy had swiftboats to the seaward side of the fishing village of My Lai. In the Gulf of Tonkin a destroyer, the *New Jersey*, was standing by and the Air Force had promised air support with F4 Phantom jets.

On their way in to the landing zone one helicopter pilot reported a stray shot. But there was no resistance once they hit the ground. Captain Medina sent his 1st and 2nd platoons into the village known as My Lai-4. The 3rd platoon was held back to mop up after the first two moved in.

As the soldiers approached the village they accidentally fired on each other. Confused, the troops thought they were under enemy fire, which convinced them they had come to the right place – a VC stronghold.

The villagers understandably turned and fled. They had good reason. But the ill-trained GIs took this as confirmation that the villagers were VC and gunned them down as they ran.

The 2nd Platoon swept through the north of the village, hurling grenades into the straw-roofed huts and shooting anyone who came out. They raped the village girls, then shot them.

After half an hour Captain Medina ordered the 2nd Platoon to move on to the hamlet of Binh Tay, where they gang-raped several more girls before rounding up ten to twenty women and children and killing them. Meanwhile, the 1st Platoon, under twenty-four-year-old Lieutenant William L. Calley Jr, swept through the south of My Lai-4 shooting anyone who tried to escape, bayoneting others, burning houses, destroying crops and shooting livestock. Calley objected to his men raping women instead of getting on with the slaughter, though he later admitted tearing a girl's blouse off. He ordered one man, who was holding a grenade to a girl's head and forcing her to fellate him, to pull his pants up and get on with the killing. Calley believed that the girls would prefer to be raped than killed, but, as far as he was concerned, a soldier with his pants down was not doing his job.

While his men were merely degenerate, raping,

sodomising and then killing their victims, Calley was on a holy mission. He believed he was there not to kill people, but to use his M-16 assault rifle to destroy the evil philosophy, Communism, inside them. And he had biblical text for his crusade. God had told Saul to go the Amalekites 'and destroy them all that they have, and spare them not; but slay both man and woman, infant and suckling, ox and sheep, camel and ass'. Calley's mission in My Lai was to destroy it utterly.

As they swept on through My Lai, Calley's platoon was high on killing. Even the cool-headed Calley could not remember whether they were being fired on. But he knew his job was to keep on killing everyone before they had a chance to get a Kalashnikov rifle out and shoot back.

He did not mind shooting old men. Old men in America would pick up a gun to defend their families, he reasoned. And women? He had heard that women fought in Viet Cong units. Children, too, blew up American soldiers. They stole the explosives from American mines to build booby-traps and moved the Americans' own minefields, making the US Army maps useless and the countryside a death trap. Ten-year-olds stole rifles, grenades and ammunition to supply the Viet Cong. In ten years time, today's babies would be just as deadly. So Calley had no qualms about killing them too.

The fact that there were only old men, women and children in the village simply confirmed, in Calley's mind, that they had found a hotbed of Communism. The young men were away fighting with the Viet Cong. The people left behind handled intelligence, supplies and logistics. They were just as deadly as men carrying guns – and they deserved to die.

When the platoon reached the east end of the village, Calley ordered the survivors be rounded up. They were herded into an irrigation ditch. There Lieutenant Calley opened fire on the defenceless villagers. He commanded his men to join in. They emptied clip after clip into the tangle of human flesh until they ran out of ammunition. Eventually, all the bodies lay motionless.

For a moment there was quiet. Then a two-year-old child, miraculously unharmed, crawled out from under the bodies. He scrambled out of the ditch, crying, and tried to run away. Calley grabbed him, pushed him back into the ditch and shot him.

As the 1st Platoon prepared to move on to My Lai-5, the 3rd Platoon moved into the village. They shot the wounded to put them out of their misery, burned the remaining houses, killed the rest of the cattle and shot anyone trying to escape. A group of women were rounded up and sprayed with machine-gun bullets. The helicopter gunships that ringed the village cut down anyone who tried to get away.

Helicopter pilot Hugh Thompson was decorated for valour against hostile forces in My Lai. But the hostile forces he fought against were his own side – Americans. He and his crew had had to threaten to fire on Calley's men to stop them killing even more.

Thompson's suspicions were aroused when he flew in over My Lai and saw the bodies of a large number of women and children. But despite the casualties, his helicopter was not being fired on by the enemy. The only people down below who were shooting were Americans.

He saw a wounded woman. She was unarmed. An American captain walked up to her, nudged her with his foot, stepped back, then blew her away.

Thompson saw the bodies in the irrigation ditch – but there were others still alive in a bunker. He set his helicopter down and went up to Lieutenant Calley, who was in charge. Thompson asked if he could help get the civilians out of the bunker. Calley replied that the only way to get them out was with a hand grenade.

Back at his helicopter, Thompson ordered his doorgunners to open fire on Calley's men if they started shooting Vietnamese again. Then they began to ferry the women, children and old men to safety.

Later he flew over the irrigation ditch again and spotted a child alive among the bodies. He picked her up and carried her away from My Lai. Thompson had a son of about the same age.

Altogether between 172 and 347 Vietnamese were killed in the village of My Lai, and maybe as many as 500 were killed in all in that area before Calley received a radio message from Captain Medina telling him to spare some of the people. It would not look good if there were no survivors.

When Lieutenant Calley reported back to Captain Medina, it was clear that all of the Vietnamese that had been killed were unarmed. They were old men, women and children. Calley was asked for a body count. He told Captain Medina thirty or forty, ten of which he claimed to have killed himself.

Were they VC or were they civilians? he was asked.

'How do you tell?' said Lieutenant Brooks, who led the 2nd Platoon.

'They're all VC. Or they're all civilians,' said Calley.

Captain Medina reported a body count of ninety VC, no civilians. Then the divisional press officer blithely announced 128 enemy killed, thirteen Viet Cong suspects detained and three weapons captured. *The New York Times* reported the figures without a murmur. No one seemed to comment that it was rather unlikely that 128 Viet Cong soldiers – or even thirteen suspects – would have had just three weapons between them. And no one seemed to think it strange that, in this vicious fire-fight with the VC's crack 48th Battalion, there was just one American casualty – and that self-inflicted.

But by 1968 the Vietnam War had already got out of hand. America, the superpower, was getting its ass kicked by a nation of peasants. Billions of dollars worth of the world's most sophisticated military hardware was being thwarted by men who wore black pyjamas, sandals cut from old car tyres and carried rifles that were twenty years out of date.

While the generals deluded themselves with body counts that had been plucked from thin air and claimed that all they needed was more firepower, the footsoldiers – the 'grunts' – on the ground turned to random killing and drugs. They shot water buffalo and old women just for the fun of it and killed their officers if they thought they might lead them into danger. The most common method of disposing of an overly officious officer was a fragmentation grenade tossed into their quarters, a practice that had become known as 'fragging'.

Discipline broke down. Grunts smoked marijuana, took heroin and LSD, used the explosives from the claymore mines as fuel for cooking and went on patrol in T-shirt and shorts.

While Charlie Company was slaughtering unarmed women and children and Captain Medina and Division were making up the numbers of enemy dead, the Viet Cong battalion in My Lai-1 moved on unscathed. But no one in the military paid that, or the massacre of innocent civilians, a second thought. It was just another ordinary day in the drug-crazed nightmare that was the Vietnam War.

The random massacre of civilians was not uncommon during the Vietnam War. But unfortunately for Lieutenant Calley, the massacre at My Lai had had witnesses.

Two pressmen – army reporter Jay Roberts and combat photographer Ronald Haeberle – had been assigned to Calley's platoon. They were appalled by the ferocity of the carnage. One woman was hit by such vicious crossfire that bone flew off her, chip by chip. Another woman was shot and her dead baby shot to pieces with M-16 rounds. Another baby was slashed with a bayonet. They saw a child who was escaping from the carnage brought down by a single shot.

But the two journalists were reporting the war for *Stars and Stripes*, the army newspaper, so they could hardly write up what they had seen and decided to stay quiet. At the time Haeberle says that he did not consider what he witnessed to be an atrocity.

He did not even process his pictures until he got back to the States. When he did, he put together a slide show. It showed troops shipping out from Hawaii, soldiers distributing medicine in the villages in Vietnam, then finally the My Lai massacre. It was only when his audience began to ask why GIs were killing old men, women and babies that he began to realise the enormity of what he had seen.

While the US Army were proudly proclaiming their great victory at My Lai, the Viet Cong distributed a pamphlet denouncing the atrocity. Rumours also spread through the army. They reached high enough up the chain of command for senior commanders to decide that something must be done about it. They ordered an internal investigation, which decided that there was no basis for further action.

However, this whitewash did not quiet the deep sense of unease that some of the men from Charlie Company felt. As the date of their return to the US came ever nearer, the gloss began to wear off their 'great victory' at My Lai. Many of them wondered how they were going to live with what they had done.

The problem was there was nothing they could do with their growing sense of disquiet. They knew they could not speak out without inviting murder charges. Even Michael Bernhardt, who had refused to take part in the massacre, felt constrained, out of loyalty to the men in his platoon. But they all felt they had to tell someone.

One man who would listen was Ronald Riden-hour, a GI who later became a journalist. He met with the men from C Company and compiled the evidence they gave him. He decided not to take the information to the army, fearing another white-wash. But when he returned to America after his tour of duty, he could not forget what he had heard. In April 1969 he wrote a letter outlining what he knew and circulated copies to thirty prominent politicians.

Congressman Morris Udall of Airzona pressed the army to send investigators to interview Riden-hour. The Senate Armed Services Committee took up the matter and, on 12 December 1969, ordered an in-depth investigation to be conducted by Sena-tor F. Goward Herbert and Senator Leslie Arends, the senior Republican on the committee. This, in turn, led to the establishment of the Peers Inquiry in November 1969 which eventually named thirty men guilty of commission of an offence or omission of duty.

Meanwhile Lieutenant Calley was still in Viet-nam. After My Lai, Calley got to like Vietnam, though he never learnt the language and hated Vietnamese food. He applied to become a welfare officer charged with 'winning the hearts and minds' of the Vietnamese people. This was not as easy as it sounds. When he took soap bars to the children, they saw the brightly coloured wrappers, thought they were sweets and ate them.

Calley bought sewing machines for prostitutes so that they could set up a clothing workshop, and pigs for farmers. But he found that the villager elders were making a hundred dollars a week from the prostitutes he was helping and selling the livestock he supplied.

He also arranged film shows for the locals – and showed them John Wayne's gung-ho Vietnam movie *Green Berets*. He felt no guilt. He thought he had done nothing wrong.

Calley's tour of duty ended in November 1968, but he extended it. Then, in May 1969, he got orders transferring him to the Chemical, Biological and Radiological Warfare School at Fort McClellan, Alabama. Special instructions told him to report to the office of the US Army Inspector General when he arrived back in America. Calley assumed that he was to be assigned there after he has completed his training at Fort McClellan.

Calley made no real effort to get back to the States and was still considering extending his tour of duty in Vietnam again when he was told that Division wanted to see him. He borrowed a jeep and drove to headquarters. There he was given his personnel records and his aeroplane ticket to Washington, D.C. His plane left in under an hour, he was told. Calley rushed to pack a bag. He kissed the Vietnamese girl who cleaned his quarters on the forehead and assured her that he would 'come right back'.

Calley arrived at the Inspector General's office convinced that he was going to be given a medal. He was told to sit down and wait. Eventually a full colonel saw him. There was a court reporter in the colonel's office and Calley was informed that this was a formal investigation for the personal use of the Chief of Staff. The colonel asked whether he wanted an attorney.

'Do I need an attorney?' asked Calley.

The colonel explained that he was investigating an operation that had taken place over a year before in or around the village of My Lai-4.

'At the conclusion of this investigation,' the colonel said, 'you will possibly be charged with murder.'

'Do you mean you pulled me out of Vietnam for this?' Calley said. He thought it was the silliest thing he had ever heard.

He agreed however to have an attorney present. The attorney advised him not to answer any questions. Calley blustered that he would answer anything he was asked. But the attorney warned him that he may face the death sentence. It was only then that Calley saw what a serious position he was in. He realised he was being railroaded.

Back at his hotel, Calley examined his conscience. Killing was wrong, he realised that, but others had killed too. It was a war. He even pictured in his mind's eye the bodies stacked up in My Lai. It did not bother him.

William 'Rusty' Calley was from Miami where he was registered for the draft. In the early 1960s he worked as an insurance investigator and moved to New Orleans, then to Houston and San Francisco where he lived just up the hill from the city's growing hippie community. His job was to check out damaged houses to see if they were really worth the amount being claimed for them.

The Vietnam War itself was a mistake – for the Americans, at least. The Vietnamese had started fighting their colonial occupying power, the French, in 1936. During World War II, with American support, the Vietnamese fought the Japanese invaders. In return the Americans adopted the policy that there should be no recolonisation of Southeast Asia after the war. But Britain wanted its colonies back in Burma and Malaya. The British had taken the Japanese surrender in Vietnam. So they re-armed the Japanese soldiers to hold Vietnam until the French returned.

France fought in Vietnam until 1954, when they were decisively defeated by the Vietnamese at Dien Bien Phu. Peace talks were held in Geneva and it was decided that the country should be divided into two administrative regions until an election united the country. Until then, the South would be run by the French, who still occupied much of the region, and the North would be administered by the Vietnamese Communists where their greatest strength was.

One of the signatories to the Geneva Peace Accords was America. But the Americans' attitude towards the Vietnamese had changed since World War II. They had seen eastern Europe, China, North Korea and the Caribbean island of Cuba fall to Communism. In Vietnam, they were determined to put a stop to it.

Knowing that Vietnam's communist leader, Ho Chi Minh, would win any nationwide vote, the Americans argued that Communist intimidation would prevent fair elections. Instead, they backed the establishment of a republic in the South.

President Kennedy gave military support to the fledgling republic but soon found casualties were high. President Johnson believed that the only way forward was a full-scale American military presence. So America manufactured an excuse. They claimed that two Vietnamese gunboats had attacked an American destroyer in the Gulf of Tonkin. No matter how absurd this sounds in retrospect, Congress passed the so-called Gulf of Tonkin Resolution, granting President Johnson the money to go to war. And in 1965 US Marines staged an amphibious assault on the beaches at Da Nang. They were greeted by local girls with garlands of dahlias, banners proclaiming 'Vietnam Welcomes the US Marine Corps', and the mayor of Da Nang with his new Polaroid camera. Meanwhile, further forces arrived by ship in Da Nang's deep water port and by plane at the 3,000-yard runway.

With the mighty fire-power at the disposal of the US forces, it seemed inconceivable that America would not win a quick victory over the ill-equipped Communist forces. But the enemy proved elusive. They were battle-hardened from nearly thirty years of fighting. They had a huge underground defensive installation that had been begun during their thousand-year struggle against the Chinese. They knew how to survive in the jungle, could march all day on a handful of rice and melt into the local populace like tears in a bucket of water.

In 1965 the only opposition to the war was by veteran pacifists. But the student organisations set up to fight racial segregation in the American South soon became a handy vehicle for the anti-war movement. Students had good reason to be against the war. They were vulnerable to the draft and would be expected to go and fight.

Then Martin Luther King turned against the war, bringing to the struggle a large number of civil rights activists and liberals. Still the majority of the American people supported the war. How could a superpower like America be defeated by one of the poorest countries in the world?

Then in February 1968 the Communists went on the offensive. Under cover of the celebrations for the Vietnamese New Year, Tet, the Viet Cong attacked. They overran every major city in South Vietnam, even briefly occupying the compound of the American Embassy in Saigon.

The US military retook everything the Viet Cong had gained in a matter of weeks, but the damage had been done. The debacle had been seen on coast-to-coast TV across America. Veteran news anchorman Walter Cronkite – who, until Tet, had supported the war effort – changed his mind. The war, he said in his nightly comment on the news, was now unwinnable.

With Cronkite, half of middle-America turned against the war. Demonstrations became routine and were often violently suppressed. Conscripts burnt their draft cards. And some – in imitation of Buddhist monks in Vietnam – burnt themselves.

The dubious moral standards of the Vietnam War soon reached home. Those who had marched off to war for their country came home tainted. Many found themselves vilified as 'baby killers' when they got off the plane in their uniform back in the United States. Friends shunned them. Even their families did not want to hear what had gone on in Vietnam.

Of the three million Americans who served in

Vietnam, around eighty per cent of them are reckoned to have made a successful transition back to civilian life. But as the war dragged on, more and more men came home with the famous 'thousand-yard stare'.

One Vietnam-War veteran, who later become the Lieutenant-Governor of Massachusetts, recalled waking up screaming after dozing on a domestic flight soon after returning home.

'The other passengers moved away from me,' he said, 'a reaction I noticed more and more in the months ahead. The country didn't give a shit about the guys coming back or what they'd gone through. The feeling toward them was: "Stay away – don't contaminate us with whatever you brought back from Vietnam" '.

Many found it hard to make the transition. Some embraced the criticism and joined an organisation called Vietnam Veterans Against the War. Even veterans disabled by the war turned out on crutches and in their wheelchairs to protest.

The Vietnam War returned an unusually high number of men who were not easily assimilated back into normal life. As many as 700,000 suffered from the 'Vietnam syndrome' – officially diagnosed in 1980 as Post Traumatic Stress Disorder. PTSD is a similiar condition to shell shock, which was diagnosed in the veterans of World War I. More Vietnam veterans have now committed suicide than were killed in the whole of the war.

Many veterans had picked up a drugs habit in Vietnam. The pressure at home made it easier to disappear in the junkie's underworld – back in what Vietnam vets called 'The World'. And financing a habit was all too easy for a man who knew how to handle a gun.

Blacks who had earned respect for their performance in the paddy fields found themselves back in the ghetto with no hope of a job. But they were highly trained killers. They had little choice but to turn to crime.

Moral doubts about the war, the blatant illegality of its conduct – especially its incursions into Cambodia and Laos, countries neighbouring Vietnam with which America was supposed to be at peace – and the culture of protest back in the States made it easy for veterans, who already found themselves marginalised, to see themselves as outlaws and act accordingly.

The idea of Vietnam veteran turned urban crazy soon surfaced in the movies and on TV. Two particular images caught on. One came from the movie *Taxi Driver*. The Vietnam crazy quickly became a stock villain in cop operas like 'Kojak'. The other was John Rambo, the Sylvester Stallone character who first appeared in the film *First Blood* in 1982. Former Green Beret John Rambo finds it hard to make the transformation from Special Forces hero to peace-time America. He becomes a survivalist, living in the forests, only to be wronged by the local sheriff. In response he wreaks havoc on the local town.

And in *Rambo II* in 1985 he gets a chance to get his own back on the Vietnamese. 'This time,' he asks, 'do we get to win?'

In July 1966 Calley got a letter from the draft board asking why he wasn't in Miami where he was registered and demanding that he report there in person. With full-scale engagement in Vietnam, large numbers of men were needed by the Army, Air Force, Navy and Marines. Although over eight million Americans volunteered for service during the Vietnam War years, more were needed.

The draft system had been put in place by the 1948 selective service legislation. Under this system, during the seven-and-a-half years of the Vietnam War, 26,800,000 young Americans found themselves eligible. Some 2,215,000 men were actually forced into service, largely blacks and poor whites. This was no accident.

The Johnson administration insisted that the preferential drafting of the socially disadvantaged gave them opportunities for housing, healthcare, education and training. Black rights groups said it was genocide.

As the war became more unpopular, draft-card burning and draft dodging seemed to become the order of the day. Draftees turned up in Canada. They proclaimed their opposition to the war from safe havens in Britain and Sweden. These men had a high profile but, in fact, as few as 570,000 were technically 'draft dodgers'.

More than 15,410,000 men were disqualified or managed to qualify for some sort of exemption or deferment. They married or applied for college. They found sympathetic doctors or even mutilated themselves to avoid being called up. Others joined the national guard, the state-based reserve. Only the desperate headed for the Canadian border.

Calley was not desperate, nor was he against the war. And he figured he was tired of California anyway. He had few friends there and was lonely.

So he bundled his belongings into his old Buick and headed for his home state.

Unfortunately, he was half-way across New Mexico when his water pump broke down. Calley was broke. He had just $4.80 in his pocket. He went to the army recruitment office in Albuquerque and asked them to wire the Miami draft board for the fare home. The recruiter told him that draft boards don't work that way. Calley was stuck.

However, the kindly recruiter said he could help him out. If Calley was to enlist for three years, that would solve all his problems. The draft board would no longer be after him and he would have no need to make it half-way across the country. How would he like to be an airborne ranger?

'What's that?' asked Calley.

'That's someone who jumps out of airplanes,' he was told.

Calley said he did not like the sound of that. He would rather sit in an air-conditioned office, he said. The recruiter signed him up as a trainee clerk.

Calley took basic training at Fort Bliss, Texas, then he went to clerical school at Fort Lewis, Washington. But in March 1967 he was sent on to the Officer Candidate School at Fort Benning, Georgia – or Fort Benning School for Boys, as they called it.

The rapid expansion of the US Army between 1965 and 1968 had put a massive stress on the officer corps. By 1967 only seven per cent of officers were West Point graduates. The Army tried to make up the balance with recruitment from the ROTC – the Reserve Officer Training Corps in 268 universities and colleges. However, as the war became more and more unpopular – especially among students – the numbers joining the ROTC fell off.

The Army had no choice but to turn to its own Officer Candidate School which drew mainly from men of lower social and educational quality. Calley's own defence counsel said that Calley would never have qualified as an officer if it had not been for the war. OCS training had bowed to modern management methods, rather than the old-fashioned 'death or glory' training. Sergeants got so-called 'Shake 'n' Bake' courses. These turned privates into NCOs in just twenty-one weeks. Even so, there were insufficient NCOs and many squads were led by senior – Spec 4 – privates. So leadership was shaky through every layer of the command structure. After the Vietnam War, the Army began a new course on 'leadership ethics'.

The OCS pupils at Fort Benning in 1967 behaved as if it were a public school. The men referred to it as their 'alma mater' and sang the school song. They smuggled in pizza, Coke and candies and had midnight feasts. These 'pogie bait' parties, where they even had pizza fights, had to be cleaned up so not a trace was left by reveille.

Meanwhile they were being taught to kill. Instructors would show them how to smash a solar plexus, spear lungs with broken ribs, garotte the enemy with a jungle vine and slit a man's throat without a sound. Calley preferred using his M-16. Shooting people with an assault rifle, he figured, was less gruesome than killing them by hand.

The officer candidates all thought they were going to be Audie Murphy – the World War II hero who went on to be a movie star. And two vital concepts were drummed into them: get a big kill ratio in Vietnam – that's the ratio of the number of Americans killed to the number of enemy troops killed – and get a big body count.

They were told that there would be civilians there, but only in the capital, Saigon. They were shown newsreels of cheering crowds and imagined that the people in Saigon would welcome them as saviours. But out in the country they had to watch out. They must be sharp, be on guard every moment.

'As soon as you think these people won't kill you, zap!' they were told. 'In combat you don't have friends, only enemies.'

They were told this over and over and the message made a deep impression on Calley. Once he got to Vietnam, he decided to act as if he was never secure, as if everyone in Vietnam would do him in, as if everyone there was bad.

An OCS graduate, even though he could not read a map, Calley was commissioned and, as a lieutenant, he moved on to Charlie Company, First Battalion, 20th Infantry in Hawaii. There, Calley practised amphibious assaults on the beaches and climbed the Kahukus mountains – some of the steepest, meanest mountains in the world – in infantry exercises.

Lieutenant Calley and Charlie Company were fit and ready for combat with the toughest, meanest, ugliest, most battle-hardened enemy in the world. But no one had told them how to deal with the old people, the women, the children and the babies.

Before Charlie Company left Hawaii en route to

Vietnam, Lieutenant Calley gave his men a three-minute talk called 'Vietnam, Our Host'.

'Wake up!' he told his men. 'We're going to Vietnam! Wake up! Because it's our host . . .' Then he gave them the standard line about it being their duty to make the world safe for democracy. This was followed by a reading of the Standard Operating Procedure – the Pentagon's list of do's and don't's.

'Don't insult the women. Don't assault the women. Be polite,' he read.

Charlie Company was bussed out of their Hawaiian base at four o'clock in the morning to avoid the anti-war demonstrators who picketed the base and threw stones at the army buses. They headed to the airport by way of Lua Lua Lei Ammunition Depot and Pearl Harbor. Pan Am flew them out. They landed in the country – in Vietnam – on 1 December 1967. Calley was so unfamiliar with the world he was thrown into, that he thought, at first, that he was somewhere in India. He was expecting hand-to-hand combat that day. He stood at the back of the truck taking Charlie Company from the airport like the meanest son-of-a-bitch there was. His M-16 was slung low. He pulled his helmet down low over his eyes and scowled.

The Vietnamese could not have been less impressed. They had seen it all before. Every GI who arrived in Vietnam thought they were the roughest, toughest son-of-a-bitch who ever walked the earth. They were there to take on Charlie, the most ruthless, evil enemy that had ever lived. Everyone of them was John Wayne in Vietnam, ready to end the war in a single day. The local people paid so little attention that, while Calley was thinking heroic thoughts about defeating Communism with one hand tied behind his back, he noticed a Vietnamese woman squat down beside the truck to take a crap.

As Charlie Company travelled south by train to the area of operation, Calley was shocked to see how poor the country was. He saw a shanty land, houses made out of cardboard and tin, 'no nice sections anywhere'. It made him feel superior.

'I'm the big American from across the sea,' he thought. 'I'll sock it to these people here.'

He got on well with the children, however, as did most of the Americans, at first. They had trouble keeping them out of the camp. Pretty soon they realised that anyone, even the kids, could be the enemy.

The 'boomboom girls' also came to the camp, to solicit trade. Battalion gave orders that he should 'shoo' them off. GIs were not to associate with the Vietnamese.

Calley warned his men not to go near them. But he soon found that even the guards were disappearing with the girls. Eventually he was forced into negotiating a standard rate with the local *mamasan*, and set four of the girls up in one of the bunkers in the camp.

The straitlaced Lieutenant Calley himself succumbed to the charms of the local 'boomboom' girls – or at least the mamasan, whose name was Susie. He introduced himself to her as 'Rusty'.

When she first visited his quarters, in her long white Saigon gown, she sat on the Vietnamese mat he had on the floor. Calley found the situation awkward. He could hardly chat her up like she was some girl he had met at a cocktail party in Miami. He put some paraffin in a C-ration can to create a more romantic ambience. When he reached for some cigarettes, she jumped up, upsetting the lamp. The paraffin splashed on her hair. She ran to wash it in the river outside, but the paraffin immediately turned into wax. Back in his room, Calley helped comb it out. He felt that he wanted to kiss and caress her. His resolve was just weakening when one of Susie's girls ran in. One of Calley's men had hit her, protested the prostitute. For twenty dollars she had screwed all the GIs there, but they wanted her to do it again and she had refused. Calley took the girl's side, but Susie told the girl to go back.

Alone again, Calley smoked a Pall Mall while the two of them cuddled up. Eventually Susie took the initiative and lay down on an airbed on the floor.

Afterwards they talked – as much as they could with a vocabulary limited to 'You GI', 'You number one', 'You number ten'. Nevertheless the conversation came round to the war.

'You no like VC, why?' asked Susie.

Calley told her that the VC were bad.

'VC no hurt me, VC no hurt you. You nice to VC, he nice to you.'

Patiently, Calley explained that the VC were bad for the Vietnamese people.

'Same, same,' said Susie. 'VC Vietnamese, Vietnamese VC.'

Calley became frustrated that he could not explain the difference between Communism and democracy. Susie had heard of neither. Later Calley found that he was relieved that he could find no way to communicate with her. Say he had asked her to choose between the two and she chose Communism, what would he do then? Should he kill her, or capture her and send her to a POW camp? He knew that that was where his duty lay.

Out in the paddy fields, Calley and his men were inept. On night patrols, they made so much noise that the VC for miles around knew they were there. They set up ambushes that no one walked into. On patrol his platoon was often fired on but they never saw who did it. They searched local villages but found no culprits. And no one co-operated.

They asked: '*VC adai*?' Where are the VC?

The villagers always answered: '*No bitt*.' I don't know.

Pretty soon the GIs realised that the local Vietnamese must have known. If they were not actually Viet Cong themselves, they were protecting the Viet Cong. Charlie Company no longer played with the children or treated the local people with any respect. They took what they wanted and burned villages at the slightest excuse.

Although they grew more cynical, they did not become any better soldiers. On their first patrol near My Lai, Calley's platoon was shot at by a sniper. Instead of walking under the shadow of the levee along the river bank, Calley had led his men along the top of it. The radio operator who shared Calley's quarters was shot and killed. Even by calling in a million-dollar artillery barrage, Charlie Company did not manage to dislodge the sniper.

For three days Charlie Company tried to enter My Lai, but were driven back. Two men were killed by booby traps. Another was hit by sniper fire. Calley's platoon blundered into a nest of booby traps. When they had extricated themselves unscathed, two more men were cut down by sniper fire. Men were dying but, as always, the enemy was unseen.

On their next patrol they were heading for a muster point when an explosion ripped through the early morning air. A man screamed. Then there was another explosion and another scream. There was another explosion, then another, then another. They had strayed into a mine-field. As men rushed forward to rescue their wounded buddies, they stumbled over more and more mines. Severed limbs flew through the air. Medics crawled from body to body, but every movement set off more explosions. They were trapped in the mine-field for more than two hours. By the time they got out of it, they had lost thirty-two men.

Two weeks before the My Lai massacre, the company was mortared and most of the grunts' personal possessions were destroyed. Then just two days before the fatal search-and-destroy operation, four of Calley's men – including one of the company's last experienced NCOs – were blown to bits by a booby trap. In just one month, Charlie Company had suffered forty-two casualties out of a field strength of less than a hundred. And they had still not seen the enemy.

What they had seen, however, were atrocities committed by their invisible enemy. Calley had seen the total collapse of a local anti-Communist village chief when an earthenware jar of what looked like stewed tomatoes was left outside his door one morning. The VC had delivered it. In it there were fragments of hair and bone. It was the village chief's son.

One of Calley's men had been captured. For the whole of one night they had heard him screaming, even though he was seven kilometers away. Calley and his men thought the VC had amplifiers. They didn't. The man's penis had been torn off and he had been skinned alive. Only his face was left intact. The raw flesh of his entire body had been soaked in brine.

Calley also witnessed the random violence of his own side. He had seen GIs casually fire on each other for no reason. They tossed canisters of CS gas into their officers' quarters if they did not want to go out on patrol. He had seen Americans shoot down Vietnamese civilians out of boredom or for target practice. And he'd heard from helicopter pilots of 'turkey shoots' where helicopter gunships would go 'squirrel hunting' in civilian areas. Calley was a man with a mission, but he found himself in a moral vacuum.

Pending a court martial, Calley was sent to Fort Benning, Georgia, instead of Fort McClellan.

'You'll have a better chance there,' the colonel told him. Fort Benning was an infantry base. He would have an infantry jury of combat officers who had served in Vietnam. At Fort McClellan, Alabama – or Fort Houston, Texas – he would be tried by doctors, clerks and WACs, people who had never seen combat.

Eighteen months after the massacre Calley was charged with murder. The news split America in two. Those who supported the war protested that he was only doing his duty. Those who were against it said that Calley was a scapegoat – massacres like Vietnam were happening every day. It was President Johnson, Secretary of Defense Robert McNamara and General Westmoreland who should be on trial. But eighty per cent of those polled were against his conviction.

Calley's commanding officer, Captain Ernest Medina, was charged with premeditated murder and commanding an unlawful act – homicide. These charges were then reduced to involuntary manslaughter in failing to exercise proper control over his men. But the jury were not convinced that Medina knew what his men were doing in My Lai-4 and acquitted him. Medina is now an estate agent in Mainette, Wisconsin.

Forty-six members of Charlie Company were under serious investigation for the crimes of murder, attempted murder, rape and sexual assault. The Army's Criminal Investigation Division – the CID – found that there was enough evidence to charge eighteen men. But the men had, by then, left the army and were no longer under military jurisdiction. They were never charged and never faced trial.

The CID also had evidence that at least fifteen men from Charlie Company had been guilty of serious sexual offences. Girls were stripped, raped, sodomised and stabbed and shot in the vagina. Two men were charged but the charges were quietly dropped and the matter was covered up.

Twelve other officers and men were charged with other offences, including murder and one charge previously used during the Nuremberg trials –

violating the laws and customs of war. Only five of them were tried. None was found guilty.

Calley's divisional commander, Major-General Samuel W. Koster, and eleven other senior officers were charged with participating in a cover-up of the massacre. None was found guilty.

Of the sixteen charged, only five were court-martialled, and only Calley was found guilty. Calley alone carried the can.

Calley did not have any problems with his comrades at Fort Benning. Every day, in the officers' club or at the PX, they would tell him they were behind him all the way. Senior officers treated him with respect. They had seen him on TV.

He received around 5,000 letters. Some were offensive, but the overwhelming majority backed him. Some told of similar atrocities perpetrated by American soldiers in World War II and Korea. Sometimes they were from the perpetrators themselves.

Before his trial, the Jacksonville branch of the American Legion in Florida – Calley's home state – raised $20,000 for his defence. People patted Calley on the back and said: 'Good luck, son.'

He was a national celebrity and sold his story to *Esquire* magazine. Calley likened himself to Christ being crucified. Even *that* he would accept for the good of the American people, he said. *The Battle Hymn of Lieutenant Calley*, on the Plantation label, sold 200,000 copies.

Calley was a bit wary about going out, though. Those people who recognised him were supportive, but his girlfriend found the attention hard to handle. His father backed him one hundred per cent, but his fourteen-year-old sister Dawn was asked at school: 'What do you think of your brother murdering all those people over in South Vietnam?'

She burst into tears.

'I don't think he would do it,' she sobbed.

When he heard about this incident, for the first time Calley felt ashamed. He started to sleep badly, believing that someone might break into his quarters at night and kill him.

By the time he came to trial, the proceedings had degenerated into a media circus. Reporters would shout: 'Lieutenant Calley! Are you sorry you couldn't have killed more women and children?'

What was on trial was not just Lieutenant Calley, but America's whole conduct of the war.

In November 1970 the trial began in 'Calley Hall', the courthouse at Fort Benning. Thirty seats were set aside for TV reporters and newspapermen, twenty for spectators and five for Calley's supporters – two of which he gave away to the wives of the attorneys for the prosecution and the defence.

It took three days to pick a jury. Twenty-five officers had to be rejected. They were prejudiced in favour of Calley – or, at least, against the Army for trying him. Under cross examination, one captain even said that he thought the Army was trying to railroad Calley.

The prosecution simply spelt out what exactly had happened. There were enough eye-witnesses to call.

Calley was terrified that he might cry or go to pieces. He believed that, in him, the whole of the American people were on trial and he was determined not to let them down. He argued that in accepting that there would be civilian casualties in an operation like the search-and-destroy mission in My Lai, his superiors had tacitly ordered him to wipe out the village.

Was what he had done any worse than dropping 500lb bombs on the Vietnamese or burning them with napalm? The atomic bomb had killed women and children in Hiroshima, hadn't it? And General Sherman had worried little about civilian casualties in his March to the Sea during the American Civil War.

The US Army was like a chisel that was kept sharp for the American people to use, he argued. It was his duty as a soldier to carry out the will of the American people. He would wipe out South America, if the majority of the American people told him to – 'or massacre a thousand Communists'.

After four months of testimony, on 16 March 1971, the third anniversary of the My Lai massacre, Lieutenant William Calley was found guilty of murdering at least twenty-two civilians. The Governor of Indiana ordered the flags on state buildings to be flown at half-mast. The draft boards of Huron County, Michigan, and Athens, Georgia, resigned in protest. The Texas Senate demanded a presidential pardon. And even the liberal democrat governor of Georgia, Jimmy Carter, ordered an American Fighting Man's Day the week Calley was convicted and asked those who supported Calley to drive with their lights on. Governor Carter went on to become president of the United States.

Calley was right, though. Over the My Lai massacre, America put itself on trial. Since the massacre, it had voted President Nixon into office on the pledge to pull America out of Vietnam. The war dragged on for another four years, but Calley's trial meant that the American military could no longer depend on the wholehearted backing of those they were supposed to serve.

Lieutenant Calley was sentenced to life imprisonment with hard labour. On review this was reduced to twenty years, then ten years. He was finally paroled on 19 November 1974 after serving three-and-a-half years under house arrest – less than two months for each murder he was convicted of and less than four days for each of the civilians killed at My Lai.

Calley is now a successful businessman, running his father-in-law's jewellery business in Columbus, Georgia. He believes that he was no worse than most – and better than many of the officers and men who served in Vietnam.

'I was like a boy scout,' he wrote in his autobiography *Body Count*, 'and I went by *The Boy Scout Handbook*.'

He believes that he was trustworthy, loyal, helpful, friendly, courteous, kind, obedient, cheerful, thrifty, brave, clean and reverent. What he did in My Lai was, he believes, his duty to God and to country. Still there were some 300 dead civilians in a ditch and one two-year-old boy who could have got away, if Calley had not dragged him back into the ditch and shot him.

Calley's atrocity at My Lai was undoubtedly just the tip of the iceberg. In Stockholm an International War Crimes Tribunal was set up. Excluding My Lai, 241 allegations of war crimes were made. Seventy-eight were substantiated. Some thirty-six cases involving sixty-one individuals brought convictions. In all, 201 army personnel were convicted of serious offences against civilians. Ninety Marines were found guilty of the same offences, but Marine records do not distinguish between crimes committed in combat and those off-duty.

But what My Lai had done was change the mood in America. It tore the nation apart, dividing those who supported the war and those who were against it. It also put mass murder on the TV every night. Soon random violence spread through America like a cancer. In April 1968 civil rights campaigner and anti-war activist Martin Luther King was gunned down. In June, anti-war presidential candidate Robert Kennedy was shot. His assassin, Jordanian Sirhan Sirhan, could give no reason for the killing. And in August, anti-war demonstrations outside the Democratic Party convention in Chicago turned into a full-scale riot. The division in the country over the war was so deep that young people and students who were against the war dropped out of mainstream society and established a counter-culture. And in that counter-culture, one young cultist managed to build up a commune of young followers who allowed him to become a spree killer by proxy.

Although Charles Manson is serving life imprisonment for murder, he did not wield a knife or gun himself. But in 1969, on his orders, eight people were hacked to death in a meaningless orgy of violence that left America – and the rest of the world – reeling.

Born in 1934 in Cincinnati, Ohio, Manson was

the illegitimate son of a teenage prostitute. Unable to support herself even through prostitution, his mother, Kathleen Maddox, left her son with his grandmother in McMechen, West Virginia. Later he was sent to the famous orphans' home, Boys Town in Nebraska, but was soon kicked out for his surly manner and constant thieving. He became a drifter and was arrested for stealing food in Peoria, Illinois. Sent to Indiana Boys School in Plainfield, he escaped eighteen times. In 1951 he was arrested again for theft in Beaver City, Utah, and served four years in federal reformatories.

Released in November 1954, he married and was then arrested for transporting stolen cars across a state line. This time he served three years in Terminal Island Federal Prison near Los Angeles.

Released in 1958, Manson became a pimp and was arrested repeatedly under the Mann Act for transporting women across a state line for immoral purposes. Then he took to forging cheques, was caught and sentenced to ten years in the federal penitentiary on McNeil Island in Washington State.

Being small, just five foot two inches, he had a hard time in prison. He was raped repeatedly by other prisoners. This left him with a lifelong hatred of blacks. To survive, Manson became shifty, cunning and manipulative. Released in 1967, he discovered that he could use what he had learnt in jail on the long-haired flower children who inhabited California at the time. His contempt for authority and convention attracted them to him and he developed a taste for middle-class girls who had followed the fashion and dropped out of mainstream society.

His hypnotic stare, his unconventional lifestyle and the strange meaningless phrases he babbled made him appear the perfect hippy guru. He travelled with an entourage of young girls – all his lovers – and docile males who would do anything he asked. These hangers-on he called the 'Family'. And the Family was at war with the world. They numbered as many as thirty at one time. Patricia Krenwinkel was a typical recruit. She was from a normal middle-class family. A former girl scout, she had had a good education and a good job at a Los Angeles insurance company. She was twenty-one when she met Manson on Manhattan Beach and abandoned everything. She walked out on her job and ditched her car. She did not even bother to pick up her last pay-check when she moved in with the Family on Spahn Movie ranch, a collection of broken-down shacks in the dusty east corner of the Simi Valley where they hung out.

Twenty-year-old Linda Kasabian left her husband and two children and stole $5,000 from a friend to join the Family, where she saw her seamy life through a constant haze of LSD. Leslie Van Houten was just nineteen when she dropped out of school. She then lived on the streets on a perpetual acid trip until she met Manson. A more pernicious influence was Susan Atkins, a twenty-one-year-old topless dancer and bar-room hustler. She was a practising Satanist and brought Devil worship to the receptive minds of Manson's Family. She became Manson's closest aide. But, like the others, she had to share his sexual favours. Manson tried to satisfy his insatiable sexual appetite with his female followers, one or two at a time – or even with all of them together. He promised each a baby in return for their devotion.

One of the few men in the commune was a twenty-three-year-old former high-school star from Farmersville, Texas, Charles 'Tex' Watson. Once he had been a top student. In Manson's hands he became a mindless automaton.

Surrounded by compliant sycophants, the drug-addled Manson began to develop huge delusions. His own name, Manson, became significant: Manson, Man-son, Son of Man – that is, Christ, or so his demented logic demanded. He was also the Devil, or so worshipper Susan Atkins told him.

Into his delusions, Manson dragged the lyrics of Beatles songs. Unaware that a helter skelter was a harmless British funfair ride, he interpreted the track 'Helter Skelter' on The Beatles' White album to herald the beginning of an inevitable race war. The blacks would be wiped out. Along with them would go the pigs – the police, authority figures, the rich and the famous, what Manson called 'movie people'.

Manson fancied himself as something of a pop-star himself. He played the guitar – badly – and wrote a song whose lyrics consisted of the two words 'you know', repeated. The tune was not much better, a series of seemingly random notes. The Family loved it. Manson took what he believed was his potentially chart-topping composition to Gary Hinman, a successful West Coast musician. Manson, Susan Atkins and Robert Beausoleil – another Family member – badgered Hinman in an attempt to get the song recorded. Hinman humoured them, even letting them stay briefly at his expensive home. Manson then learned that Hinman had recently inherited $20,000. Naively believing that he kept the money at home, Manson sent Susan Atkins and Bob Beausoleil to get it – and to kill Hinman for refusing to help Manson make 'You Know' a hit. Atkins and Beausoleil held Hinman hostage for two days while they ransacked the house. The money was not there. Eventually, out of frustration, they stabbed Hinman while he was still tied up.

To give this senseless murder some spurious significance, Susan Atkins dipped her finger in Hinman's blood and wrote 'political piggie' on the wall. The police found Beausoleil's fingerprints in the house and tracked him down. In Beausoleil's car they found the knife that killed Hinman and a T-shirt drenched in Hinman's blood. Beausoleil was convicted of murder and went to jail without implicating Atkins. The loss of a foot soldier, Beausoleil, bothered Manson not at all. The murder simply incited Manson to plan new acts of violence.

Manson continued to try to have his dire composition recorded and released. Next he approached Terry Melcher, the son of Doris Day. Melcher was a big player in the music industry but, somehow, he failed to see the potential in Manson's material. Plainly he had to be shown that Manson, the Son of Man, was serious.

Manson formed his followers into a death squad. Dressed in black, they were trained in abandoned buildings in the arts of breaking and entering. These bizarre rehearsals were known to the Family as the 'creepy crawlies'. Manson also indoctrinated his drug-crazed followers in the necessity of killing anyone who stood in his way. On 23 March 1969 he drove his followers to Melcher's remote home in the Hollywood Hills to reconnoitre. Melcher no longer lived in the same house in Cielo Drive in Benedict Canyon. But that did not matter to Manson. The people he saw going into the house were 'movie types'. Their slaughter would act as a warning to Melcher.

On 8 August 1969 Manson's death squad was despatched to Benedict Canyon. He sent Tex Watson, Susan Atkins, Patricia Krenwinkel and Linda Kasabian. Armed with a .22 revolver, a knife and a length of rope, they were ordered to kill everyone in the house and 'make it as gruesome as possible'.

Manson had not been wrong about the new people who lived at the end of Cielo Drive. They were 'movie people'. The new resident was film director Roman Polanski, although he was away shooting a movie in London at the time. His eight-months-pregnant wife, movie star Sharon Tate, was at home though. So was Folger's coffee heiress Abigail Folger, her boyfriend Polish writer Voyteck Frykowski and Sharon Tate's friend, celebrity hairdresser Jay Sebring.

Kasabian claimed she lost her nerve at the last minute and remained outside. But the rest of the death squad entered the estate. The first person they met was eighteen-year-old Steven Parent, who had been visiting the caretaker. Parent begged for his life, but Watson shot him four times, killing him instantly.

Inside the house, the three killers herded Sharon Tate and her guests into the living-room. They were told that the house was simply being robbed and no harm would come to them. While they were being tied up, Sebring broke free, but was shot down before he could escape. Realising that they were all going to be killed, Frykowski attacked Watson. He was beaten to the ground with the pistol butt and kicked. Then the girls stabbed him to death in a frenzy. There were fifty-one stab wounds on his body. Folger also made a break for it. She was out of the back door and halfway across the lawn before Krenwinkel caught up with her. She was knocked to the ground, then Watson stabbed her to death.

Sharon Tate was by then the only one left alive. She begged for her life and the life of her unborn child. The killers showed no mercy. Susan Atkins stabbed her sixteen times. Tate's mutilated corpse was tied to Sebring's dead body. Then the killers spread an American flag across the couch and wrote the word 'pig' on the front door in Sharon Tate's blood. At their leisure they changed their bloody clothes and collected their weapons. On the way back to the Spahn Ranch, they threw them into a ravine in the San Fernando Valley. They also stopped for a wash with a hosepipe in a garden, but the owners chased them away.

Next day, Manson got stoned on dope and read the lurid reports of the murders in the press. To celebrate, he had an orgy with his female followers. But soon he craved more blood.

On 10 August, Manson randomly selected a house in the Silver Lake area and broke in. Forty-four-year-old grocery store owner Leno LaBianca and his thirty-eight-year-old wife Rosemary, who ran a fashionable dress shop, awoke to find Manson's pistol in their face. He tied them up, telling them they would not be harmed. He intended only to rob them.

He took LaBianca's wallet and went outside to the car where the rest of the death squad was waiting. With them was twenty-three-year-old Steve Grogan. Manson sent Tex Watson, Leslie Van Houten and Patricia Krenwinkel into the house with instructions to murder the LaBiancas, saying that he was going to the house next door to murder its occupants. Instead, he drove off.

Watson did as he was told. He dragged Leno LaBianca into the living-room and stabbed him to death, leaving the knife sticking out of his throat. Meanwhile, Van Houten and Krenwinkel stabbed the helpless Mrs LaBianca while chanting a murderous mantra. They used their victims blood to write 'Death to all pigs', 'Rise' and 'Helter Skelter' on the walls. Watson carved the word 'War' across LaBianca's stomach, again leaving the knife sticking in the dead man. Then the three killers had a midnight snack and took a shower together.

Although the killers thought of their senseless slayings as a joke, they knew that there was a danger that they might get caught and the Family began to break up. To support herself, Susan Atkins turned to prostitution and was arrested. In prison, she boasted to another inmate about the killings. Under interrogation, she told the police that Manson was behind them. He and several other members of the Family still at the Spahn Ranch were arrested, but they were released again due to lack of evidence.

Then on 15 October 1969 Manson was arrested again. This time he was charged. Most of the Family were in custody by then. Tex Watson had fled back to Texas and resisted extradition. Finally he was returned to California and the trial went ahead. Manson and his followers took the proceedings as a joke and showed no remorse. Basking in the publicity that surrounded the case, Manson portrayed himself as the most evil man on Earth and boasted that he had been responsible for thirty-five other murders. He, Beausoleil, Atkins, Krenwinkel, Van Houtèn and Grogan were all found guilty and sentenced to the gas chamber. But in 1972, the death penalty was abolished in California and the sentences were commuted to life imprisonment. Manson and his followers are eligible for parole. None of them has been granted it.

Even though Manson and the most bloodthirsty of his followers were behind bars, the American public did not sleep easy in their beds. Hippy communes had sprung up all over California and there might be others like Manson. On 19 October 1970, prominent eye surgeon Dr Victor Ohta was found dead in his swimming pool in Santa Cruz with his wife, secretary and his two young sons. Each had been tied up and shot. His palatial house had been set on fire. When the fire brigade was called, they found their way blocked by Dr Ohta's Rolls Royce in the driveway. Under a windscreen wiper was a note which read: 'halloween 1970 ... today world war 3 will begin as brought to you by the people of the free universe'. The killings were all too frighteningly reminiscent of Manson.

Four days later twenty-four-year-old John Linely Frazier was arrested. He was a recluse with record of drug use who lived in dilapidated cowshed just down the hill from the Ohta home. A paranoid schizophrenic, he claimed that the Book of Revelations had told him to rid the world of those guilty of 'polluting and destroying the earth'. His bizarre behaviour had forced his mother and wife to seek psychiatric help for him. But, at that time, liberals opposed the warehousing of mental patients in what they termed 'snake pits'. Ronald Reagan, then Governor of California, was only too eager to slash the mental health budget and had closed down the mental hospitals. The community treatment centres he promised in their place never materialised and the patients were thrown out on to the streets. Although Frazier was clearly psychotic the court found him sane and sentenced him to death in the gas chamber. His sentence, too, was reduced to life in prison.

But the drug-taking counter-culture was not having it all its own way. The authorities, in the person of the National Guard, went in for their own bit of spree killing at Kent State University. Around 12.25 p.m. on Monday 4 May 1970 the Ohio National Guard opened fire on anti-war protesters who were holding a demonstration on the campus. Four students – Allison Krause, Jeffrey Miller (a registered Republican), William Schroeder (a member of the ROTC) and Sandra Lee Sheuer (who was passing on her way to class) – were killed. Ten other students were wounded.

Anti-war protesters had already hounded President Johnson from office. He had been replaced by Richard Nixon, who rode into the White House on the promise of ending the Vietnam War. Instead he escalated it by invading neighbouring Cambodia and bombing neutral Laos. Demonstrations exploded on campuses across America. Nixon called the demonstrators 'bums'. The previous year he had ostentatiously watched a college football game on TV while 250,000 fellow Americans demonstrated in Washington against the war. As Governor of California, Ronald Reagan justified the shooting and killing of a demonstrator at Berkeley by saying 'once the dogs of war are unleashed, you must expect these things will happen'.

The anti-war protest at Kent State started at noon on Friday 1 May 1970 when a group of history graduate students calling themselves World Historians Opposed to Racists and Exploitation – WHORE – organized a rally at the Victory Bell in the middle of the campus on a large area of grass called the Commons. Around 500 people attended and witnessed the burial of a copy of the constitution, symbolising its murder by Nixon. Jim Geary, a student who had won the Silver Star with the 101st Airborne Rangers in Vietnam, burned his discharge papers. The organisers called for another demonstration to be held at the same place at 12 o'clock on Monday 4 May, to protest against the war in Vietnam, the invasion of Cambodia and to push for the closure of the university's Reserve Officers Training Corps (ROTC). The president of the university monitored the protest, decided that it was peaceful and left that afternoon for a weekend in Iowa.

That Friday night started as all Friday nights did at Kent State. The students went drinking at Big Daddy's, the Cove and Ron-de-Vou along the Strip. But the topic of discussion that night soon changed from the New York Knicks–Los Angeles Lakers basketball game to Vietnam and the invasion of Cambodia. Out on the street, beer glasses were thrown at passing police cars. A crowd began shouting: '1-2-3-4, we don't want your fucking war.' Soon a human chain blocked Water Street, stopping the traffic. Drivers were asked their opinion of the escalation of the war. A bonfire of rubbish was lit in the middle of the street and a group of protesters started trashing the street, doing $10,000 worth of damage.

Mayor Leroy Statrum, who was out of town when the trouble started, returned just after midnight. He declared a state of emergency and imposed an 11 p.m. curfew on the town and a 1 a.m. curfew on the campus. He also closed the bars, which forced more students out on to the streets. Deputies tried to disperse the swelling crowds with tear gas. They forced the students off the streets and back up on to the campus. By 2.30 a.m. peace was restored.

On Saturday 2 May, the Ohio National Guard told city officials that if they were called in they would assume total control of the university. Neither the university authorities nor the city officials challenged this. Rumours spread that the disturbances had been stirred up by the anti-war terrorist group, the Weathermen, who were planting bombs in federal buildings at the time, and the mayor called in the National Guard.

That evening around 1,500 students milled around the campus shouting political slogans, letting off firecrackers and throwing rocks. The old wooden barracks that housed the university's ROTC became a target. 'Burn it!' people shouted. The windows were smashed and burning rubbish was pushed inside. Soon the building was ablaze. When the fire department turned up, their hoses were cut. The fire appeared to go out of its own accord, then suddenly blazed up again as the live ammunition stored in the barracks exploded. At around 10 p.m. the National Guard went in with tear gas and drawn bayonets and cleared the campus.

On the Sunday morning, the Governor of Ohio, Jim Rhodes, visited Kent State and declared that the events of the previous two nights were 'probably the most vicious form of campus-oriented violence yet perpetrated by dissident groups and their allies in the State of Ohio'. The 'troublemakers,' he said, were 'worse than the brown shirts and the Communist elements. They are the worst type of people we harbour in America.' And he pledged to use 'every form of law' to control them. It was the last weekend of his campaign for the Republican nominaton in the elections for the Senate.

That evening the students gathered at the Victory Bell again. They were told that the curfew had been moved forward from 1 a.m. to 9 p.m. At nine o'clock the Ohio State Riot Act was read and they were given five minutes to disperse. The crowd broke into two. One group headed towards the university president's house. The other group went down into the town where they sat down and sang

'Give Peace a Chance' while a helicopter with a searchlight trained on them circled overhead. The students wanted to talk with President White or Mayor Statrum and present their demands – the withdrawal of the National Guard, the lifting of the curfew and an amnesty for those students who had been arrested. At 11 p.m. the Riot Act was read again.

On Monday 4 May between 1,500 and 3,000 students gathered at the Victory Bell for the rally called on Friday. But the governor had, illegally, banned all demonstrations, even peaceful ones, and ordered that the area be cleared. At 11.50 a.m. a military jeep arrived carrying National Guardsmen and a campus policeman. Through a bullhorn, the policeman announced: 'This crowd must disperse immediately. This is an order.'

The students responded with shourts of 'Sieg Heil' and 'Pigs off campus!' And they rang the Victory Bell, which usually only sounded after football games.

The National Guard commander, General Canwith, ordered his men to load their rifles with live ammunition and put on their gas masks. He then ordered the hundred troopers to the top of a grassy knoll, known to young lovers as 'Blanket Hill'. From there they began firing tear-gas canisters into the crowd. But the students threw the canisters back. Others threw rocks and stones.

When the guardsmen ran out of tear gas, around forty of them moved down the hill to confront the demonstrators. The crowd was angry and the troopers were forced back. Several times the troopers on top of the knoll assumed the firing position in an attempt to scare the students. A single shot was heard. Then there was a salvo. In just three seconds, the troopers loosed off sixty-one shots. No warning was given. The students did not even know that the guardsmen's weapons were loaded.

'They're firing blanks,' said one student. 'Otherwise they would be aiming in the air or at the ground.' Some of the guardsmen may have. But others, almost unbelievably, fired directly into the crowd. Screams and moans filled the air. Four were dead. Ten were wounded. One student was paralysed from the waist down when a bullet lodged in his spine. Ignoring his cries for help, the guardsmen marched away. The days when hippy anti-war protestors put flowers in the barrels of soldiers' guns were dead and gone.

President Nixon's reaction to news of the shootings was 'when dissent turns to violence it invites tragedy'. Over 150 colleges were closed or on strike in the days after the killings and 100,000 protesters marched on Washington. But in New York a gang of beefy construction workers broke up a student demonstration on Wall Street while the police looked on.

The Weathermen set up a National War Council. They bombed the house of a judge trying black radicals, planned an attack on an army dance at Fort Dix, shook the New York City Police Department with an explosion, blew up a ladies' room in the US Senate, bombed a bathroom in the Pentagon and wounded three in a bomb attack on the Army's Mathematics Research Center in Wisconsin.

Government attempts to justify the shootings at Kent State as self-defence were blown when the results of an FBI investigation were leaked. It concluded that: 'The shootings were not necessary and not in order,' and 'We have some reason to believe that the claim by the National Guard that their lives were endangered by the students was fabricated subsequent to the event.' Even so, the guardsmen were not found guilty when they went to trial.

But eight and a half years after the shootings the defendants signed a statement admitting their responsibility for the shootings and expressing their regret. And on 4 January 1979, in an out-of-court settlement, the parents and surviving students received $675,000 from the State of Ohio.

By 1972 America's attitude to the Vietnam War had changed radically. Their fighting men were no longer considered heroes. Vietnam veterans could not find jobs. They became outcasts, spat upon, ostracised. Then one day in Harrisonville, Missouri, the Vietnam veterans struck back, with a burst of gunfire – only the man wielding the gun was not, himself, a Vietnam veteran.

The lone figure came running across the leafy square of Harrisonville. The M-1 carbine in his hands was blazing. Two policemen fell dead in front of the bank. Inside, two clerks were wounded. The gunman raced on down the street, killing the laundry delivery man in his tracks. He put two more shots through the window of the sheriff's office, wounding Sheriff Bill Gough. Then, on the steps of the Harrisonville Retirement Home, the gunman, twenty-four-year-old Charles Simpson, stopped. He put the muzzle of the rifle into his mouth and pulled the trigger one last time.

The massacre on the small town square of Harrisonville that spring afternoon was not the work of a brooding loner. Simpson was one of the group of nine long-haired young men who spent their time hanging out in the town square – under the hostile glare of the short-haired farmers who made up much of the town's population of 5,000. But Simpson and his friends were no gypsy band of hippies who had descended on the town from outside. They were local boys, born and raised in the area. They still lived with their parents. But most of them had been away, in the army, in Vietnam. Simpson himself had failed the physical. Chronic asthma had kept him out of the service. It was his greatest disappointment.

The group now drew unemployment benefit, which was sin enough to the hard-working residents of Harrisonville. And they flaunted their idleness by hanging out in the town square. Although their hair was barely down to their collars, they seemed to be the very personification of the radical youth that the townsfolk had heard so much about.

'The people in this town were scared,' said Police Chief William H. Davis Jr. 'I just can't understand these kids' thinkin' – sittin' on their can, doin' nothin'. If they had just acted decent from the start, and had haircuts and shaves . . .' Davis's men had the group under surveillance.

'These kids were interfering with the public,' the mayor of Harrisonville, M.O. Raine said. 'They'd stare at the people and scare them to death.'

The town was swept with wild rumours about sexual goings-on in the town square. Complaints mounted, particularly from women. Concerned citizens accused the group of being revolutionaries and threatened them, sometimes with guns. The town council passed a bylaw banning gatherings of more than three people in the town square. Simpson's group complained that this bylaw was enforced only against them.

The night before the shootings, the group were arrested for loitering. Simpson had been out of town, but when he returned in the morning he took his entire life savings – $1,800 – and bailed out his friends. That afternoon he, and three innocent people, lay dead.

Simpson's buddies carried his coffin to the grave three days later and raised a clenching fist salute in tribute to their fallen comrade. But they were at a loss to explain Simpson's crack-up.

'He was no more upset about the arrests than we were,' said group-member John Risner, twenty-three, who had been target shooting with Simpson shortly before he went berserk.

Simpson was a high-school drop-out who lived with his father in a rooming-house twenty miles from town. One friend described him as calm and cool, showing no sign of the violence that plainly lurked inside him. But another friend said that Simpson had been under stress for some months before the fatal incident.

'He was up at the square and he looked like he didn't feel well,' high-school chum Mike Young recalled. 'I asked him how he was, and he said, "I'm sick of the world, but it's nothing serious." Then I noticed he was crying.'

Some in Harrisonville reacted to the killing with renewed anger. But four days after the shootings, half a dozen of the town's more respectable citizens had a meeting with Simpson's long-haired friends in the basement of a local Methodist church. These soon became weekly events and attendance climbed. The town council also called in two specialists in community relations from nearby Kansas City. John Risner later reported that communication between the generations in Harrisonville was improving, making Charlie Simpson one of the only spree killers to leave behind him any positive legacy.

7

Black Power

They called it the Battle of New Orleans and it
was the first spree killing to be carried out live on
national television. On the morning of 8 January
1973, in the comfort of their own living-rooms,
American TV viewers watched as a marine helicopter attacked Howard Johnson's Motor Lodge in
downtown New Orleans which was surrounded
by more than two hundred uniformed policemen,
detectives and sharpshooters. Two dozen heavily
armed policemen stormed the roof of the high-rise
building which they believed was being held by a
militant black guerrilla unit which had held them
at bay for thirty-two hours and already killed seven
and wounded twenty-one in a spree of arson and
gun play. The police erupted from the stairwells on
to the pebbled roof in a blaze of shotgun- and rifle-
fire. Several fell wounded. As it turned out, the
police were shooting each other. The one man who
had held them off for more than a day lay dead,
his corpse riddled with more than a hundred sharpshooters' bullets and machine-gun rounds from the
helicopter. Even then, with the siege over, the police
were loath to admit that they had been held off for
so long by a single man. Rumours circulated that

one, possibly two, accomplices had escaped through the police cordon. But as the investigation continued it became clear that twenty-three-year-old Mark James Essex had acted alone. And Essex had felt he had the most powerful of motives. He was a black man in a white world.

He had not always felt that way. Essex was brought up in the quiet midwestern town of Emporia, Kansas, where racism, if not unknown, did not reach the vilest excesses of that in the southern states or the urban ghettos. His father worked as a meat packer and his mother, who had a master's degree in education, worked at the local Head Start programme. They were a God-fearing family and Essex tithed part of his part-time earnings to the local Baptist Church.

However, the spectre of the Vietnam War haunted every young man at that time. And in 1969, after a poor semester at Kansas State College, Essex joined the Navy to avoid the draft and almost certain assignment to Vietnam. He finished boot camp with an outstanding performance rating and was encouraged by superior officers to take advanced training in a speciality. He enrolled for a three-month course in X-ray procedures and oral surgery at the Naval Dental Center. Again he passed with flying colours and was posted to the Naval Air Station at Imperial Beach as a dental assistant. He got on with everyone he worked with there, though he gradually became aware of the undertow of racism. No one called him 'nigger' to his face but he was constantly harassed by petty regulations that did not seem to apply to white seamen. He wrote to his parents, complaining that the Navy was 'not like Emporia. Blacks have trouble getting along here.' He spoke of other black friends on the base who told him to wise up. This was the real world. Racism was as deeply entrenched in the Navy as it was in the rest of America. He was just going to have to learn to live with it. A friend said: 'Essex came to the Navy expecting to be treated in the same decent way he always had been treated back in Emporia, and he found it wasn't like that at all.'

Essex and three of his black bunk mates were put on report for playing their stereo too loud – although whites played their music just as loud without punishment. Essex's boss, a white dentist, spoke up for him at his hearing, claiming that the charge was racially motivated. The proceedings were halted, but Essex and his buddies were separated and assigned to different barracks. This was not the sort of justice Essex expected.

The case had made him notorious among the white seamen at the base. They rode him constantly. He was subjected to endless bed-checks, extra guard-duty and regularly told to turn his stereo down, even though the volume was so low that he could hardly hear it. Racial slurs were half-whispered behind his back. Friends said that he had been singled out as a 'cocky nigger'. He was reported for the tiniest infraction of Navy regulations while whites got off scot-free. The harassment began to take its toll on his work and he began to take sedatives.

In August 1970 a white petty officer made a remark about Essex 'smiling and shuffling'. For Essex, this mild racial taunt was the straw that broke the camel's back. He leapt on the officer and began beating him with his fists. It was the first time he had hit a white man. And for Essex, it was a liberation.

However, it did not improve his situation. Now every white man on the base was on his case. Unable to sleep, he went absent without leave for self-preservation. He went home to his parents to think his situation through. The local minister in Emporia persuaded him to return to the base and give himself up. At his court-martial, Essex explained that he 'had begun to hate all white people: I was tired of going to white people and telling them my problems and not getting anything done about it.' He was found guilty, fined, demoted and confined to barracks for thirty days. A few weeks later, he was discharged from the service for a 'character disorder'.

Essex returned home to Emporia, but having experienced the intolerable racism of the outside world he could not settle. He made several mysterious trips to New York, ostensibly to visit friends from the Navy, but he may have been in contact with various Black Muslim and Black Power organisations that were rife in the US at that time. A lot of their literature was found in his possession and he certainly had some weapons training after he left the Navy.

In the summer of 1972 he went to New Orleans to see a Navy buddy called Rodney Frank, who was a Black Muslim. He joined a vocational training course for the hardcore unemployed where he was described as 'probably the best student in the class'. In his spare time he began studying his African heritage. He took the nickname 'Mata', the Swahili for 'bow'.

The murder of two black students during a campus demonstration on 16 November 1972 seemed to push Essex over the edge. 'I have now decided that the white man is my enemy,' he wrote to his mother. 'I will fight to regain my manhood or die trying.' And he began giving his possessions away.

Essex began his war against the white world with an attack on a police station on New Year's Eve 1972. His first victim, ironically, was a nineteen-year-old black police cadet. Two white officers were also injured. Essex was pursued by the police through a disused hemp factory. He had suffered a flesh wound in the shoot-out. If the police had trouble following the trail of blood, Essex dropped a trail of bullets. The police followed him to a nearby Methodist church. They surrounded it, but the church was in a black area and they were afraid of sparking a full-scale race riot. During an agreed cooling-off period, Essex escaped.

During the afternoon of New Year's Day, several fires were set in the area which took 200 firemen to extinguish. Essex seems to have been responsible. Local grocery store owner Joseph Perniciaro reported seeing him return to the church, and more blood and bullets were found there.

On 7 January Essex walked into Perniciaro's shop and shot him in the chest. Out in the street, Essex stuck his rifle in through the window of a car and forced the driver to get out. He took the 1968 Chevrolet and made his getaway. Later the stolen car was found in the garage of the Howard Johnson Hotel.

Within an hour, a black maid in the hotel bumped into a man with a rifle on the eighth floor. She screamed. 'Don't worry,' he said. 'We're not going to shoot any blacks, just whites. The revolution's here.'

The scream brought a twenty-seven-year-old doctor, Robert Steagall, from his room. Essex shot him in the chest. Steagall's wife Betty rushed from the room and fell to her knees by her husband's body. Essex shot her in the head. The couple had come to New Orleans on their honeymoon.

Essex began to set fire to curtains and mattresses. Forty-three-year-old San Francisco broadcast executive Robert Bemish smelt smoke. He opened the door to his room and noticed 'light bulbs popping all over the place' with the heat. He was standing facing the hotel's swimming pool when a black youth with a rifle jumped out from some bushes, stared at him for a full second, took aim and fired. Shot in the stomach, Bemish fell into the pool, pretending to be dead. Air trapped inside his coat kept Bemish afloat as he lay still for two-and-a-half hours. Bemish said that his assailant had a goatee beard and was carrying a bolt-action rifle. Essex was clean shaven and was carrying a .44 Ruger semi-automatic.

Police converged on the hotel while frightened guests huddled in the corridors and the lobby. Told that a sniper was on the eighth floor, Deputy Sheriff Dave Munch raced up the stairs of the Rault Center across the street for a better look. On the eighth-floor pool deck he saw an armed black man with a companion who looked like a woman. This was the only other indication that Essex had accomplices. The sniper spotted Munch and fired at him. Twenty-three shards of shrapnel cut into Munch's flesh.

The hotel's assistant manager Frank Scheider went up from the lobby to investigate reports of a fire on the eleventh floor. He was later found dead, shot in the face at point-black range. A fireman climbing a ladder to the tenth floor was also shot.

Policeman Paul Persigo was shot in the head by the sniper as he moved across Duncan Plaza, opposite the hotel. Deputy Police Superintendent Louis Sirgo personally led a search party through the hotel. On the fifteenth floor the gunman shot him in the back. Both Persigo and Sirgo were declared dead on arrival when they reached hospital.

Downtown New Orleans became a city under siege. Smoke billowed from the damaged hotel while firemen crouched behind their fire engines. One policeman lay wounded on the grassy mall, another under a tree. Patrolman Phil Coleman was shot in the head and killed as he scrambled to the aid of a wounded comrade. The police had had two tense confrontations with local black militants in the past two years. Now they assumed that they were facing a well-equipped band of urban guerrillas.

The gunfire was coming from a concrete structure on the roof which covered the top of the stairwell. The police returned fire using grenades, mortars, rockets and even 20mm canons. They tried using tear gas but it drifted away in the wind. It was then that a Sea King armour-plated helicopter was called in. Carrying a squad of police sharpshooters, the helicopters swooped past the hotel ten times, sometimes coming in as close as thirty feet. The marksmen fired hundreds of glowing tracer bullets into the shadows on the roof – to no avail. As the helicopter veered away, police and newsmen in adjacent buildings heard cries from the roof: 'I'm still here. Come and get me, you motherfucking pigs. Power to the people.'

At 9.25 p.m. the helicopter lumbered past again. This time a slight figure, armed with a rifle, bolted into the open. The withering crossfire from the helicopter and marksmen on the two adjacent buildings tore the sniper's body apart. Bullets still ripped into him even when he went down, his body twitching as each fresh bullet hit.

The police radio crackled: 'We've got one of them.' But in the dark it was impossible to tell whether he was alone. Reports of fresh shots and taunts from the roof spread. Cold and exhausted, the police waited out the long hours of the night. It was not until the following afternoon that the police staged their assault on the roof.

There were rumours that a black couple – the other man and woman witnesses had seen – had checked into the hotel before the shooting. This would imply a premeditated terrorist plot. But a five-hour search uncovered nothing but three suitcases of .44 Magnum ammunition. Police Superintendent Clarence Giarrusso said: 'Either there was only one, or another got away. The speculation might run the gamut all the way from negligence on the part of the police to a superbrain on the part of the sniper.'

Louisiana Attorney General William Guste maintained that the shooting was part of a black conspiracy. Essex's mother maintained that he had acted alone from private motivation. 'It all started in the Navy,' she said. 'He was all right when he left.'

At Essex's run-down apartment, the police found the walls daubed with revolutionary slogans – 'My destiny lies in the bloody death of racist pigs', 'Political power comes from the barrel of a gun', 'Black war', and 'The quest for freedom is death, then by death I shall escape to freedom'. And on the ceiling, he had written for the police to read: 'Only a pig would read shit on the ceiling.'

'White Power', not Black Power, was the slogan behind a racist spree in 1977. Frederick Cowan, a thirty-three-year-old bodybuilder, liked to wear an Afrika Korps hat around his home town of New Rochelle, New York. His burly eighteen-stone body was covered in Nazi tattoos – a death's head, an iron cross and the double lightning bolts of the SS. Behind the lace curtains of his attic bedroom was a collection of World War II German guns. On the wall was a poster of Hitler.

Cowan's *Götterdämmerung* fell on St Valentine's Day. Three weeks before, his supervisor at Neptune World Wide Moving Company, where Cowan worked as a trucker's assistant, had sacked him for refusing to move a refrigerator for a customer. The supervisor happened to be Jewish. Cowan woke early on 14 February and donned a pair of brown

slacks and a khaki soldier's shirt. Under it, he wore
a T-shirt with the words 'White Power' printed
across the front. He took his arsenal down to his
car and loaded the trunk of his red Pontiac with a
rifle, four pistols and a hunting knife.

Cowan drove into the Neptune parking lot at
7.45 a.m., just as the morning shift was clocking in.
He armed himself for his own personal *blitzkrieg*,
then started looking for thirty-one-year-old
Norman Bing, the supervisor who had fired him.

Fifty-nine-year-old packer Joseph Hicks and
drivers James Green, forty-four and Frederick
Holmes, fifty-four, were all standing near the
entrance when Cowan came barging in. All three
were black. Cowan shot Hicks and Holmes in the
chest with his .308 rifle. Green ran off down the hall.
Cowan downed him with a bullet in the back. Terrified employees sprinted for cover as Cowan began
to prowl the corridors looking for Bing.

'Where's Norman?' he bellowed. 'I'm gonna
blow him away.'

Bing ran from his office and hid under a wooden
desk, where Cowan failed to spot him.

At 7.55 a.m. the first patrol car came speeding
into the depot. Officer Allen McLeod, a thirty-three-
year-old father of two, leapt out and yelled: 'Drop
that rifle!' Cowan dropped McLeod instead, with a
bullet in the head. Then, in blind fury, Cowan
sprayed the company's cafeteria with bullets, killing thirty-two-year-old Indian immigrant elec-
trician Pariyarathu Itty Varghese.

Soon more than 300 local policemen and FBI
agents had surrounded the warehouse. Cowan's
parents and brothers were contacted. They tried,

unsuccessfully, to talk him from his lair. 'Pray for Freddie,' a distraught Mrs Cowan cried. 'He's gone crazy.'

Shortly after noon Cowan phoned the local police station and apologised for the 'inconvenience' he was causing. Then he ordered up some lunch. 'I get very mean when I'm hungry,' he explained. Then, at 2.23 p.m., there was a muffled shot from inside the building. At dusk the police edged forward into the plant. They found Cowan lying face down in the executive suite. He had a .45 pistol in each hand and had joined his idol Adolf Hitler in suicide. The force of the last shot had blown off the black beret he had been wearing. Glinting among the blood on the floor was its cap badge – the skull and crossbones of the SS panzer division.

In Cowan's room the police found seven boxes full of guns, shells, knives, pictures and posters of Hitler and Himmler and a belt buckle enscribed, prophetically: 'I will give up my gun when they pry my cold dead fingers from around it.' In the margins of a Nazi propaganda book, Cowan had scrawled: 'Nothing is lower than black and Jewish people except the police who protect them.'

Police also turned up Cowan's membership card to the anti-Semitic, anti-black National States Rights Party. It's leader, J.B. Stoner, also blamed the police. 'The FBI caused niggers to start harassing Cowan on the job,' he told *Newsweek* magazine. 'Apparently, the FBI's to blame for the whole thing.'

According to friends and relatives Cowan had been a bright boy and a good student at the local Catholic Parochial School. He only went bad after

Loner Michael Ryan aged 11 standing apart from his class-mates, frowning deeply. He went on to blast 16 people to death in the picturesque town of Hungerford. *(Photograph: Press Association)*

Charles Starkweather with girlfriend Caril Fugate, a junior high school pupil. Starkweather was charged with the killing of 10 people, including Fugate's mother, step-father and step-sister. *(Photograph: Associated Press)*

Former military cadet Harry de la Roche murdered both his parents and two brothers while he was home from school during 1976's Thanksgiving weekend. *(Photograph: Associated Press)*

The Reverend Jim Jones, founder of the People's Temple sect, interviewed in Guyana shortly before the mass-suicide of 900 of his followers at Jonestown. *(Photograph: Associated Press)*

Richard Speck *(right)* butchered eight student nurses after a drinking binge in Chicago. *(Photograph: Associated Press)*

James Ruppert leaving court after being found guilty of 11 counts of murder – those of his mother, brother, sister-in-law and their eight children. *(Photograph: Associated Press)*

Charles Manson's 'family' arguably committed the most infamous murders of the 1960s when they massacred pregnant filmstar Sharon Tate and her friends in California. *(Photograph: Associated Press)*

Nineteen-year-old Julian Knight *(right)* shot dead six people and injured at least 18 others in a Melbourne street. Two days after his arrest he suffered a nervous breakdown and had to be confined to a padded cell. *(Photograph: Associated Press)*

a hitch in the US Army, when he was stationed in Germany.

'I don't remember him collecting the Nazi propaganda until then,' said his brother James. 'We never expected this. We thought it was just a hobby.'

Some of his drinking buddies at the Galway Bay bar had more sinister memories of Cowan, whom they called 'Fritz' or 'Reinhardt'. Collecting Nazi memorabilia seemed to be a vocation to him. After a few beers he would curse: 'Fuck the Jews, fuck the niggers.'

'I should have been born forty years ago, so I could have been in the SS,' he told one regular.

The Neptune World Wide Moving Company seems to have been blissfully unaware of Cowan's spare-time activities. Under 'psychiatric disorders' in his company medical report, it simply says: 'No.'

But Cowan's spree was just one of a spate of racist attacks, usually directed at young black men. In 1981 US Army private Joseph Christopher was sentenced to sixty years to life in prison for the racially motivated slayings of three blacks in Buffalo, upstate New York, during a twenty-six-hour spree in September 1980. New York State Supreme Court Justice Frederick M. Marshall handed down the sentence. Christopher had stalked the streets with a sawn-off .22 calibre rifle and terrorised Buffalo's black community. At a preliminary sanity hearing, Christopher was ruled mentally unfit to stand trial. But after two months of psychiatric care, he was declared competent and the trial proceeded. He was found guilty on three counts of second-degree murder.

Avowed racist, Joseph Paul Franklin, was convicted on federal charges in the sniper slayings of two young black men in Salt Lake City, Utah, in 1980 and sentenced to serve two consecutive terms of life imprisonment – the maximum penalty under federal law.

Thirty-year-old drifter, Franklin, a former Ku Klux Klansman and a member of the American Nazi Party, was convicted by an all-white jury of violating the civil rights of two blacks by shooting them to death on 20 August 1980 as they jogged in a Salt Lake park. The victims were eighteen-year-old David Martin and twenty-year-old Ted Fields, who had been jogging with two white women.

There was an uproar at his sentencing when Franklin tried to physically attack the federal prosecutor – a black man – and had to be restrained by ten federal marshals. Franklin screamed that his conviction was a 'farce' and called the judge 'nothing but an agent of this Communist government'. Throughout his trial, Franklin had maintained that the charges were 'trumped up because of my racist views'.

Franklin had been brought up in Mobile, Alabama, the heart of the deep South. As a boy he had been beaten by his mother. He dropped out of school at seventeen and began getting into frequent scrapes with the police. His juvenile rap-sheet included arrests for assault, carrying concealed weapons and disorderly conduct.

He became an evangelical Christian, then a Nazi, then a Ku Klux Klansman. At one time he told friends that he was going to join Ian Smith's Rhodesian Army. Instead he started drifting from state to state, driven seemingly by his twin passions

– a love of guns and a hatred of blacks. In 1976 he was charged with throwing the chemical Mace over a black man and white woman in Maryland, but jumped bail before he could stand trial. He also sent a threatening letter to President Carter and was arrested in Tampa, Florida shortly before the president was scheduled to arrive on his election campaign.

Franklin passionately disapproved of 'race mixing' and, according to prosecution witnesses, had boasted of the killings, though the prosecution could produce no eye-witness nor the murder weapon at the trial. Franklin was caught in possession of a rifle similar to the one used in the sniper attack, and owned a small arsenal of weapons. A car matching the description of Franklin's souped-up Camaro was seen in the area at the time of the killings and the police matched tyre treads. However, the defence maintained that Franklin had a visual impairment and could not have fired the six rapid shots that killed the two victims.

After a three-week trial, the jury deliberated for less than two hours. Franklin was also wanted in connection with the sniper slaying of a black man and a white woman in a parking lot in Oklahoma City in 1979 and the shooting of the publisher of *Hustler* magazine Larry Flynt the year before, after the soft-porn magazine published a photo spread showing a white woman with a black man. Flynt's spine had been severed and he was confined to a wheelchair.

Then, on 2 June 1981, while in jail, Franklin was arraigned in South Bend, Indiana on charges of shooting Vernon Jordan, black civil rights leader, on 12 June 1980. Jordan was shot at while he was getting out of a white woman's car at a motel parking lot after addressing the local chapter of the Urban League in Fort Wayne, Indiana. He was critically wounded. Franklin had checked into a nearby motel a week before and left town immediately after the incident. At the time of the arraignment Franklin was in the prison hospital, recovering from stab wounds inflicted in February 1982 in a racially motivated attack by fellow inmates of the federal penitentiary at Marion, Illinois.

Since the Vietnam War, a large number of Asian refugees have settled in America. They too have become an object of hate. In 1989 Patrick Purdy walked into a schoolyard in Stockton, California and opened fire on Asian children, killing five and wounding seven. And James Huberty claimed the biggest death toll at that time – twenty-one – when he took out the fact that he had lost his job on the Mexicans who were eating at a McDonald's in San Ysidro, California in 1984.

8

Forty Whacks

Some spree killers turn on their own families. The most famous, of course, was Lizzie Borden. The old nursery rhyme went:

Lizzie Borden took an ax
And gave her mother forty whacks;
And when she saw what she had done,
She gave her father forty-one.

In fact, she did not. Or at least that is what the jury thought. At the end of her trial in June 1893 she was found not guilty and lived on in New England until 1927.

A shy, plump, upperclass spinster, Lizzie Borden had lived a quiet life in her parents three-storey home in Fall River, Massachusetts, up until the time of the murders. On the ferociously hot day of 4 August 1892, her father, sixty-nine-year-old Andrew Jackson Borden and her stepmother, sixty-four-year-old Abby Durfee Gray Borden were found hacked to death by hachet blows. Lizzie discovered her father's body in the living-room, but she was not alone in the house at the time. The maid, Bridget Sullivan, was taking a nap in her room. Lizzie sent Bridget to a neighbour, Mrs

Churchill, to summon help. Mrs Churchill found Mrs Borden dead in an upstairs bedroom. The medical examiner diligently counted the hatchet blows to the victims' heads. Mrs Borden had nineteen and Mr Borden ten – not forty and forty-one as the rhyme says.

The story soon circulated that Lizzie had wanted her stepmother and her father dead so that she could inherit her father's money. This was untrue. Both she and her sister Emma benefitted equally from her father's will, which had been written ten years before and had remained unaltered. And both daughters enjoyed a healthy allowance. Other rumours said that Lizzie had long been trying to poison her parents with prussic acid. As the family all ate from a common platter, this too is unlikely.

At thirty-two, Lizzie had lived the sheltered life of an over-protected child. She suffered nightmares and told acquaintances of her strange fears. The only reason charges were brought against her was that she was unable to establish where she was when her parents had been murdered. Initially she said that she had been in the barn, looking for a fishing sinker. On other occasions she said she had been in the yard, picking pears, or eating them in the barn. No one could believe that she would be in the barn on such a fiercely hot day.

Lizzie was arrested and charged with the wanton murder of her parents. The maid, Bridget Sullivan, turned states evidence against her. This may have been to deflect any suspicion that might be levelled at her. Sullivan was alone in her room and could easily have crept down the back stairs and despatched her employers.

However, it came out that Andrew Jackson was not well-liked in town. He was a uncaring landlord and a penny-pinching businessman. There had also been a series of thefts from the Bordens' house in the months before the murders. On such a hot day, the doors had been left open and it would be easy for an intruder to have slipped into the house unnoticed. It was even said that Lizzie's sister Emma, who was out of town in nearby Fairhaven at the time, could have rented a buggy, driven to the house, killed her parents, and driven back to Fairhaven. She would have benefited equally from the inheritance. Indeed, Emma had rented a buggy that day and one witness said they had seen her outside the house shortly before the murders.

But two vital pieces of evidence saved Lizzie. The hachet blows to the victims' heads had sprayed blood all over the living-room and bedroom. Lizzie was seen immediately after the slayings and there was not a spot of blood on her. One bizarre suggestion was that she had committed the murders naked, quickly washed the blood off, and slipped back into her original dress. But the bathroom had been examined directly after the discovery of the bodies. There was no sign of blood, or water – so there had been no quick wash.

And where was the murder weapon? Defence counsel, former Masschusetts Governor George D. Robinson, held up the Bordens' household hachet that had been found in the cellar. It was without a handle, rusted and covered in cobwebs. There was not a spot of blood on it.

The jury decided that there was a possibility that someone else could have crept into the house and killed Andrew and Abby Borden. Lizzine was set free. With their inheritance, Lizzie and Emma bought a huge mansion called Maplecroft where they nursed stray animals. When Lizzie died on 2 June 1927 she left the bulk of her estate – over $350,000 – to animal shelters.

At the time of the Vietnam War, there was another family slaying at Fayetteville, North Caroline. This one, like many spree killings, had military connections. Fort Bragg, the largest military base in the world and the home of America's Green Berets, is in Fayetteville.

On 17 February 1970 a dozen members of the military found a scene of devastation at the home of Dr Jeffrey MacDonald, a medical officer with the Green Berets. MacDonald's wife, twenty-six-year-old Colette, and their two daughters, Kimberly, aged five, and Kristen, aged two, had been beaten and stabbed to death. Dr MacDonald was found semi-conscious and badly wounded. He claimed that he had been sleeping on the couch when a band of drug-crazed hippies invaded his home and killed his family. One of the assailants was a young woman wearing a floppy hat and a short skirt who chanted: 'Acid is groovy, kill the pigs!' America was still suffering the trauma of the Charles Manson slayings, which had occurred less than a year before.

The army initially charged MacDonald with the murders, but the charges were dismissed in October 1970. MacDonald left the army and went to start a new life in Long Beach, California, where he took a senior post in a hospital. However, MacDonald's father-in-law Alfred Kassab was convinced that MacDonald had murdered Colette and the two children. He petitioned the Attorney General.

MacDonald was charged again, this time by the civil authorities, and came to trial in Raleigh, North Carolina, in July 1979. The prosecution maintained that Dr MacDonald was a drug abuser who was having an extra-marital affair. The defence brought to the stand Helena Stoekley, the woman they contended had chanted 'kill the pigs'. She was a known drug abuser and had been diagnosed as a paranoid schizophrenic. But she claimed that she had never seen MacDonald before and had never been inside the MacDonald home.

Dr MacDonald was found guilty of second-degree murder on 29 August 1979 and was sentenced to three consecutive terms of life imprisonment at Terminal Island, California. In July 1980 the convictions were overturned by a federal appeals court on the grounds that MacDonald had been denied his constitutional right to a speedy trial. But this ruling was itself overturned by the United States Supreme Court in 1982. Then in 1989 the documentary filmmaker Ted Landreth aired *False Witness*, which alleged that the MacDonald murders had been committed by drug users in the Fayetteville area and cast doubt on the testimony of Helena Stoekley.

In other cases, however, there can be no doubt that the one survivor massacred their entire family. On the evening of 13 November 1974 the Suffolk County Police Department received a phone call from a man who identified himself as Joe Yeswit.

'A kid came running into the bar,' the caller said. 'He says everybody in his family had been killed, and we came down to look.'

The location was Ocean Avenue in the affluent suburb of Amityville, Long Island.

The first policeman on the scene was Patrolman Kenneth Greguski. He found a group of young men milling around the driveway of a large suburban house. One of them was crying. 'My mother, my father are dead,' he sobbed. He gave his name as Ronald DeFeo Jr, aged twenty-three.

Inside the house, Greguski was quite unprepared for what he found. Until then the only crime in the sleepy suburb some thirty-five miles east of New York City was that of vandals ripping boats from their moorings around Great South Bay. The blood-stained bodies of a man and a woman lay face down on the bed in the master bedroom. In a smaller room, Greguski found two young boys who had also been shot. In a third bedroom, a young girl had been shot in the face. Greguski then climbed the stairs into the attic, where he found the body of an older girl face down on the bed.

The victims had been Ronald DeFeo Sr, a wealthy car dealer aged forty-three, his wife Louise, their two daughters Allison, thirteen, and Dawn, eighteen and their sons John, seven, and Mark, twelve. Ronald DeFeo Jr, sobbing in the driveway, was the family's sole survivor.

DeFeo told the detectives that the murders were the work of Louis Falini, a friend of his father. DeFeo Jr had fallen out with Falini over a botched paint job for the DeFeo family firm, a Brooklyn Buick dealership, and cursed him. DeFeo Sr had then reprimanded him for insulting Falini. 'He's a Mafia hitman,' DeFeo Jr claimed his father had said.

DeFeo also claimed that, on another occasion, his father had had a run-in with Falini and had yelled: 'If anything happens to my son, I'll kill you and your whole family.'

Ronald Joseph DeFeo had been born on 26 September 1951 in Brooklyn, New York. His father was then a twenty-year-old textile worker. His mother, Louise, was nineteen. Her father owned a car showroom in Brooklyn. He offered DeFeo Sr a well-paid job there as service manager.

The family moved out into the bayside village of Amityville to a large house they named 'High Hopes'. They had enough money to spoil their children, but their eldest, Ronald Jr, responded only with sulks and tantrums. At school his classmates called him 'Butch' and the nickname stuck. His classwork was poor and he dropped out at sixteen without graduating.

Drifting through a number of lowly paid manual jobs, he began to get a taste for girls, drink and drugs – all bankrolled by hand-outs from his father. His drug habit started with pills, marijuana and LSD, but soon he moved on to heroin and amphetamines. He also got into trouble with the police and was on probation for stealing an outboard motor.

In an effort to bring his son under control, DeFeo Sr gave Ronald a job in the family firm – as a mechanic and general dogsbody at just eighty dollars a week. This again was topped up by his father's generous handouts of up to $500 a week.

Neighbours speculated about how a service manager could live so well. There was some speculation at the trial that DeFeo Sr had been swindling his father-in-law, and that DeFeo Jr had attempted a bogus heist of the company payroll.

Although the DeFeos had left Brooklyn for the suburbs, they had brought its aggressive ways with them. Neighbours complained of their shouting matches. In 1973, during a fight between his parents, DeFeo had pulled a gun. He pointed it at his father and pulled the trigger. It misfired. The effect on DeFeo Sr was salutary. He became a devout Catholic and built several shrines in the garden of his home.

DeFeo Jr got on no better with his mother, whom he described as 'lousy cook'. His brothers were 'a couple of pigs'. He liked his sisters no better.

In 1974 DeFeo discovered that, when he stopped taking drugs, he became violent. Then he had problems with girls. He found that they turned him off and he turned to heroin for succour.

In the rambling eight-page statement he gave to the police after the massacre, he said that he had spent the afternoon drinking with friends in a bar, then shot up some heroin. He returned to the bar later – he had arranged to meet a friend named Bobby Kelske there. DeFeo was detained at Suffolk County's Fourth Precinct overnight.

When Bobby Kelske was interviewed he said that when he had arrived, DeFeo was complaining to four or five others that he could not raise anyone at home. He had not got his own keys, he said, and he was 'going to have to break a window to get in'.

DeFeo sped off in his Buick, but within minutes he was back. He stood in the doorway screaming:

'You gotta help me. Someone shot my mum and dad.'

Kelske also told the police that DeFeo was a gun fanatic and that, a couple of weeks before, he had been trying to buy a silencer.

Suffolk County's ballistic expert said that all the victims had been slain with a .35 calibre Marlin rifle. But no such weapon had been found on the scene. Then, in an alcove in DeFeo's bedroom, the police found two cardboard boxes. Their labels showed that they had contained Marlin rifles – a .22 and a .35.

At 9 a.m. three homicide detectives pushed open the door to the room where DeFeo was sleeping.

'Did you find Falini yet?' DeFeo asked when they woke him.

The detectives explained that they had people out on the streets looking for him. Then Detective Harrison said: 'But to tell you the truth, I think you're the guy we want.'

During questioning that morning DeFeo gave several different versions of the killing. But each time, Falini was the culprit.

'That Falini loved it,' DeFeo claimed. 'He was like a mad dog. The gun was smoking and the barrel was hot.'

In one version, Falini had an unnamed accomplice. DeFeo claimed that he had been awoken with a gun to his head. 'You're gonna live with this for the rest of your life,' Falini had told him. 'This is for what you did to me.'

DeFeo claimed that he was then forced at pistol-point from room to room while Falini murdered four of his family. Then DeFeo himself had been forced to shoot his father and his brother Mark.

The detectives patiently pointed out the inconsistencies in his story. Then Detective Dennis Rafferty said to DeFeo: 'It didn't happen that way, did it?' DeFeo cradled his head in his hands and Rafferty said quietly: 'Butch, tell me what happened.'

After a moment, DeFeo confessed.

'It all started so fast,' he said. 'Once I started, I just could not stop.'

At 6 p.m. DeFeo was charged and gave a full confession. He said that he had fallen asleep in front of the TV set. When he awoke, he went to his room, loaded his .35 rifle and shot his father and mother in their bed. He shot Allison in the head, then moved on to his brothers' room and shot them where they lay.

Dawn had been woken by the noise. He assured her that everything was all right. When she went back into her room, he followed and shot her.

Carefully, he collected the spent cartridge cases. Back in his room, DeFeo changed. He stuffed the clothes he had been wearing, the rifle, spare ammunition and the cartridge cases into some pillowcases, and he carried the pillowcases out to the car. The rifle he dumped in the bay. Everything else was dropped down a drain in Brooklyn. Then he had breakfast in a diner before reporting for work.

The police found the ammunition and clothes in a sewer on the corner of East 19th Street, in Brooklyn. And a police scuba diver retrieved the rifle from the small village dock at the end of Ocean Avenue.

The case took a year to come to trial. DeFeo

planned to plead insanity. He began to act up in prison, setting fire to his cell, ripping up his mail and threatening to commit suicide. But he boasted to a cellmate that, once he had beaten the rap, he would have an inheritance of over $100,000 to spend.

DeFeo also tried to plea-bargain. He told the prosecution that he had had accomplices and named then – Bobby Kelske, his girlfriend Sherry Klein and another couple. They had been ransacking the DeFeo home when Mr DeFeo Sr had disturbed them. DeFeo himself had not actually pulled the trigger, he said, and one of the other gang-members had gone on to kill his mother, sisters and brothers.

In another version of this story, DeFeo had been doing the ransacking himself when his father discovered the hiding place for his loot. DeFeo had killed his father to silence him, then gone 'berserk' and killed the rest of the family.

The first witness at DeFeo's trial was Patrolman Greguski, whose eyes streamed with tears when he described what he had found in DeFeo's home that night. DeFeo smirked. Later he played the bewildered madman.

The defence psychiatrist said that DeFeo was mentally ill, a paranoid schizophrenic who believed that people were out to kill him and that his only recourse was to kill them first. He did not know what he was doing on the night of the crime, the doctor said.

When DeFeo took the stand he was shown a picture of his mother lying murdered in her bed.

DeFeo claimed not to know 'this person'. He had never seen her before, he said.

He recognised a similar picture of his father and admitted killing him, in self-defence. He denied having any accomplices, then said that his evil sister Dawn had made him do it. She had decided to kill everyone in the house and had put the rifle in his hands. 'Very, very calmly' he had gone to his parents' room and had shot them. Then he dropped the gun, but Dawn had picked it up. He heard shots and realised that she had killed the other children, he said. This made him mad. He grabbed the gun and shot her. On top of that, Dawn had had an accomplice. He even claimed that he was not sure that his family were all dead. 'One of them might come walking in here any minute,' he said. 'Then we'll see who the laugh is on.'

The jury were not impressed. They found him sane and guilty on all six counts of murder in the second degree. He was sentenced to twenty-five years to life on each count, which he is serving in Dannemora Correctional Facility, New York. He will be eligible for parole in the year 1999.

After sentencing, when the clerk of the court took down DeFeo's details – 'Name?', 'Date of birth?', 'Citizenship status?' – he asked: 'Are your parents living or dead?'

'Dead,' came the chilling reply.

Once DeFeo was safely in the state penitentiary the DeFeo's family home, 'High Hopes', was sold to a family who lived there for less than a month. They fled, claiming that the house was possessed by evil forces. This story led to the book and film *The Amityville Horror*. However, people have lived there since and say that the house is perfectly normal.

Less than six months after Butch DeFeo's Amityville massacre, another killer wiped out his entire family – the largest mass murder of a single family in American history. It was Easter Sunday 1975, the day after James Ruppert's forty-first birthday. Ruppert had never married and shared his mother's small wood-frame house in a leafy, middle-class neighbourhood of Hamilton, Ohio. Short, bookish with thick spectacles, Ruppert had trained as a draughtsman but, at that time, he was out of work and short of money. He stayed in bed, hung over and depressed.

His mother, sixty-five-year-old Charity Ruppert, was downstairs at 635 Minor Avenue preparing a big family dinner. Her elder son Leonard, his wife Alma and their eight children – aged between seventeen and four – were driving over from nearby Fairfield after they had been to morning mass.

At 4 p.m. James Ruppert came downstairs and chatted with his brother Leonard. The children were in the garden, hunting for Easter eggs. Ruppert said that he was going to target shooting and went upstairs to get his gun. When he came down again carrying a rifle and three pistols, the whole family was gathered in the kitchen. His mother was cutting sandwiches. Leonard and Alma were sitting together at the kitchen table.

'How's your Volkswagen?' Leonard asked his brother.

Ruppert answered with his gun. One shot sent Leonard tumbling back from his seat. Alma was the next to die. Ruppert's mother lunged at him in a desperate effort to save her family. She died next. Then the eight children were killed one after the other. James Ruppert fired thirty-one times in all. One child was shot just once in the chest. The others were shot three times each, to make sure they were dead. It was all over quickly. Eleven were dead in all. Nobody ran. Nobody screamed. The neighbours heard nothing.

Three hours later Ruppert picked up the phone and called the police. 'There's been a shooting here,' he said.

When the police arrived they found six blood-stained bodies in the kitchen and five in the lounge. The only sign of a struggle was one overturned wastepaper bin.

Ruppert put up no resistance, but he refused to talk, indicating that he intended to plead insanity. This left the police baffled.

'We can't seem to find a motive for this,' Hamilton Police Chief George McNally told reporters.

Neighbours knew little of Ruppert, except that he was intelligent, an avid reader and a bit of a loner. His uncle, Rufus Skinner, claimed that the two brothers had been very close and that they had done everything for their mother since their father died in 1947. Ruppert's only friend, Arthur Bauer, said: 'He's not violent at all. I can't believe he did it.'

At his trial Ruppert entered a plea of insanity. His attorney claimed that he had been insane for ten years. Psychiatrists said he was in a 'paranoid psychotic state' which loosened his hold on reality. Ruppert, it was said, believed that his family, the police and the FBI were involved in a long-term conspiracy against him. This delusion led him, suddenly, to strike back against his persecutors.

The prosecution disagreed. They said that the motive was simple – the $300,000 in property, life assurance, investments and other savings that he stood to inherit from the death of his entire family. Hence, the prosecution said, the plea of temporary insanity. If found not guilty due to insanity, Ruppert would be sent to a mental hospital. But, eventually, he would walk – with $300,000 in his pocket. Found guilty he would be in for life and Ohio State law would deprive him of his inheritance. Psychiatrists for the prosecution maintained that Ruppert was sane – and in control – when he slaughtered the rest of his family.

The picture was painted of James Ruppert as a sickly child, whose widowed mother lavished her love on her elder son Leonard. James began to feel like an outcast in his own family. He was shorter than Leonard, less bright, less adept at school. While Leonard had a successful career with General Electric and a hugely successful family life, James – on the threshold of middle age – found himself by comparison a failure. He became a heavy drinker and was threatened with eviction by his own mother because, while he could pay for alcohol, he had no money for rent.

James Ruppert claimed that his brother had beaten him when they were children and had taunted him for his weediness – taunts which had found a deadly echo in an innocent enquiry about his broken-down Volkswagen. By the mid-1960s, when James was thirty, he began to believe that Leonard was a major figure in the conspiracy against him:

his brother and his mother had begun whispering to the FBI that Ruppert was a Communist and a homosexual.

Ruppert took comfort in his small collection of guns. He would sit on the banks of the Great Miami River and take pot-shots at floating tin cans with his .357 Magnum. People had seen him doing this two days before the massacre. A gun-store assistant also remembered Ruppert asking about buying a silencer.

Twenty-eight-year-old Wanda Bishop said that she had met Ruppert in a cocktail lounge the night before the shootings. He had complained about being unemployed and his lack of money. His mother, he said, was planning to evict him from his rent-free room at home. She had told him that if he could afford to buy beer seven days a week, he could afford to pay rent.

Ruppert claimed that Leonard's casual enquiry about his VW was the breaking point. Leonard had been trying to sabotage it, he was convinced, and he had asked the question with 'a mocking smile'. This was the final straw. He killed Leonard and his family so that Leonard would never hurt him again.

The three-judge panel found Ruppert guilty on all eleven counts of murder and sentenced him to life imprisonment. Later he was granted a new trial on a technicality. This time he was found guilty of the murders of his brother and mother, but not guilty on the nine other counts due to insanity. Even so, Ruppert's inheritance was lost.

DeFeo and Ruppert were both, in the words of Hamilton Police Chief George McNally, 'gun freaks'. But another family killer, Harry De La Roche Jr, had more conventional associations for a spree killer. He was a cadet at a military academy, and was home for the Thanksgiving holiday when he suddenly went berserk and wiped out his entire family.

Thanksgiving is celebrated in America every year on the third Thursday in November. As a national holiday it is more important than Christmas. Families get together and eat turkey, cranberry sauce, baked yams and pumpkin pie.

On the Sunday of 21 November 1976, eighteen-year-old Harry De La Roche Jr flew home to New Jersey for the Thanksgiving holiday. For three months he had been an unwilling student at The Citadel, a military college in South Carolina. He was not happy there.

De La Roche was an introverted and sickly child. He had problems with his ears that made them so sensitive that certain sounds made him scream in agony. At four he underwent a major operation on his ears and throat. He was shortsighted and weedy – the smallest boy in his class at high school. To compensate he wore an army jacket and combat boots. But still he was bullied. Too small to defend himself, he nursed grudges. He was never able to forgive and forget.

His father had a hot temper and would hit his sons over any minor infraction. But De La Roche formed a close relationship with his younger brother, Ronald, and the two boys would cover up for each other's drinking, cigarette- and marijuana-smoking, and late-night excursions.

De La Roche loved animals and the countryside.

He also joined the Civil Air Patrol and enjoyed it. The family thought that he would pursue a military career. De La Roche went along with this, probably to please his father. He had long decided to work things out on his own and never let anyone know how he felt inside.

He was disappointed when he was turned down by grander military establishments, including West Point. But the family were proud that he was accepted by The Citadel. De La Roche hated it. It was far from home and too much like being back in school. He was picked on, teased and mocked.

Thanksgiving was De La Roche's first trip home since enrolling. He was determined to tell his parents that he was never going back to The Citadel, but he dreaded his father's reaction.

The whole family drove to New York's Kennedy Airport to meet him. His father, Harry De La Roche Sr, took the wheel of the family's green Ford station wagon for the drive home to 23 East Grand Avenue, Montvale, fifteen miles across the state line in New Jersey. Harry's mother, Mary Jane, admired her son's new dress uniform and his two young brothers, Ronnie and Eric, teased him about the weight he had put on. But the family were proud of him and happy to see him again.

They asked him about his life at college, but he refused to answer. 'I'll tell you later,' he said. In a letter posted the previous week he had said that he would tell them all about it on Thanksgiving night, and not before.

De La Roche had tried his hardest at The Citadel. He had changed his name to 'Bill' and was determined to make a new start. Craving a life full of friends, he found himself excluded, the object of derision. Seething with pent-up rage, he found it hard to buckle down to the strict discipline expected of raw recruits. Before leaving The Citadel for Thanksgiving, De La Roche had told his tutors that his mother had contracted terminal cancer and he was needed at home. He would not be back.

Back in Montvale, De La Roche had been in the heart of the American dream. His father was illegitimate and fatherless. He had began work as a sewing-machine repairman and worked his way up to a senior position in the export sales division of the Ford Motor Company in Newark. Although his wife's family never accepted him – the source of numerous rows – Harry De La Roche Sr was a model citizen: a church-goer, an organiser of the local Boy Scouts troop and coach to a number of local teams.

He also had great ambitions for his sons. Instead, in Harry Jr, he had raised a spotty, myopic dullard. There were only two things he had ever done right in his life. One was to be accepted at The Citadel; the other, against all the odds and after years of diligent practice, was to become a first-class shot.

It was Harry Sr who had taught his sons to shoot. The $50,000 family home was littered with guns. De La Roche's father even kept a .22 pistol next to his bed. Harry Jr loved to touch them.

He spent the time in the run-up to Thanksgiving smoking pot. Over the Thanksgiving meal questions about his life at The Citadel came up, but De La Roche was evasive. He kept telling his family that he would tell them later.

De La Roche was scheduled to fly back to South

Carolina on Sunday. By Saturday evening, when the time came to pack, he still had not got around to telling his parents how he felt. Instead he went out for a drive with a friend in his mother's white Falcon. They went for a meal at a Burger King in Rockland County, then De La Roche dropped his friend off and headed for New York City on his own. He sat in a bar until 2 a.m. nursing a beer, then drove home through a thick fog.

In the still Autumn night the fog lay thick across New Jersey. Montvale slumbered under its blanket. It swirled down East Grand Avenue as De La Roche drove by.

Two hours later it had still barely lifted when, at 4.10 a.m., Patrolman Carl Olsen saw a white Falcon run a stop sign. The car slewed to a halt outside a bar on Park Avenue. Olsen pulled alongside. The driver, a young man with glasses, leapt out and ran over to the patrol car.

'Quick,' yelled the young man. 'Quick, come up to my house. I've just found my parents and my younger brother dead and my middle brother missing.'

Patrolman Olsen went back to 23 East Grand Avenue with De La Roche and while the young man slumped on the sofa in the living-room Olsen searched the house. Upstairs he found Harry De La Roche Sr's body lying face down on one of the two twin beds. Mrs De La Roche was also dead, her head on a bloody pillow. Olsen also found the blood-soaked body of twelve-year-old Eric. There were signs that a life-or-death struggle had taken place. All three had been shot. Back downstairs,

Patrolman Olsen had just one question for De La Roche: 'What the hell happened here?'

De La Roche lit a cigarette from the butt he had just finished. He told Patrolman Olsen that he had returned home after an evening out with an old high-school friend to find the porch-light out. Normally it was left burning. Upstairs he found his youngest brother and his parents dead. His other brother, Ronald, was missing. Numb with shock, he had driven off to find a cop.

Downtown at police headquarters, De La Roche explained that his father had caught his middle brother smoking pot. There had been a fight about it. De La Roche Sr had threatened to turn Ronald in to the police. To prevent that, Harry Jr said he had planned to refuse to return to The Citadel – wasting his father's money – but he never got the chance. By the time he could make his announcement, his family were dead.

Later that day Ronald's body was found stuffed in a trunk in the attic at East Grand Avenue. He had been shot. There was no sign of a gun. The trunk lid was closed and boxes of Christmas decorations had been piled on top. All this ruled out suicide.

Confronted with this new evidence, De La Roche confessed to massacring his family. In a second sworn statement he described how he had crept into his father's bedroom and picked up the .22 pistol his father kept by his bed. De La Roche could not make up his mind whether to kill his father – and end a life-time of oppression – or not. He claimed to have held the pistol to the old man's head for fifteen minutes before screaming 'I can't go back' and pulling the trigger.

The noise woke his mother. De La Roche shot her. Then he fired again into his father's body. In the next bedroom De La Roche's two brothers were now awake. Fifteen-year-old Ronald cowered in his bed, where he was shot. But his younger brother Eric fought for his life. He ran at De La Roche, who shot him twice in the face and once more in the chest. Even then Eric did not stop screaming, so De La Roche battered him around the head with the pistol butt until he was silent.

That afternoon, when De La Roche was formally charged with four counts of murder, Bergen County prosecutor Joseph C. Woodcock found him 'extraordinarily calm'. But a few weeks later De La Roche told the family priest, Pastor Roy Nilsen, that he had not killed his family alone. In fact, he claimed, his brother Ronald had shot his parents and brother Eric after their father had caught him taking drugs. De La Roche admitted then shooting his brother in rage. Nevertheless, Harry De La Roche Jr was arraigned for all four murders.

After thorough psychiatric examination, both prosecution and defence agreed that De La Roche was not insane. But by the time the case came to trial, the defence team had little option but to plead 'general insanity'. The prosecution agreed that he was sick, perhaps even needed hospitalisation. But, legally, he was sane and the four murders were premeditated. The jury found him guilty on all four counts of murder in the first degree. He was sentenced to life imprisonment on each count, the sentences to run concurrently.

The day after the verdict, at De La Roche's request, he was taken in handcuffs to the cemetery where his family had been buried. It was twelve degrees below zero. As a prison officer brushed the snow from the grave stone to reveal the family name, De La Roche began to cry.

Brenda Spencer, one of the few women to turn to spree killing, showed no such remorse. Her stated reason for killing two and wounding nine in a senseless shoot-out was made world famous by The Boom Town Rats in their song 'I Don't Like Mondays'. Sixteen-year-old Brenda must have been thrilled. The Monday before the shootings she had said that she was going to do 'something big to get on TV'. She succeeded beyond her wildest dreams.

In 1978, the year before she resolved her inner conflicts with a gun, Brenda's parents had divorced. Brenda lived with her father in San Diego, California, and soon showed signs of severe disturbance. She played truant from school, committed petty thefts and was caught taking drugs. She watched violent videos and enjoyed shooting birds. She also shot out the windows of the Cleveland Elementary School across the road from her father's house with an airgun. Nevertheless, for Christmas, her father bought her a .22 semi-automatic rifle and 500 rounds of ammunition.

Early in the New Year Brenda began to make plans. She moved her weapons into the garage and dug a hide-out in the garden. Then on Monday 29 January she got Burton Wagg, the principal of Cleveland Elementary, in her sights as he walked across the playground. When he opened the school gates to allow the waiting children in, she opened fire. Wragg and the school janitor, Michael Suchar, were killed. The first policeman to arrive on the scene, thirty-year-old Robert Robb, found eight children aged from six to twelve wounded. He was wounded in the neck as he tried to tend a victim.

After a twenty-minute spree, Brenda Spencer blithely chatted on the phone to the police. Who was she trying to kill in Cleveland Elementary? she was asked. 'No one in particular. I kinda like the red and blue jackets.'

She told reporters: 'I just started shooting. That's it. I just did it for the fun of it.' Then she uttered the immortal line: 'I don't like Mondays. I did this because it's a way to cheer up the day. Nobody likes Mondays.'

While Brenda was chatting, kids in the bullet-torn school across the road were huddling on the floor. She held the police off for six hours, then meekly gave herself up. She walked calmly out of the house and put her gun on the ground. Then she turned and went back in. When she re-emerged she handed 150 rounds of .22 ammunition over to the waiting police.

Next day teachers at Cleveland Elementary encouraged their students to talk about the tragedy. 'Why did she do it?' asked one bewildered eight-year-old. No one had an answer.

Brenda Spencer was not the only woman to go spree killing. In 1979 forty-three-year-old 'Willie' Williams shot two men who shouted at her son during a bar-room row. Her common-law husband said that she had not been taking the medication prescribed by a psychiatric centre. In 1985 twenty-five-year-old Sylvia Seegrist shot and killed three people, injuring seven others, in a Philadelphia shopping mall. And in Illinois in 1988, thirty-year-old divorcee Laurie Dann shot seven people, one fatally, and attempted to kill hundreds of others.

Laurie Dann, née Wasserman, was the daughter of a respectable accountant and was brought up in the exclusive North Shore area of Chicago. Although she was unattractive as a child, Laurie's parents lavished the attention of America's plastic surgeons upon her. And by the time she graduated from high school, Laurie was as cute as a Barbie doll. However, she did not have the academic ability or social skills to match her looks. She failed to cut it as a cheerleader. Even the boys were not fooled.

At college in Arizona, where she studied to be a primary school teacher, she pursued men with a passion. Most did not want to know. They found her slavish and possessive. And when her relationship with a pre-med student broke up, she fled home to Illinois. Enrolling in psychology at nearby Northwestern University, she supported herself by working as a waitress at Green Acres Country Club. There she met young, dynamic sales executive Russell Dann. They fell in love and married in 1982.

Even during their honeymoon in the Virgin Islands, Russell Dann began to notice that something was very wrong. Though she had held herself together during their courtship, suddenly Laurie seemed totally devoid of self-confidence. Back in Chicago she felt herself totally out-classed by the other women in the Dann family. They were all successful in business and accomplished sports-women. Laurie dropped out of college and soon found that she was unable to hold down a job. She killed her days sleeping, shopping, watching TV and having lunch with her mom.

When the marriage began to come apart at the seams, Laurie sought psychiatric help, but soon dropped out of therapy. In desperation her husband found her a new house, full of the latest gadgets, in the hope that it would help. Laurie found herself more than ever out of her depth, storing money in the microwave and canned food in the dishwasher. She also did the unthinkable. In a social gaff that would reverberate around North Shore for years, she served frozen vegetables instead of fresh at a dinner party – unforgivable in those circles.

The couple separated. Laurie went back to her parents, but Russell paid for her to go back to teacher training college, this time at the National College of Education in Evanston. Nevertheless the divorce became messy, with petitions and counter-petitions mounting up in the courts. She complained that Russell was harassing her, even accusing him of breaking into her parents' home. Meanwhile, Russell, and other acquaintances, were pestered by phone calls, usually in the middle of the night, where the mysterious caller hung up as soon as the phone was answered.

In May 1986 Laurie bought a gun – a .357 calibre Magnum – and one hundred rounds of ammunition. When Russell got to hear of it, he called the police. They persuaded Laurie to lodge the gun in her father's bank deposit box – but they were not allowed to inspect it there.

Laurie found a new boyfriend, a little younger than herself. But he was disturbed by the fact that she compulsively washed her hands all the time. Meanwhile, allegations continued to fly between Russell and Laurie. He claimed that she had broken into his home and stabbed him with an ice-pick one night. While she alleged that he had tried to petrol-bomb her parents' home and had sexually assaulted her one night while she was having a bath. According to her statement, she had heard a noise in the house, had put on a dress and some underwear and gone to investigate. Russell had grabbed her, she said, dragged her into the bedroom and torn her dress and her panties off with one yank. Then he stuck a steak knife into her vagina and threatened to 'cut her all the way up' unless she signed the divorce papers. But there was no evidence to support either side and no charges were filed.

After her divorce Laurie moved on to campus at Evanston. She lied her way into several babysitting jobs, but her clients found her reliable and had no hesitation recommending her to their friends. However, she was forced to move out of the college dormitory after she was suspected of being behind a wave of petty pilfering.

Back home again, she kept up the babysitting. But complaints started rolling in of bizarre thefts from the homes of her employers. Those who complained suffered the same pestering phone calls.

In November 1987 Laurie bought her second handgun – a .32-calibre Smith & Wesson revolver. And in December 1987 she bought her third – a .22-calibre Beretta semi-automatic pistol. Her phone campaign became more serious. She threatened Russell's family and friends with death. And former employers were told: 'Your children are going to die.'

Laurie's father arranged treatment for her with the experimental drug clomipramine at the University of Wisconsin Hospital in Madison. She was also treated with lithium carbonate and swallowed birth control pills, antibiotics and aspirins in large quantities. Other drugs were prescribed for depression.

Laurie began stealing. Her thefts included poisons from the university hospitals and a book on their effects. She was arrested for shoplifting and released on bail. She put on more than thirty pounds, but still managed to find herself a boyfriend – a weedy student who wore combat fatigues and read *Soldier of Fortune* magazine. Laurie's own reading included true-crime books and soft-porn magazines like *Penthouse*. But soon her telephone-threat campaign reached such a pitch that the FBI were called in. They recorded Laurie making hysterical death threats to Russell's sister and Laurie was indicted.

The day before the grand jury hearing Laurie took the Greyhound bus home to Chicago. There she called two local primary schools, where acquaintances including Russell Dann's sister had their children. Pretending to be calling from a modelling agency, she invited cheerleaders she had known from high school to bring their children over to those schools for auditions that Friday. Laurie herself arranged to take the two youngest children of a former employer.

That Friday morning Laurie spiked a pack of Rice Krispies with arsenic and sent it to a former room-mate at college. She injected lead into orange juice cartons and sent them to other people she knew – including both her therapist and her ex-husband – as 'free samples'. She also drove around delivering poisoned foods through people's letter-boxes. Fraternity and sorority houses at Northwestern University got similar deliveries.

Then Laurie went to pick up the two kids she had arranged to take to school, leaving behind in the kitchen, in exchange, more poisoned cookies. She even managed to slip a few drops of arsenic into a jug of milk.

Laurie and the two kids arrived at the Ravinia Elementary School at around 9 a.m. There were some 300 children inside. Laurie left the two boys in the back of the car, and walked into the school unchallenged. With her she had a bag which contained highly flammable liquid, acids and other toxic chemicals. She hid in the playhouse and lit the draw-string as an elementary fuse. Fortunately the bag was spotted and the staff extinguished the flames before the contents went up.

Outside the nearby Kennedy School Laurie tried to murder the two children in the car with poisoned milk – but they refused to take more than a tiny sip because the arsenic made it taste so bitter. So Laurie took a can of petrol from the boot of the car and, with the two boys, walked over to the school entrance. But they would not let her in with the can.

Frustrated, Laurie took the two children back to their mother. There she poured petrol on the basement carpet threw a lighted match at it, and locked the mother and two children in. They managed to escape through a tiny window, suffering some nasty cuts and bruises.

At nearby Hubbard Woods Elementary School Laurie gained admission by giving the impression she was still a teacher training college student, and was allowed to sit in on the class of teacher Amy Moses. However, Laurie could not sit still. She went out into the corridor, grabbed six-year-old Robert Trossman from the drinking fountain, bundled him into the boys' toilet and shot him point-blank with a pistol she had concealed in her shorts.

Back in Amy Moses' elementary class, Laurie ordered the children into one corner. Amy Moses tried to grab her gun and shout for help, but Laurie broke free. She shot eight-year-old Mark Teborek in the neck. Then, coolly and deliberately and at point-blank range, she shot seven-year-old Kathryn Miller, and eight-year-olds Peter Munro, Lindsay Fisher and Nicholas Corwin. Blazing with two guns, Laurie made her escape. But the police spotted her speeding car. She lost them in a surburban area and screeched to a halt in the driveway of a mock-Tudor mansion. There she took off her shorts and tied a bin-liner around her as if it were a Superman cape.

She entered 2 Kent Road by the back door, claiming that she had been raped. She had shot her assailant and the police were after her, she said. Twenty-year-old Philip Andrew and his parents Ruth and Raymond were half-believing her when she waved her pistols in their direction and took them hostage.

Laurie called her mother a few times, but their conversation did not calm her. Meanwhile the police were combing the area. Philip Andrew managed to persuade her to release his parents and to hand over one of her guns, the Beretta. He unclipped the magazine. Then, for no apparent reason, Laurie shot him in the chest. Critically wounded, Philip managed to edge his way out of the back door and was almost shot by the patrolmen – who were now surrounding the house – because he was carrying a gun.

Laurie's parents were brought in to make an appeal to her through a police bullhorn. There was no reply from the house. Laurie had already put her .32 calibre Smith & Wesson in her mouth and pulled the trigger. Later that day an assault team cautiously worked their way through the twenty-two-room mansion to find Laurie in the top-floor bedroom with her brains blown out.

The only other fatality from her murderous rampage was eight-year-old Nicholas Corwin who died in his classroom at Hubbard Woods Elementary. But if Laurie Dann had succeeded in all her plans her death toll would have been one of the highest in the bloody history of spree killing.

9

Dying for Sex

Spree killing, though largely a North American phenomenon, could not long be contained within the borders of the USA. Although Canada shares much with its more populous neighbour, it has a much more peaceful and law-abiding ethos. Its capital, Ottawa, differs particularly from most American cities in having virtually no dirt and no poverty. It has a high proportion of bureaucrats, little night-life and could justly be described as boring. But this has at least one major advantage: compared to other major cities, its crime-rate is low, with half a dozen or so murders a year. So Ottawans were completely unprepared for the events of 27 October 1975.

The morning passed normally enough. Then, at 1 p.m., the Ottawa fire department received a call to investigate what seemed like a fairly routine domestic fire. A woman reported that clouds of smoke were pouring from a second-storey window of her home. Ten minutes later two fire trucks halted outside 5 Warrington Drive in a quiet suburban area of Ottawa, and were met by the housewife who had called them, Mrs Mary Poulin. Black smoke was issuing from the back door of the house, but there were no flames. The fire, it seemed, was in the basement, where her teenage son Robert lived. Two firefighters, Lawrence Bowes and Raymond Flavel, donned oxygen masks and made their way down the stairs. The smoke was so thick that they had to feel their way. But even through the breathing gear they noticed an unpleasant smell, like burning meat.

As the firemen entered the basement bedroom, they saw the charred body of a girl spread-eagled on what remained of the bed. She was naked except for a blood-stained blouse. Her head was covered with a plastic bag.

The intense heat quickly forced the two firemen to retreat into the fresh air. Visibly shaken, they asked another officer to call the police department – and report a murder.

The rest of the crew put the fire out, leaving the basement flooded with several inches of water. When the police waded back into the bedroom, they found the dead girl had been handcuffed to the bedpost by her left wrist. Handcuffs hung from the other bedpost, suggesting that her right wrist had also been fastened at one time. There were ski bindings around the posts at the foot of the bed. These seemed to indicate that her feet had also been tied. In fact she had been tied down and raped. The blood-stains on the remains of her plaid blouse quickly led investigators to believe that the girl had then been stabbed to death.

There was a trail of half-charred sex magazines running up the stairs. They had been doused with three gallons of camping fuel and set alight. The arsonist had plainly intended to burn the whole

house, not just the bedroom. However, the insti-
gator had forgotten to open the tiny bedroom
window. Starved of oxygen, the fire had effectively
snuffed itself out.

Suspicions quickly turned to eighteen-year-old
Robert Poulin. Mrs Poulin said she had last seen
him that morning before she left for her job as a
lunch supervisor at a local elementary school. He
had come upstairs at about 11 o'clock and asked
her to make him a peanut-butter sandwich, then sat
watching a quiz show on TV. She noticed nothing
strange about him. Nor had she any idea of his
plans for the day, although she knew he was due
to attend a theology class at the St Pius X High
School.

In classroom 71, students were listening to Father
Robert Bedard. The lesson that day was about Jesus
Christ and the problems of modern society. At 2.30
p.m. the door of the classroom creaked slowly open.
The students at the back glanced around and saw
a foot edge around the door, followed by the barrel
of a shotgun. Carrying it was a young man who,
from his smiling face, seemed to be in a kind of a
trance.

He raised the shotgun and started to fire. The
noise of his pump-action shotgun was no louder
than the popping of a balloon – then the air was
filled with screams. Father Bedard flung himself to
the floor, shouting at his students to do the same.
For some, it was already too late. The firing continued for about two minutes. Then it stopped. The
deathly silence that followed was punctuated by
the sound of just one more shot, this time outside
the classroom.

Then panic erupted. Students were smashing the windows with chairs and hurling themselves out. But Father Bedard remained calm. He got up and walked cautiously to the classroom door. Outside, the gunman lay sprawled on the floor. Half his face was blown away. A sawn-off Winchester shotgun lay beside him. The dead man was little more than a teenager. Despite the boy's appalling self-inflicted disfigurement, Father Bedard recognized him as one of his students – Robert Poulin.

Apart from Poulin, who died instantly when the final cartridge blew off the top of his head, only one person died as a result of the murderous classroom assault. Seventeen-year-old Mark Hough suffered critical wounds to the back of the head and neck. He died four days later.

Six other students were wounded, three of them seriously. All of them were men. They were rushed to hospital. Barclay Holbrook was wounded in the lung area. Two others, Mark Potvin and Terry Handenberg, also had neck wounds. The other three were released almost immediately.

Soon after the firemen had extinguished the blaze, Mrs Poulin learned of her son's death. When her husband Stuart, a teacher in the local primary school, was called home, his immediate fear was that the body in the basement was one of their three daughters. In fact all three were safe.

Robert Poulin did not have a girlfriend, so investigators were baffled. However, Poulin's sister said that he had been interested in a seventeen-year-old Sri-Lankan girl named Kim Rabot, who lived a few doors away. Poulin's sister had once invited Kim over to the house at Robert's request.

The last person to have seen Kim alive was her thirteen-year-old brother John. He had been with her at the bus stop on their way to school at 8.30 a.m. that morning when Robert Poulin had approached them. Poulin had told Kim that he had something to show her. A gentle girl who disliked hurting anyone's feelings, Kim had agreed to go with him.

Poulin had taken Kim to his basement room where he threatened her with the shotgun. He forced her to undress and handcuffed her to the bed. Then he raped her. At one point he untied her feet and unhandcuffed one wrist to turn her over. A post-mortem showed that she had been raped and sodomised. Finally he had stabbed her fourteen times with a hunting knife.

When Mrs Poulin had gone downstairs to the basement at around 10 o'clock that morning a bizarre incident had occurred. The curtains that closed off Poulin's bedroom were drawn. So she called out: 'Knock, knock, can I talk to you for a minute?'

Poulin said: 'Yeah, but don't come in.' His mother respected his privacy.

Poulin came upstairs an hour later for his peanut-butter sandwiches. Then he had returned to the basement, spread the magazines up the stairs and set the room alight. He strapped his hunting knife across his chest, put his 12-bore shotgun in a blue duffle bag and cycled across town on his ten-speed bicycle to his 2 o'clock theology class.

At St Pius X High School, instead of going straight into class, he went to the school cafeteria, carrying the blue duffle bag. The school's physical education teacher saw him there. Poulin, he said, looked 'scared'. Indeed, with one rape and murder already behind him, Poulin had already burnt his boats. Shortly before 2.30 he crossed the hall, pulled the gun from the duffle bag and dropped the bag to the floor. Then, like a sleepwalker, he turned the handle of a classroom door and slowly pushed it open with his foot.

Robert Poulin, born in 1957, was described as a 'strange, quiet boy'. At school he was conscientious and hardworking. When he was twelve his third sister, Jody, was born, and Poulin moved into the basement to make room for the new baby. He lived there alone. It was only after his death that his secret life was discovered. He had a passion for war games and played out heroic battles on the basement floor, manoeuvring huge numbers of troops and artillery. His other obsession was sex. The walls of the basement were plastered with pictures of naked girls, and there were piles of soft-porn magazines stacked on the floor. His diaries and notebooks revealed that he was also a desperately lonely boy, yearning for sexual contact and deeply tormented by his inability to talk to girls. One entry read: 'Today is September 5, 1972, a Tuesday ... There are some girls at school that I would love to be good friends with but I know that I am still too shy to go up and talk to any of them. I wish I could overcome this fear of women.'

There were also fragments of essays entitled 'Chance to be a Hero' and 'Inquiry Not Under Arrest'. These described Poulin's shyness and inability to deal with women.

Among his possessions the police found a box

containing women's bras, panties and negligées, and a pink blow-up sex doll with a pouting mouth and artificial vagina. There was a condom-type vibrator device, and no fewer than four pairs of handcuffs. The police also found a collection of pornographic books, some of which showed women tied up and handcuffed to bedposts.

One notebook contained the names, addresses and telephone numbers of eighteen girls. Police checked with the girls to see if any of them knew Poulin well. None of them did. But several had received 'heavy breather' phone calls. Plainly Poulin's tormented sex dreams were not entirely a matter of lurid fantasy.

In a neatly typed diary entry, dated 7 April 1975, Poulin spelt out his intentions. He had just flunked a biology test. 'For the last couple of weeks,' it read, 'I have been fairly depressed . . . [and] thought of committing suicide, but I don't want to die before I have had the pleasure of fucking some girl. So I decided to order a model gun from an ad in Gallery magazine (April 1975). With this I was going to threaten a girl in one of the dark streets around here and rape her. I planned to carry my father's scout knife strapped to the inside of my right leg. If the girl caused me any trouble I would kill her, for I was planning to kill myself anyhow, and I have nothing to lose. After that, I would wait for a reason for killing myself. The day I would kill myself would be a Sunday, for if I was going to die, the people that made up my family were going to suffer.'

Plainly Poulin's mind was becoming rambling and unhinged. At first he thought of taking his father's rifle and killing his whole family, but then decided that 'death is pure bliss and I would not want them to be happy'. Instead he planned to douse the contents of the house with petrol and set it alight before shootng himself. He even planned to burn the place down soon after his parents' payday so that they would lose the largest possible amount of money.

Then Poulin was brought back from the brink. His diary went on to relate that he had found an ad for 'Everything' Dolls in *Playboy* magazine and sent off $29.95 for what he hoped would be a lifelike doll of a girl. With his hopes high, he wrote: 'Now I no longer think that I will have to rape a girl, and I am unsure whether or not I will still commit suicide.' Then on 5 May 1975, he noted: '"Everything" Doll arrived – a big disappointment.' Clearly, sex with a plastic blow-up woman was not everything he had hoped for.

In the months immediately before Poulin's rampage there were a number of sexual assaults and attempted rapes in the area of Poulin's house. The perpetrator was a man wearing a balaclava. This may have been Poulin. According to his diary, in his planned rape he would use a balaclava to disguise his identity. The attacker was the same general height and build as Poulin.

In early October, in desperation, Poulin ran a small ad in the *Ottawa Journal* for a week. It read: 'Male, 18, looking for companionship. PO Box 4021.'

This did not work out as he expected either. He had received three replies – all from homosexuals. Poulin had replied to one, but had left the letter unposted. He wrote: 'I have never had a homosexual experience, though the thought has crossed my mind before. However, I'm not only interested in sex but in sharing other pastimes and hobbies. My favourite hobbies are, in order: war-gaming, reading (science fiction) and collecting (a variety of things, including stamps and models). I hope you have the same sort of hobbies, especially war-gaming.'

It is a measure of Poulin's utter loneliness that, with his strong heterosexual orientation, he was even prepared to experiment with homosexuality in order to find a friend.

Poulin came from a military family. His father had been an air-force pilot. Poulin's goal was to make a career in the army. But earlier that year he had applied for officer training in the Campbell Highlanders militia and, after an hour-long interview, had every reason to believe he had been accepted. But the three-man board had decided that he was too immature. Instead, he joined the militia as a private. Two weeks before the murders, he dropped out of training. He had lied about his interest in school sports and had been found out by the authorities.

This was the final blow. He went to a local store with the remains of his savings and paid $109 for a Winchester shotgun. Then, in his lonely basement, he sawed off the barrel.

Poulin's rampage was not the only killing spree that had hit Canadian schools. Five months before, sixteen-year-old Michael Slobodian went on a shooting frenzy in Brampton, Ontario. On 28 May 1975, Slobodian went to school with two rifles concealed in a guitar case. He left a suicide note in which he wrote that he intended to kill two teachers who had told him off for poor attendance, and 'anyone who got in his way'. He shot seventeen-year-old John Singer in the washroom. Thirteen people were injured as he sprayed bullets around the building. Twenty-five-year-old Margaret Wright, the art teacher, was killed. Then Slobodian shot himself.

Immediately after Poulin's killing spree, a spate of violence erupted in the schools of Ottawa. One student attacked a teacher with a razor. Another beat up a counsellor with an iron bar. And six months later a bomb went off in a high school.

In May 1975, twenty-year-old Russell Lee Smith ended an argument with his girlfriend by shooting her in the head. He shot and wounded two other men who had been involved in the argument, then drove his dead girlfriend's body to a hospital at Dayton, Ohio. On the hospital ramp he shot and wounded one person before driving away. He shot and wounded the driver of another car on the highway and in the parking lot of a movie theatre he shot a family of four, critically injuring their six-year-old daughter.

Smith then moved his rampage to a residential area, where he knocked on doors and shot at anyone who answered. He kidnapped a girl at gunpoint from a restaurant. While making his getaway, he stopped a car with a young couple in it and kidnapped a second girl. He killed the first, then drove the second to a wooded area where he raped her. The police turned up and Smith turned the gun on himself. At the time, Smith had been on probation for a murder he had been convicted of four years before.

Just a week before the Poulin spree, there was another mass murder which had a sexual motive. On 18 October 1975 twenty-nine-year-old Erwin Charles Simants broke into the house of the Kellie family in Sutherland, Nebraska. He raped ten-year-old Florence Kellie, shot her, then shot the other five members of the Kellie family who came running when they heard Florence's screams. Simants was arrested the next day and confessed to sexually violating Florence again after she was dead and attempting to violate the dead body of fifty-seven-year-old Audrey Marie Kellie. In January 1976, Simants was found guilty on six counts of murder and sentenced to the electric chair. The execution was delayed twice, then the verdict was overturned because the local sheriff had visited members of the jury. At a retrial, Simants was found to be not guilty by reason of insanity.

In 1980, twenty-three-year-old Andrew Weiss killed four people with a rifle, handgun and a butcher's knife in a house in Augusa, Maine. Weiss left a note at the scene of the massacre explaining the crime. It read: 'By the time you get this I will be out of the county. I killed Greg' – York, thirty-one, who had been stabbed in the back five times and shot in the head with a handgun three times – 'for getting me addicted to coke. I shot Lynn' – Weiss's twenty-four-year-old fiancée Lynn Girouard who had to be identified from dental records – 'because she too was addicted and was having an affair with Bobby' – Lizotte, shot once in the head and stabbed four times in the back. 'I shot Jerry' –

Nelson, shot twice in the head with a highpowered rifle – 'because she saw me do it.' Weiss was found in a room in a Holiday Inn in Massachsetts, dead from a drug overdose.

Sex was also behind the worst mass murder in Canada's history – but not because the perpetrator wanted it. He claimed his motive was the fight against feminism. It happened at the University of Montreal, which stands on the slopes of Mont Royal, overlooking Canada's largest city, on 6 December 1989.

It was the last day of the Autumn term and the atmosphere was festive. In room 230 on the first floor, sixty engineering students were just about to finish their last class. Just before 5.10 p.m. the door flew open. A young man marched into the room carrying a green bin-liner. 'Okay,' he shouted in French, 'Everybody stop what they're doing.'

As he spoke, he reached into the bin-liner and pulled out an automatic rifle. Nobody moved. The young man was bearded and wore blue jeans, an anorak and a red baseball cap. He looked like a student, like them, and everyone suspected this was some kind of end-of-term practical joke.

A moment later they discovered it was anything but a joke. The young man raised the rifle and fired into the ceiling. 'Move!' he yelled. 'Split into two – the girls on the left, the guys on the right.'

The students did as they were told. The girls – there were just nine of them – moved to the far side of the classroom away from the door. 'All right,' said the gunman. 'The guys can leave.' But the girls were told to stay exactly where they were.

Still thinking this was some kind of student rag,

the men filed out. The gunman kicked the door closed behind them.

'Do any of you know why I'm here?' he asked. Someone said no.

'I'm here to fight against feminism,' he said.

'But we are not feminists,' protested twenty-three-year-old Natalie Provost. 'We're just engineering students.'

No sooner were the words out of her mouth than the gunman started to spray the girls with bullets, raking the weapon back and forth. The girls' screams were barely audible above the sounds of automatic fire. Six fell dead. The other three were badly wounded.

When he thought he had finished them off, the gunman lowered his rifle and marched out into the corridor. Some of the men students were still there. He fired. They scattered. He did not seem to want to kill the men: 'I want the women,' he yelled.

With his back to the corridor wall, he slipped another clip of ammunition into his gun. Then he moved forward cautiously down the corridor. At the slightest sound, he turned and fired. Every so often he said: 'I want the women.' When one appeared, his action was swift. A moment later, she too fell dead by a photocopier.

One eye-witness to the carnage was Daniel Depuis, a student aged twenty-four. He had been on the third floor when he heard about the gunman. Someone warned frantically: 'Don't go down. He's shooting at everything that moves.' But curiosity drove Dupuis to make his way down the stairs to the first floor. He caught a glimpse of the killer who was descending to the foyer.

Dupuis went into room 230. One girl was sitting at a desk, bleeding profusely from a gaping shoulder wound and crying hysterically. Dupuis made a tourniquet in an attempt to staunch the blood. Another girl was lying on the floor nearby. Half her head had been blown away. He knelt beside her and took her hand.

'If you can hear me, squeeze my hand,' he said. To his surprise she gave a small squeeze. Outside in the corridor, Dupuis tended two girls who were lying together, groaning. One of them died in Dupuis' arms. The other girl was dead by the time the ambulancemen came.

Downstairs in the cafeteria the gunman began shooting again. Three more women were cut down under the Christmas decorations. Other students ran for the exit. The gunman turned and marched back upstairs.

On the second floor, in room 311, two women students were presenting a project on metallurgy. As soon as the gunman entered the room, he started firing. Both women fell, shot, followed by two women in the audience. Some students dived under their desks. Others ran for the door.

The gunman walked towards the front of the class, where one of the girls who had been addressing the class was moaning and crying for help. A bullet was embedded in her lung. The gunman put down his rifle and pulled a hunting knife from his belt. He stabbed her three times, until she gasped and stopped moving.

The gunman then removed his anorak and carefully wrapped it round the end of the gun barrel. In the eerie silence, some fearless students peered out from beneath their desks. They saw the gunman put the gun to his head and pull the trigger. His baseball cap – with the top of his skull in it – flew across the room.

Students rushed to help those who had been hit. The last victim, Maud Haviernick, was dead from a stab to the heart. So was her co-presenter, twenty-one-year-old Michele Richard. Several other students in room 311 were seriously wounded.

Photographer Claude Rivest, who managed to slip past security guards, found two wounded girls lying at the top of the stairs. He also discovered a dead female student under the table in the cafeteria.

The dead and wounded were already being lifted on to stretchers when the police arrived. A telephone call had alerted them at 5.17 p.m., just three minutes before the gunman ended his life. At 5.26 p.m. Lieutenant Claude Lachapelle of the homicide squad arrived. He ordered that the university guards were to admit no one else – there could be another gunman inside. Even ambulance crews were not allowed to move the wounded until the police were sure that the killer was dead.

Lachapelle made his way up to classroom 311, where the gunman lay spread-eagled, his brains exposed. His red baseball cap and the top of his skull, still covered with curly black hair, lay on the other side of the room. The rifle, a .223 calibre Ruger semi-automatic, lay beside him. Lachapelle could not figure out why the killer had gone to the trouble of placing his anorak over the end of the barrel to prevent the blast burning his flesh when he intended to blow his brains out.

The dead man appeared to be a typical student.

He was slightly built and about five feet six inches tall. A three-page letter, handwritten in French, was found in his pocket. It started: 'Forgive the mistakes – I had only fifteen minutes to write this.' He went on to explain his actions.

'Please note that if I am committing suicide today ... it is not for economic reasons ... but for political reasons,' he wrote. 'For I have decided to send to their forefathers the feminists who have always ruined my life. It has been seven years since that life ceased to bring me any joy, and being totally bored, I have decided to put an end to those viragos ...

'Even if a mad-killer label is stuck on me by the media, I regard myself as a rational and intelligent person who has been forced into taking extreme action ... Being rather backward-looking by nature (except for science), the feminists always have a talent for enraging me. They want to keep the advantages of women ... while grabbing those of the men.'

More rambling anti-feminist rhetoric was followed by a list of fiteen local women. 'These nearly died today,' the note ended. 'Lack of time (because I started too late) has allowed these radical feminists to survive.'

At the bottom of the letter, there was a signature. It read: 'Marc Lepine'

Within an hour of the shooting, a news flash about the massacre was carried on the radio and TV, though early reports put the death toll at only two or three. Immediately the engineering building was besieged by reporters and frantic parents. The director of public relations for Montreal police,

Pierre Leclair, stood on the steps of the building, doing his best to answer the questions. Then someone came out of the building and whispered in his ear. Leclair went pale. He apologised to the crowd, turned and went slowly into the university building. He had been asked to identify the body of his own daughter, twenty-three-year-old Maryse.

At the City Hall, Councillor Therese Daviau was attending a meeting when news of the deaths at Montreal University began to come through. Her twenty-one-year-old daughter, Genevieve Bergeron, was an engineering student there. At first Therese was not too concerned – Genevieve was most probably at choir practice. However, during an adjournment, Councillor Daviau learned that more than two or three had been killed. There had been a massacre.

She rushed to police headquarters to try to find out more – but most of the victims had still not been identified. By 11 that night, she was in a state of terrible anxiety. She sent a male friend over to the university where the grim task of identifying the bodies had begun in earnest. An hour later he rang back. He had just seen Genevieve's body among the dead.

Families all over Canada soon had the same story to tell. At first, they had believed it to be a hundred-to-one chance that their daughter was one of the victims, then they learned the worst. Even the citizens of Montreal who had lost no one in the tragedy exhibited all the symptoms of people in a state of deep shock. They could not believe that their university had been the scene of the worst mass murder in Canadian history. A local politician asked simply: 'How could such a thing happen in our society?'

It was not until the following day that the full death toll became known. Marc Lepine had killed fourteen women. Thirteen other students, several male, had been wounded, some seriously. All the victims were engineering students except for Maryse Laganiere, a twenty-five-year-old office worker. Still nobody understood why he had done it.

Newspaper reporters soon found that Lepine rented a five-room apartment at 2175 Rue Bordeaux, a few miles away from the university. A woman who lived in the flat below remembered how Lepine played his music so loudly at night that the police had been called on three occasions. Lepine himself had always avoided her. He ran up the stairs to his second-floor apartment if he saw her come into the building. The other tenants simply described him as an eccentric loner who seldom spoke.

Chantal Dumais, a girl who rented a flat across the street from Lepine, had even more disturbing memories. She described how she could see into Lepine's dining-room from one of her windows. He kept a human skull on the bookcase, she said. She often sensed that someone was watching her. One evening she had forgotten to close the curtains while undressing when she realised that she could be seen from Lepine's flat. She quickly closed the bedroom curtains. As she did so, she heard a sound from Lepine's apartment like someone blowing his nose loudly. Then she heard someone laughing. The eerie sound was repeated every night for weeks after.

A girl who knew Lepine said that he was bored, lonely and sex-starved, completely unable to attract a steady girlfriend. Former school-mate Jean Belanger, Lepine's closest and probably only friend, said that Lepine was extremely shy and had never had any girlfriends.

'It's not that he wasn't interested,' Belanger said. 'But the way he approached women wasn't exactly the way women like.' Lepine had not had any friends of either sex after he and Belanger parted company.

When journalists tracked down Lepine's mother, forty-three-year-old nurse Monique Lepine, they found a broken woman. She had survived a disastrous seven-year marriage to Marc's father, a brutal Algerian named Raschid Liass Gharbi.

Gharbi was convinced that women were fundamentally inferior to men. Their true role was as servants. His mood changes were sudden and violent.

'He would speak of love . . . then, out of nowhere, I would receive a blow in the face,' Monique Lepine recalled. He also hit his two children in the face, often making their noses bleed. Afterwards, he would not allow his wife to comfort them.

Gamil Gharbi – who later changed his name to Marc Lepine – suffered more than his elder sister Nadia and was terrified of his father. The fear did not go away even after his parents were separated. If he realised that his mother was driving him over to see his father, he would grab the steering wheel. Once he almost caused a crash.

Raschid Gharbi vehemently denied any responsibility. He had never beaten anyone, he said. The worst punishment he had ever meted out was to make the children stand to attention for ten minutes with their arms by their sides. But other relatives said they had seen Gharbi repeatedly slam his young wife against the wall in front of the children.

After their divorce Monique began to use her maiden name, Lepine. Her son started using it too, and called himself Marc instead of Gamil. Even though they were free of the violent Gharbi, the family was not happy. Monique had to work long hours to support Marc and his sister. The children were alone together a great deal and Nadia treated her shy younger brother with open contempt.

Early on at school Lepine had shown great promise, but gradually he lost interest in his studies. An obsession with war films took over and he dreamed of joining the army. But when he applied, he was turned down. He also failed to get a place to study engineering at the polytechnic.

With no close friends and no girlfriend, Lepine lived completely alone. At the age of just twenty-five, he was slowly overtaken by an overwhelming sense of madness and defeat. But no one ever discovered why he believed feminists had ruined his life.

10

In The Name of God

On 18 November 1978 the Reverend Jim Jones sat on his crude wooden throne deep in the jungles of Guyana. He was surrounded by nearly 1,000 of his followers. He had bad news for them. Most of them were about to die.

Although Jim Jones was not the type of spree killer who climbed a tower with an assault rifle, he was responsible for one of the biggest single incidents of mass murder in history, claiming over nine hundred lives in a matter of minutes.

Jones had brought the congregation of his People's Temple – largely poor black Americans with an upper echelon of radical middle-class whites – with him from the United States to found a new utopia in the backwoods of South America. There, he promised, they would be free from the racist and capitalist oppression that they believed dogged their every move in their homeland.

But even in Guyana they were not free. Several members of Jones's People's Temple had left the sect in America – traitors, Jones called them – and had told the press bizarre tales of the goings-on in Guyana. They claimed that the bisexual Jones sexually dominated his flock. He had forced them into gruelling manual labour in appalling physical conditions. They were disciplined in humiliating rituals and were not allowed to leave.

A support group, the Committee of Concerned Relatives, had been formed. One of these relatives, Sam Houston, a journalist with Associated Press, accused the cult of murdering his son. He had left the Temple after a violent argument with Jones. The next day he had died in a grisly railroad accident near the waterfront in San Francisco.

One of Houston's drinking buddies was Congressman Leo Ryan. Several of the Temple's members came from Ryan's congressional district in south San Francisco. Houston had persuaded Ryan to investigate the sect and find out what was going on in the Temple's South American settlement, Jonestown.

On 24 October 1978 Ryan received authorisation from the House Foreign Affairs Committee to go to Guyana. With legal action threatening to cut off the sect's American funds, Jones had no choice but to comply with the visit. However, Jones tried to lay down conditions. He would not allow Ryan into Jonestown if he brought any 'traitors' or the press with him.

The feisty congressman would have none of this. He turned up in Guyana with four members of the Committee of Concerned Relatives, reporters and photographers from the San Francisco dailies and the *Washington Post* – and an NBC film crew. If he was not allowed into Jonestown, Ryan informed Jones, film of him being turned away would be shown on NBC's network, coast to coast across

America. A full-scale congressional investigation was sure to follow.

On the afternoon of 17 November Ryan's party flew to the airstrip at Port Kaituma, a few miles from Jonestown. They were picked up by one of Jones's adopted sons, Johnny. Congressman Ryan, the relatives and the party of journalists entered Jonestown just before sunset on the back of the Jonestown dump truck.

The reception was surprisingly friendly. Although Jones retired scowling to his hut, sect members had been instructed to smile. Dinner was served at eight and, afterwards, the Jonestown band began to play.

Congressman Ryan made a speech. It was pure political genius. Without a word of criticism against Jones, he told the Templars how much he enjoyed the band and that Jonestown looked like a pretty nice place to live.

'From what I have seen,' said Congressman Ryan, 'there are a lot of people who believe this is the best thing that ever happened to them.'

There was only one thing wrong with Jonestown, he said – it wasn't in his congressional district so its members couldn't vote for him.

The Templars, who despite their smiles and Sunday-go-meeting clothes were deeply resentful of outside interference, broke into spontaneous applause. The tension was broken. The band struck up again. The young people took to the dance floor. The older ones joined in clapping. Everyone seemed happy. But as the dance floor emptied that night, a young black woman, Monica Bagby, passed a note to NBC journalist Don Harris. It asked him to arrange for her and her friend Vern Gosney to leave Jonestown with Congressman Ryan the next day.

The next morning things really started falling apart. At daybreak, nine sect members seized their chance to escape. They set off through the jungle towards the village of Matthew's Ridge, some twenty miles away.

Dodging the official tour of Jonestown, some journalists began poking around on their own – almost provoking a riot. And Don Harris began interviewing Jones on camera. Jones talked openly about his mistresses and denied press reports that there was any ban on sexual intercourse among his followers. It was 'bullshit,' he said, 'thirty babies have been born since the summer of 1977.'

But this was not the smooth polyester-suited pastor who had charmed politicians in California and had once dined with the president's wife Rosa-lynn Carter and flown in the private jet of presiden-tial hopeful Walter Mondale. Jim Jones was now fat, pale and sweaty. After only a few minutes of persistent questioning, he began to crack.

'The only thing I regret is that somebody hasn't shot me,' he ranted. 'We're a small community, we're no threat to anyone, but they won't rest until they destroy us. I wish they would just shoot me and get it over with. But I guess the media smear is what they use now – in the long run it's as good as assassination.'

Other reporters began pressing Jones about the son he had had with one of the cult members who had defected and which Jones refused to return to its mother. Why did the Jonestown security guards carry weapons and why were threats made to those who wanted to leave?

'It's all lies,' responded Jones wearily. But immediately he was caught in a lie. One of his henchmen brought news that Edith Parks, the grandmother of a family that had been planning to escape for some time, had asked Ryan that they be taken out of Jonestown. Jones went to see them.

'I am betrayed,' he wailed. 'It never stops.'

Seizing their opportunity, another twenty people asked Ryan to take them with them. Jones, by this time, was hysterical.

'I've given my life for my people,' he cried. Aides calmed him down and persuaded Jones to let them go. Such a small number of defections – compared with the huge number that stayed – was not important. Even so, the atmosphere in Jonestown began to turn ugly.

As the defectors left, a husky young man in his late twenties, Don Sly, pulled a knife from his pocket and grabbed Congressman Ryan. Two of Jones's aides pulled Sly off, cutting his arm in the process. The blood spurted over Ryan.

At the last moment, another defector, Larry Layton, announced that he was 'pissed off with Jonestown' and joined the departing party. The earlier defectors were terrified. Layton was known as Jones's 'robot'. Layton was searched before he boarded the plane at Port Kaituma. But somehow he had managed to smuggle a gun on board. The Jonestown tractor then turned up, blocking the runway. In its trailer there were twenty heavily armed men.

Inside the plane Layton started shooting, hitting

Monica Bagby in the chest. The men from the trailer then opened up. Three of the defectors were hit.

Out on the runway, Congressmen Ryan and three of the NBC crew including Don Harris were caught in a hail of bullets. Once they were down, the Jonestown gunmen made sure they were dead with a shot in the head as they lay on the ground. Three other journalists were wounded. The tractor and trailer then pulled away.

Meanwhile, back in Jonestown, Jim Jones called his followers together. He explained that one of their number, Layton, had shot the pilot of Ryan's plane in the head and that the plane had crashed in the jungle. This had been the original plan. The twenty men on the trailer were sent in case anything went wrong.

Jones said that the CIA would force the left-wing government in Georgetown to send soldiers of the Guyanese Defence Force against them. These soldiers were their black socialist brothers. They could not fight back. The only answer was a solution for which they had long prepared – they should all kill themselves.

One of the Templars asked whether it was not too late to escape to the Soviet Union. The Russians would not take them now, said Jones, though he had already despatched two of his henchmen to the Soviet Embassy in Georgetown with a suitcase containing half-a-million dollars in cash.

Jonestown medical staff prepared two fifty-gallon drums of Kool-Aid, laced with valium and cyanide. His followers were well prepared. Jones assured them that they would 'meet again in another place'. The Templars queued up for their lethal drink in an orderly fashion. Mothers gave the cyanide to their children. Infants had it squirted in their mouths from a syringe. Even Jones's own children were happy to take the poison.

The congregation had long been told that swallowing the poison would lead to a painless death. But when the children went into convulsions, panic broke out. Jones managed to calm the congregation.

'They not crying out of pain,' he said. 'It's just a little bitter tasting' – and the adults calmly went on taking their poison from paper cups. They went out into the fields and lay down and died. Then came the turn of the armed guards. They too took their poison without resistance.

When they were all dead, Jones took a pistol and blew his brains out. Annie Moore, one of the Jonestown nurses, shot herself in the head with the same gun moments later.

Mass suicides are not unknown in history. During World War II, the Japanese citizens of Saipan hurled themselves from the cliffs of their rocky island rather than suffer the ignominy of defeat. But a parallel that would strike a closer chord to the victims of Jonestown is probably the suicide of the Zealots at Masada.

The Zealots were a Jewish sect that fought against the occupation of Palestine by the Romans in the first century AD. Masada was an ancient mountain-top fortress where these Jews made their last stand.

Occupied by the Romans after the death of King Herod in 4 BC, Masada was captured by the Zealots in a surprise attack in 66 AD. When Jerusalem fell and the Temple was destroyed, it became the last remnant of Jewish rule in Palestine. For two years, a Roman army of 15,000 besieged a Jewish force of just 1,000 men, women and children there.

Overwhelmed when the Romans built a ramp and set fire to the fortress's wooden walls, the Zealots preferred suicide to surrender. Only seven women and children hidden in a water duct survived.

However, Jim Jones had left a bizarre suicide note – a ghoulish tape-recording of the final meeting and the grisly mass suicide itself. On it, Jones exhorts his followers to 'take the potion like they used to take in Ancient Greece; it is a revolutionary act.'

Like so many spree killers, he was deeply egocentric.

'The world was not ready for me,' he said to his followers. 'The best testimony we can make is to leave the goddamn world.'

And he did not care how many people he took with him.

'I don't care how many screams you hear ... how many anguished cries; death is a million times preferable,' he said.

Even children's.

'Can some people assure these children of the relaxation of stepping over into the next plane?' he asked.

The one thing the tape didn't do was to explain to a shocked world how a charismatic leader had driven 914 people to kill themselves.

Jim Jones was born and brought up in Lynn, Indiana, a town about the size of Jonestown, which depended for its existence on one thriving local industry – coffin-making. Jones's father had been gassed in France during the First World War and returned to Lynn to become the local bar-fly. Jim Jones described him as a 'mean old redneck racist'. It was only after his death that his son discovered he had been a lifelong member of the Ku Klux Klan.

Jones's mother shocked small-town Indiana by wearing trousers and smoking in the street. She fancied that she had travelled the world in a previous existence, subscribed to *National Geographic* and filled her son's bedtime stories with tales of her adventures with headhunters up the Amazon, spells, omens, the transmigration of souls and black magic. She believed that dreams were a vision of the future and told her son that he was destined to help the poor and weak. He would be a man who would leave his mark on the world.

Although Jones does not seem to have caught religion from the family, this was the 'born-again' bible belt of Indiana and he could not help but be influenced. At the age of twelve, in a loft surrounded by pictures of the Good Shepherd and his grisly death, Jim Jones began preaching his hellfire-and-damnation sermons. He earned a reputation as a healer of ailing pets and held mock funeral services for dead cats. Others saw a more sinister side to his interest in animals.

'Some of the neighbours would have cats missing and we always thought he was using them for sacrifices,' a contemporary recalled.

While most of his contemporaries went into the white world of banking, business, farming or teaching, Jones worked as a porter in a hospital near

Indianapolis where his colleagues were mainly poor and black. There he met and married a skinny, pale student nurse, five years his senior.

At this time Jones wanted to become a doctor and enrolled at the University of Indiana in Bloomington. After a year he dropped out, intent on being a preacher.

After recruiting from door-to-door for a Methodist mission, he became an unordained supply preacher. But his ministry was not a success. The largely white congregation objected to the blacks Jones was bringing in. They did not like his wild, declamatory preaching style – nor did they like being told that God had been a fellow passenger on the train he'd taken to Philadelphia one day. The church elders threw him out and closed down his church as if it had been desecrated. At the age of twenty-two, unfinanced and unordained, Jim Jones founded the Community National Church in a rundown section of Indianapolis. Although the Community National sounds like a savings bank, it was very much a shoestring operation. Jones supported it by importing and selling monkeys – at twenty-nine dollars each.

But Jones was not the prototype American tele-evangelist who preached God, the Flag, family values and the American Way. In 1953 he joined the Communist Party. That year he also conceived the idea of 'revolutionary death' when atom spies Julius and Ethel Rosenberg were executed. The arrest and trial of these two Jewish Americans had split America in the early 1950s. They were accused and convicted of selling the secrets of America's atomic bomb to the Soviet Union.

This was at the height of the McCarthy-ite era, when fanatical anti-Communist Wisconsin Senator Joe McCarthy even accused former president Harry S. Truman of giving succour to Communists in his administration. He was supported by much of middle America who wanted to rid America of all those they saw as traitors – Communists, blacks, Catholics and Jews.

The Rosenbergs protested their innocence and many east- and west-coast liberals viewed their trial as anti-semitic rather than anti-Communist.

Sentenced to death in March 1951, their appeals for clemency fell on deaf ears. President Eisenhower said that by giving atomic secrets to the Soviets they had committed a crime worse than murder because it could cause the death of 'millions of innocent people all over the world'.

On 19 June 1953 they were strapped into the electric chair and executed. That day over 5,000 people gathered in New York's Union Square to protest against the executions, denounce President Eisenhower and pray for the couple's two surviving children.

The execution of the Rosenbergs, Jones concluded, shattered the illusion that America was the 'last best hope of mankind'.

'I wish I could have died then,' Jones said later. 'Hell, you can only have so many revolutionary deaths . . . so, hell, death isn't a problem for me any more. I was in this goddamn miserable coma . . . I don't know why I lived.'

Jones described himself privately as a 'socialist' – though his political philosophy seems to owe more to Robin Hood than to Karl Marx. The poorer, the weaker his followers, the more atttention he lavished on them. One early member recalls: 'He had a lot of them, the kind of people most folks don't want to have nothing to do with. Fat, ugly old ladies who didn't have nobody in the world. He'd pass around hugs and kisses like he really loved them, and you could see on their faces what he meant to them.'

Jones's success at building a truly multi-racial congregation – one of the first in America – attracted unwelcome attention. Segregationalists called him a 'nigger-lover' and threw dead cats into his church. His windows were broken and explosives went off in his yard. But the more opposition he faced, the harder he tried. He even adopted eight Korean and black children. His unwavering stand against racism lead to his appointment to the newly created City Human Rights Commission, reporting directly to the mayor, in 1961.

By 1957 he had collected $50,000 and set himself up in a lavishly converted synagogue on North Delaware Street, Indianapolis. This was the first People's Temple Full Gospel Church.

Around the same time, Jones made several pilgrimages to the Peace Mission of Father Divine, the most successful ministry to the urban poor in the country. He learnt at the master's feet. The keys to Father Divine's success were his absolute insistence on his own divinity and extravagant demonstrations of the power of faith. Jones quickly learnt the lesson and began putting on his own displays of healing.

In carefully contrived theatrical settings, he got

believers to spew up chicken livers claiming they were cancers, raised perfectly fit young people made up to look like paralysed ancients from their wheelchairs and astounded his congregation with his mind-reading powers. He had a photographic memory and had already begun detailed files on all his followers.

Jones also noted that Father Divine, though black with an exclusively black following, surrounded himself with an inner circle of attractive, middle-class white women. But Jones did not follow his mentor's example of compensating himself for long days at the ministry with Cadillacs and forty-room mansions.

Instead, Jones took his young family off for two-years' missionary work in the favelas of Belo Horizonte in Brazil. There he met hardened Marxists for the first time and added a fresh dollop of Communist philosophy to his gospel of social change through Christian love. On the way back to America he stopped in British Guiana, soon to become the independent country of Guyana.

Back in the USA, everything had changed. His fight to unite black and white was no longer a single-handed struggle. For the first time he heard Martin Luther King expound his vision of a future America where racism would no longer be an issue. But what made a more powerful impact were the words of Malcolm Little, aka Malcolm X, who asked: 'What has Christianity done for black people – except oppress them?'

Malcolm X rejected Christian love and even broke with the Black Muslims. Armed insurrection was the only answer. And in a country that was dominated by a vast majority of whites, for black people this amounted to 'revolutionary suicide'.

The Vietnam War, civil rights marches in the South and race riots across the USA convinced Jones that he must take his followers to a 'promised land'.

Then in 1964 *Esquire* magazine published an article pinpointing safe havens from nuclear holocaust. One of these was not Redwood Valley near Ukiah, California. But Jim Jones picked this as the place to be anyway.

He relocated the People's Temple there, bussing hundreds of followers across the country. Some stayed behind. But those who went had to sell their property and became totally dependent on Jim Jones and the Temple.

From Redwood Valley, the Temple spread into San Francisco and Los Angeles. Jones opened food kitchens and day-care centres. Soon he was wielding political power. He could deliver his several thousand members as a block vote. Virtually every liberal office holder – from the lieutenant governor of the state of California down to the district attorney – was offered the chance to address the congregation. They quickly became beholden to Jones. In gratitude San Francisco mayor George Moscone appointed Jones chairman of the city's Housing Authority.

Even national politicians cultivated him. During the 1976 presidential campaign, he had dinner with Rosalynn Carter. For his part, Jones could use his influence to secure preferential treatment for his congregation with welfare agencies, housing authorities and even in court.

In California Jones met an ambitious young lawyer named Tim Stoen. Stoen had just married his young wife Grace. He had been disillusioned by the assassination of President Kennedy and was searching for a revolutionary way ahead. Jones promised just that. His multi-racial congregation and free-wheeling Christian-Marxist philosophy seemed to represent the wave of the future. Jones's political influence could also secure Stoen the plum job of assistant DA in San Francisco.

The price of Stoen's participation was his wife. On 25 January 1972 she bore a son, John-John. Although the birth certificate lists Tim Stoen as the father, in a private affidavit he admits that he had requested that Jones sire a child by his wife 'with the steadfast hope that said child will become the devoted follower of Jesus Christ and be instrumental in bringing God's kingdom here on earth, as has been his wonderful natural father'. Jim Jones, Tim Stoen said, was the 'most, compassionate, honest and courageous human being on earth.' The affidavit was witnessed by Marceline, Jones's wife. Grace Stoen's feelings were not recorded.

Already Jones was using his congregation as a harem. Young women followers seemed to consider it a privilege to satisfy his sexual cravings. It was the least they could do for the great man. One of Jones's secretaries kept a special appointments book for these dalliances. Jones himself boasted of his prowess, claiming an almost superhuman potency, technique and endurance. At one time he even sought psychiatric advice on how to bring his libido under control.

Jones used sex not just for pleasure, but for

power. It weakened the bond between married couples and bound both individuals closer to the Temple. No sex was allowed with outsiders – and any relationship inside the congregation needed the Temple's approval. Jones had at least three children by members of the congregation, though one woman had an abortion rather than bear his child.

Sex was frequently a topic of discussion at meetings of the all-important Planning Commission. This was an inner circle of around a hundred members, largely the better-educated middle-class whites.

Meetings would drag on to the early hours with Jones exhorting the members to new heights of revolutionary zeal. He would rail against bourgeois sexual attitudes and force members to publicly confess their sexual fears and fantasies. Long periods of celibacy were sometimes demanded. Jones took no sensual pleasure in sex, he claimed, he used it as a revolutionary tool. On one occasion he forced a white man to perform cunnilingus on a black woman publicly during a meeting to prove that he was free of racial prejudice. Sexual frankness and public urination, Jones contended, were symbolic demonstrations of the community's openness. However, some members were disturbed by the pleasure Jones seemed to take in exhibiting himself.

Jones's sexual activities were not confined to women. Men in the congregation were encouraged to sleep with him too – as a revolutionary act. In 1973 Jones was arrested for making blatant homosexual advances to an undercover police officer in the men's room of a movie theatre during the matinee of *Jesus Christ – Superstar*. It was part of a police vendetta against Jones and the Temple. A few weeks earlier they had been called to a traffic accident outside the Los Angeles branch of the Temple. One of Jones's stooges was supposed to be critically injured, but a few words from the pastor were enough to revive him. But the police barged in, sirens blaring. Temple officers tried to keep them back and a fight broke out. The next day Jones used his political clout to have the officers reprimanded.

But the LAPD's attempt to disgrace Jones backfired. Such was his political influence that not only did he get the charges dropped but the arrest record was sealed by a Los Angeles judge.

While things were becoming more open inside the community, Jones began to take a more paranoid view of the outside world. He believed that his phone was being tapped by the FBI and he was being followed by government agents.

Ex-members' houses were watched to make sure they were not talking to government agents or hostile journalists. Their private lives – and sometimes even their garbage – were combed for potential blackmail material. The Mertles were typical victims.

In 1968, newlyweds Elmer and Deanna Mertle had been invited to visit the People's Temple in Redwood Valley. They found there a friendship and community they had not experienced before. Both came from fatherless homes and found a convenient father figure in Jim Jones – who was already styling himself as 'Dad'.

Deanna found her Seventh Day Adventist beliefs challenged. Christianity was a 'slave religion', she was told, and the Bible is full of logical contradictions. She read her Bible again and found that it was.

Elmer was more attracted by Jones's politics. He liked the way, after their first visit, everyone greeted them by name. They and eventually their children were fussed over like they really belonged.

One night Deanna had a dream. She and Elmer were being threatened by a terrible monster. Jones saved them. Soon after, they sold their home and moved into a farm Jones had found for them nearby. Within a few weeks he had also found them jobs.

By 1975 the Mertles were members of the Planning Commission, but were becoming increasingly disturbed by Jones's bizarre behaviour, and when their 6-year-old daughter was spanked for a minor infraction, they decided to leave. This was not as easy as they thought. Two of their children lived in the homes of other Temple members and felt more commitment to Jones than to their natural parents.

Their home and everything they owned belonged to the Temple. It was their only source of income. They had been completely supported by – and surrounded by – the Temple for five years and had little or no contact with the outside world.

The Mertles were lucky though. Elmer's mother gave them a profitable rest-home she owned in Berkeley and the money to buy a house. But when Deanna Mertle called one of Jones's aides to tell him they were leaving all hell broke loose.

A delegation came round and tried to persuade them to change their minds. Others searched for stolen documents. Jones threatened to smear Elmer as a child molester. The Mertles responded by threatening to take lurid tales of the meetings of the Planning Commission to the press.

Eventually the Mertles had to change their names and deposited documents damaging to the Temple and sworn affidavits charging Jones with all manner of indecent behaviour in a safe deposit box to ensure their safety.

After they had left, Jones denounced the Mertles as traitors who abandoned building up a better world for worldly pleasures. They had sold out their brothers and sisters, he said, 'for a pocketful of credit cards and a fancy car'.

That same year Jones was named by the *Los Angeles Herald-Examiner* 'Humanitarian of the Year', one of the '100 Outstanding Clergymen in America' by the Foundation for Religion in America and appointed chairman of the San Francisco Housing Authority by Mayor George Moscone.

Meanwhile, Jones was about to reveal publicly his sinister hidden agenda – though the world would not take a blind bit of notice. He had been invited to speak at an anti-suicide rally in San Francisco on Memorial Day 1977. The purpose of the rally was to get the city fathers to construct an anti-suicide barrier along the Golden Gate Bridge – a favourite jumping-off point for the depressed and disturbed.

Although Jones's speech began with stern moral disapproval of suicide – suddenly, half-way through, he changed course. His condemnation of suicide became a blanket endorsement for it.

Jones had first mentioned the idea of 'revolutionary suicide' to Grace Stoen in 1973. At that time he only planned for his followers to die. He would stay alive to explain why they had done it.

In 1976 he began to put his plans into practice. On New Year's Day he coerced his followers into drinking what he told them was poison. He railed against the 'traitors' who had left the Temple and told the congregation that, if they loved him, they could only prove it by drinking the poison. Some became hysterical. But after the mock shooting of a member who tried to run away, Jones's followers meekly did what they were told. Forty-five minutes later he told them that the 'poison' was innocuous. They thanked him for testing them.

This was the first of a series of suicide rehearsals that Jones called 'white nights'.

'Everyone will die – except me. I've got to stay behind and explain why we did it,' Jim Jones told his followers.

Each time, the congregation were told that they were swallowing poison – they could never be sure that they were not. But gradually they got used to the idea of laying down their life for 'Dad' – who by now was claiming to be God, or at the very least from another planet like Superman.

Templars did not thank God, they thanked Jim Jones. At the same time, Jones gave up all belief in Christianity, even hurling his Bible to the ground during a sermon to reinforce his point.

Then things started going wrong for the Temple. The *San Francisco Examiner* carried the first stories of torture and public flogging at the People's Temple for minor infractions. Then *New West* magazine published an article attacking Jones. Once free, the Mertles dedicated themselves to fighting the

Temple. They outlined the sexual and physical abuse they had witnessed. The magazine unearthed evidence of extortion, embezzlement and blackmail. Jones had begun diverting into offshore investments. The article also outlined Grace Stoen's relationship with Jones.

Grace had run away from the Temple some time before. Now she began suing for the return of her son. Jones was determined she should not have him – he was one of the new breed that Jones was determined would inherit the earth.

Tim Stoen was still Jones's legal adviser. He told Jones that there was no point in fighting Grace through the courts. They were bound to return John-John to his natural mother – especially when Grace and the Mertles outlined Jones's bizarre sexual practices from the witness box. There was only one way that Jones could hold on to John-John. That was to take him abroad. Fighting for custody in a foreign court could be strung out for years – perhaps forever.

In 1975 Jones had paid $1 million for 27,000 acres of jungle in Guyana. British Guiana had been granted its independence in 1966 and changed its name to Guyana. Although the majority of the people in the country are ethnically East Indian, Guyana has had a socialist government run by blacks of African origin ever since. Jones found this an irresistible combination.

Seven years after his first fleeting visit in 1963, Jones went back with his plans of building a utopia there. The Guyanese government were immediately receptive. An under-developed country, they welcomed any scheme that would bring in foreign capital – especially from a source as politically sympathetic as Jim Jones.

Jones's proposal of clearing the jungle and turning the virgin land over to agriculture also coincided with Guyanese development aims. The land they leased him was along the Venezuelan border in an area that had long been disputed. Establishing a large colony of Americans there would prevent the Venezuelan army annexing the region and would provide the Guyanese government with documentation establishing that it belonged to them.

In 1976 it was still an experimental agricultural outpost, but in 1977 large amounts of building materials were shipped up the river to nearby Port Kaituma. Some 380 Templars applied for visas and headed for Guyana. John-John was among them.

But by and large the ordinary Guyanese were puzzled by the new settlers. There were two Guyanese soldiers at Port Kaituma when the shooting started. They did nothing to defend Congressman Ryan and his party. They later said that if two lots of crazy Americans wanted to shoot each other, what business was it of theirs?

Stoen's advice to flee to Guyana to prolong John-John's custody in the foreign courts eventually worked against him. He too finally defected from the People's Temple, and was reconciled with his wife. Together they tried to get John-John back. The case did indeed stall in the Guyanese courts and John-John died at Jonestown.

In 1978 another 700 set off. The entry fee to Jones's utopia was everything they owned or earned. Many chose to pay it. Others had no choice.

An unknown number of children – perhaps as many as 150 – were handed over to the Temple, along with their welfare cheques, by probation officers and the welfare agencies in Ukiah and San Francisco.

Briefly free from the discipline of Jones, Templars travelling to Jonestown got drunk in the grog shops of Georgetown. The party continued on the boat up river. One teenage girl, full of rum, had a brief fling with one of the Guyanese boatmen. Jones was furious. Once inside the compound at Jonestown, iron discipline was enforced. Casual sexual encounters were banned – and the Relationship Committee enforced three months celibacy on any couple applying to have a serious relationship.

Such prohibitions did not apply to Jones himself, of course. He moved into a hut with two of his mistresses while his wife lived nearby. One young girl who refused his advances was forcibly drugged and taken from the Jonestown hospital to Jones's hut each night. Those who found favour with Jones were given special privileges. The Jonestown doctor who supported Jones's claim that non-revolutionary sex caused cancer was indulged by a succession of teenage girls. And when Debbie Blakely left, Jones confessed that her defection was his fault – it was because he refused to have sex with her. She wanted bourgeois sex – for pleasure! – whereas for him sex was a political act.

Beatings were commonplace for minor offenses or simply because Jones thought their 'head was between their legs' – that is, they were thinking of sex – rather than of socialist work. He was especially hard on any male who was hitting on a girl he fancied. Adults were caned, or forced to fight each other until 'right triumphed', or simply beaten into bloody submission. Children were informed on for minor breaches of discipline. They were taken before a microphone at 2 a.m. and beaten – as many as seventy-five times – with a board while their cries echoed from the PA system around the compound. One was buried in a metal box for twenty-four hours. Others were lowered down a well, where they were pulled into the water by a waiting assistant.

Meanwhile, Jones became increasingly paranoid. He claimed to have killed a burglar breaking into his hut and served the man's flesh up in a stew for his followers.

While his followers toiled in the fields from sun up to sun down, Jones stayed in his hut taking drugs and monitoring the news from San Francisco and the Temple's outpost in Georgetown. He controlled the Templars' listening and doctored all news from the outside world.

He claimed that Jonestown was about to be attacked by a force of mercenaries trained by the CIA who were mustering in a staging area across the Brazilian border. Armed guards were posted around the compound, ostensibly to protect the Templars from attack. In fact, they were to stop disaffected Templars escaping.

However, when Congressman Ryan turned up only some thirty Templars wanted to leave. The rest willingly killed themselves at Jones's behest. In a horribly perverse way, Jones had succeeded. He had fused his followers into a single community. He had convinced almost a thousand people that they lived – and died – only for each other.

'We've stepped over, one thousand people who said we don't like the way the world is,' Jones's voice said on the tape. 'Nobody takes our lives from us. We laid it down. We got tired. We didn't commit suicide. We committed an act of revolutionary suicide, protesting the conditions of an inhumane world.'

Two escaped. One was Odell Rhodes, who had been a heroin addict when he first encountered the People's Temple. They had turned his life around. They got him off drugs and put him in charge of the children. He became a teacher and for the first time had some status in life.

He was happy to go to Guyana. When he heard that the CIA was going to attack he did not mind fighting and dying for the Temple. He was a Vietnam veteran. But he got fed up with the nightly meetings. After a long day in the fields he could not stand the hysteria, the sermonising, the sexual humiliation and the white nights. Instead, he volunteered to work in the nursing cottage. Not being as indoctrinated as the others, he was not prepared to take the potion.

At the final meeting, Rhodes found himself at the front – unable to move without drawing attention to himself. He was shocked how easily others took the poison. When the children started dying he volunteered to go to the hospital to get a stethoscope. He slipped out of the back way and out into the jungle.

When he reached Port Kaituma, he found it difficult to convince the police that everyone at Jonestown was dead. But eventually they put him on the phone to Georgetown, where a sceptical police inspector said he would be down the next morning with the army.

The other escapee was Stanley Clayton. He had been working in the kitchen when he had been told to forget about dinner. There had been white nights before, but no one had ever said forget about dinner. When he reached the pavilion, he saw the children dying. But he was not prepared to take his own life because a few people had left the Temple. He would rather risk getting a bullet in the back.

He pretended that he was looking for someone, slipped around the backs of the guards and made off into the jungle. He found a nearby house and told the occupants what had happened. They did not believe him. But when he said that they would be able to help themselves to the tools and supplies in Jonestown, they decided to check out what he was saying. They came back with arms full of stolen goods and a glazed look of horror in their eyes.

When Clayton made it to town, he was arrested. Rhodes had already made his phone call to the police. News of the massacre had got out and it was rumoured that one of Jones's last acts was to send out assassination squads.

The day after the massacre, Guyanese soldiers entering Jonestown found two more survivors. Grover Davis was hard of hearing and had missed the summons to the pavilion. When he finally went to see what was happening, he saw the first children in their death throes. He hid in a dry well. The next morning he climbed out and went back to his hut to sleep. He woke when the soldiers arrived and was nearly shot. They thought that he was a corpse coming back to life again.

The other survivor, Hyacinth Thrush, slept through the whole thing. She was frail and bedridden and when her breakfast did not turn up the next morning she hobbled outside to find out what was happening. By the time she had reached the door, the terrible smell explained everything. Later she said that she was sorry to have missed the opportunity to die with her brothers and sisters.

Surveying the corpses, the Guyanese army estmated that there were only 600 dead. It was hard to tell, as body was piled on body. It was only ten days later when a US Army mortuary team arrived that the death toll was finally fixed at 914.

The mortuary team and the Guyanese coroner Dr Leslie Mootoo examined the bodies for blisters on their upper arms. They were looking for evidence that the cyanide had been administered forcibly to unwilling victims. But with the exception of a few feeble old people, there were no signs of telltale blisters.

The crowd of followers had indeed been ringed by armed guards, but they did not seem to need to coerce the Templars into killing themselves. In fact, the victims seemed not just willing but eager to drink the poison. According to one witness, the first victim, Ruletta Paul, walked up to the dais with her child and took the cyanide without even being asked. 'She just poured it down the baby's throat. And then she took the rest herself. It didn't take them right away. She had time to walk outside . . . then the next woman, Michelle Wilson, she came up with her baby and did the same thing.'

And when Jones radioed to the office in George-town that liaised with the Guyanese government and instructed them to commit suicide too, the Temple's public relations officer took her three small children into the bathroom, killed them, then slit her own wrists. The others failed, however, to follow suit.

But although the deaths seemed to be voluntary, Jones had spent years cowing his followers into total submission. Not only would they do whatever he said, they would anticipate what he wanted and do it before he even asked. Had he lived, it would have been hard for Jim Jones to have denied responsibility for those who gulped down cyanide – and gave it to their children – at his behest.

Despite the fact that his father was a member of the Ku Klux Klan, Jim Jones had spent his whole life fighting against racial prejudice. He established his ministry in the ghettos and preached largely to black people. Until the People's Temple, it was rare to see black and white people worship together in America.

In the ghettos, he got junkies off the street, helped unmarried mothers, educated black children, helped house black people and provided day-care centres and food kitchens for black inner-city residents.

He saw himself as a great revolutionary leader in the mould of Martin Luther King and Malcolm X. To identify more closely with his black congre-gation, he claimed to have Cherokee Indian blood that gave him his swarthy complexion.

However, when the bodies were found, the cyan-ide had turned the skin of even his white followers black, while Jones, who had shot himself, had turned a deathly white.

Only one person went to trial for complicity in the Jonestown massacre. It was thirty-five-year-old ex-Quaker Larry Layton, a member of Jones's death squad. Extradicted to the United States, he was charged with injuring US diplomat Richard Dwyer and conspiracy to kill Congressman Ryan. But the jury in San Francisco could not reach a verdict and the judge declared a mistrial.

Even when Jones was dead, his followers were not safe. After the Jonestown Massacre, the Mertles and their teenage daughter were murdered. No one has been caught and the police have no suspects and no active leads. Although the police say they have no reason to believe that the Murtles' murders had anything to do with the People's Temple, other defectors do. Many still live in fear of the Temple's assassination squads.

Pastor Jim Powell of the First Baptist Church in the small town of Daingerfield, Texas, was a charismatic preacher too. To dramatise his sermon against the evils of Communism, he had several uniformed men come rushing into the Sunday service. So it was no surprise to the 350 worshippers when, on 22 June 1980, forty-six-year-old Alvin Lee King III came bursting in while they were singing the hymn *More About Jesus*. He was wearing Army fatigues, a flak jacket and helmet, and carrying an arsenal. This included an AR-15 rifle with bayonet fix, an M-1 carbine, a pearl-handled .22 calibre pistol revolver and a .38 calibre pistol. Slung over his shoulder was a pack stuffed with 250 rounds of ammunition.

'This is war!' he announced and opened fire with the AR-15. He loosed off five rounds in ten seconds into the stunned congregation. The skull of seven-year-old Gina Linam was smashed, killing her instantly. Seventy-eight-year-old Thelme Robinson also fell dead. And forty-nine-year-old Gene Gandy was fatally wounded just below the heart. She survived until that night.

Chris Hall, the sound recordist who broadcast Pastor Powell's sermon, leapt on King and pushed the gunman, who outweighed him by more than five stone, out into the church vestibule. King dropped his automatic and lost his helmet and his glasses. Without them, he could see no more than six feet. King unholstered his .38 and blasted blindly down the steps into the crypt as Hall made his escape.

Then fifty-three-year-old James 'Red' McDaniel charged at the gunman. He ran him out through the front door, which broke, and down the church steps. But King's .38 went off, and Red McDaniel rolled off him dead.

Forty-nine-year-old councillor Kenneth Truitt tried to run the gunman down. He was shot and killed.

Inside the church Larry Cowan picked up the M-1 that King had dropped and fired at the gunman. King dropped his .38 and ran to a nearby fire station. There he shot himself in the head with his .22, but failed to kill himself. At the church, five were dead and eleven wounded.

When policemen went out to King's isolated

farmhouse eight miles from Daingerfield, they found his wife, Gretchen, tied to a chair with rope and a telephone cord. On a table was a note. It read: 'Jeremiah says the King is the King of Kings.' In the basement the officers found a letter from the Soviet embassy in Washington, DC, informing King that he could not become a Soviet citizen. They also found records of a Swiss bank account, where he had deposited $3,000 that spring, and passports for King and his wife. 'He definitely had something planned,' said Deputy Sheriff Emit Kennedy. But no one could say what.

King was born in 1934 and raised in Corpus Christi, Texas by his parents, who owned a pawnshop, a liquor store and a jukebox leasing company. He majored in education at North Texas State University, where he met his wife Gretchen Gains. The couple were married in 1956. Ten years later the Kings, along with their daughter Cynthia and son Alvin Lee King IV, moved to Daingerfield, Texas, where King taught maths at the local high school. 1966 was also the year a terrible accident took place. While examining a loaded 12-bore shotgun in his parents' home in Corpus Christi, King dropped the gun. It went off, killing his father. The coroner ruled it was accidental death.

At Daingerfield High, King was considered brilliant but an oddball. He refused to sign the oath required of all local teachers saying they believed in God. And his teaching methods were somewhat eccentric. For example, he let students whose grades fell between the Bs and Cs cut a deck to decide whether their final grade should go up or down. Then in 1972 he resigned rather than teach retarded children and became a truck driver.

Five years later the Kings' house burned down under rather mysterious circumstances and King moved his family to a hundred-acre farm where he raised peas and cucumbers, practised judo and collected guns. As far as most people in Daingerfield were concerned, King had disappeared.

Then in October 1979 nineteen-year-old Cynthia King turned up at Daingerfield Police Station. She claimed that her father had been forcing her to have sex with him for the last ten yers. She told officers that she had finally decided to file incest charges against him at the urgings of a friend, Stanley Sinclair, twenty, the son of a Methodist minister. The following month, Sinclair was found in Houston. He had been stabbed to death.

After a change of venue, King was due to face trial in Silver Spring. He asked several members of the First Baptist Church to testify as character witnesses. All refused. The trial was set for 23 June 1980, the Monday after the massacre. King did not attend. Instead he faced five counts of murder and ten counts of assault with intent to kill. On 28 July 1980 a jury found him incompetent to stand trial and sent him to Ruskin State Hospital for the Criminally Insane. There it was determined that his IQ was 151, but he was not found competent to plead until November 1981. King was moved back to Daingerfield jail, ready to stand trial. The proceedings were scheduled to start on 25 January 1982, but on 19 January King tore a towel into strips, tied the strips together, made a noose and hanged himself from a crossbar in his jail cell.

11

The Menace Spreads

Spree killing spread over the border into Canada
again in 1984. This time the attack took place at
Quebec's National Assembly, whose debating
chamber had long been a battlefield between Eng-
lish-speaking Canadians and the French-speaking
Québécois. Just a month after security guards had
been replaced by more appealing hostesses who
ushered visitors through the hushed Renaissance-
style halls, a man with a beret rushed into the
building, spraying the crowds with sub-machine-
gun fire. School children fled for cover. One of the
hostesses fell to the ground. The gunman ran on
up to the second floor where he killed three government employees and wounded thirteen others. But
when he barged into the chamber of the Assembly,
the politicians were not there. He was too early.
The morning session had not yet started.

'I came to kill,' he yelled at staff members as he
sprayed the chamber with bullets. 'I must have
made a mistake about the time.'

That was as far as Corporal Denis Lortie got in
his attempt to destroy the province's ruling Parti
Québécois. The only person who did not flee from
the Assembly chamber was René Jalbert, the sixty-

three-year-old sergeant at arms. He approached Lortie and offered him a cigarette. Then Jalbert discovered that Lortie served in his old army regiment. He insisted that Corporal Lortie address him as major. After the police surrounded the building, he persuaded the gunman to surrender.

'He just wasn't rational,' Jalbert told reporters after his five-hour ordeal. 'He just kept talking about how he wanted to impress people.'

Lortie, a twenty-five-year-old supply technician from the Carp military base near Ottawa, had started the day by delivering a pre-recorded tape at a local radio station in Quebec City. When station employees played the tape, they heard a frightening message. Ranting about the 1977 legislation that established French as Quebec's pre-eminent language, Lortie said that he planned to eliminate the Parti Québécois – and kill anyone else who got in his way.

Lortie's attack stirred strong emotions across Canada. Quebecers had grown increasingly disenchanted with the Parti Québécois. A few locals even expressed sympathy for Lortie's rampage. One French-speaker was unnerved by it. The next day thirty-nine-year-old Quebec City resident Jean-Claude Nadeau opened fire with a 20-bore shotgun in a city street. Two people were injured, but not seriously. Nadeau barricaded himself in his home, which was quickly surrounded by the police. He surrendered twenty-four hours later.

Most Canadians were, however, horrified. They still believed that spree killing was largely confined to the US. Lortie's attack on one of their seats of government helped convince them that no one was safe. Indeed, in 1987, even a sleepy, crime-free English countryside found it was vulnerable to a killer with a gun, a grudge and no reason to live.

On 20 August 1987, thirty-three-year-old Susan Godfrey took her two children for a picnic in Savernake Forest, ten miles from the drowsy village of Hungerford in Berkshire. It was around 12.30 p.m. They had finished eating and Mrs Godfrey was strapping four-year-old Hannah and two-year-old James into the back of the family car when a man dressed in black appeared.

Incongruously for the Berkshire countryside, he was carrying a Chinese-made AK47 – a Kalashnikov assault rifle more usually seen in the hands of Third World guerillas. He took the car keys from the dashboard of the black Nissan and forced Mrs Godfrey to come with him. Less than a hundred yards from the car he emptied the entire magazine of the Kalashnikov – fifteen high-velocity rounds – into her back at point-blank range. The children were later found wandering the forest.

There seems to have been no motive for this savage murder. Mrs Godfrey was not sexually assaulted and there seems to have been no connection between her and her murderer – twenty-seven-year-old Michael Ryan – before her death. There is no evidence that Ryan had trailed the family. He had been in the forest, armed, since the mid-morning. The police could only speculate that she had surprised him during target practice. A local boy had heard a burst of semi-automatic fire from the forest at around 10.30 that morning.

But one senseless act of violence was not enough for the lonely and deluded Ryan. He drove his D-registered Vauxhall Astra back down the A4 towards his home in Hungerford.

Hungerford is an ancient market town with a population of less than 5,000. The broad market main street is dominated by the Bear Hotel and the redbrick clock-tower that tolls out the hours with a long, flat note. Hungerford was granted a charter by John of Gaunt, whose name is commemorated by a pub in the town and the secondary school Michael Ryan attended. The charter allows the owner of three cottages to freedom of the town. Ths brings with it grazing and fishing rights in the neaby River Kennet which is well stocked with trout and grayling. The owner also has to hold office on 'Tutty' (Tithing) Day and act as ale-taster, Constable and Tutty Man, parading through the streets in morning dress, kissing maidens and throwing oranges and pennies to the children.

The summer in Hungerford is quiet and still, though in August the sky is occasionally darkened by smoke from the burning stubble. The redbrick villas of the old town are a symbol of stability in the unchanging English countryside. The only lurking sense of fear emanates from the dark Victorian mental asylum that stands across the cattle grid on the Common. But on the back road from Hungerford to Lambourn there is a monument half-buried in the hedgerow. It commemorates the death of two policemen who were murdered there by a gang of robbers in 1870. It was Hungerford's only previous experience of public slaughter.

On the way back to Hungerford, Ryan stopped at the Golden Arrow filling station in Froxfield, Wiltshire. It was 12.45 p.m. The cashier mother-of-three Kabaub Dean recognised Ryan. He stopped there for petrol every other day, normally paying by credit card but never passing the time of day.

Today was somehow different. Mrs Dean noticed Ryan was hanging around nervously. He appeared to be waiting for another customer to leave. Then she saw him fiddling about with something in the boot of his car. Suddenly he pulled a gun out and started shooting at her. The glass window of her booth shattered and she was showered with glass. She dived for cover.

Ryan approached as she lay helpless under the counter. She begged for her life as he stood over her. Coldly he took aim and – at point-blank range – he pulled the trigger.

Mrs Dean heard the click of an empty gun chamber. Ryan had run out of ammunition. He pulled the trigger again and again. Mrs Dean heard four or five clicks. Then Ryan walked back to his car and drove away.

His next stop was his mother's house at 4 South View in Hungerford where Ryan also lived. There he had built up a fearsome arsenal. In a steel cabinet bolted to the wall of the house he kept at least one shotgun, two rifles, the 7.92 mm Kalashnikov, three hand-guns including a 9mm pistol and an American-made M-1 carbine and fifty rounds of ammunition which he had bought for £150 at the Wiltshire Shooting Centre just eight days before the incident.

Ryan had joined the shooting centre a month before the incident. Here he was known as 'polite' and 'unremarkable'. Those who got to know him better found him articulate, especially about his favourite subject – guns. He could reel off a detailed history of the M-1 and its use in World War II and the Korean War. He had been practising with the M-1 on the club's shooting range just the day before the shootings.

Little is known about what occurred between Ryan and his mother when he got home. Some say they got on well. Others paint a bleaker picture. But less than twenty minutes after the shooting at the petrol station, Ryan shot his mother. Her body was found lying in the road outside the house. Ryan then set the house on fire. The blaze quickly spread to the three adjoining houses in the terrace.

A neighbour, Jack Gibbs, was the next to die. He was in the kitchen of his home when Ryan began his murderous assault. Sixty-six-year-old Mr Gibbs threw himself across his sixty-three-year-old, wheelchair-bound wife, Myrtle Gibbs, to protect her from the burst of semi-automatic fire from Ryan's Kalashnikov. Four high-powered bullets passed through his body, fatally wounding his wife. She died in Princess Margaret Hospital, Swindon, the next day.

Then Ryan shot neighbours Sheila Mason and her seventy-year-old father Roland as they rushed from their home at Number 6. He gunned down eighty-four-year-old retired shop-keeper Abdur Khan who used to wander the streets of Hungerford from his home in Fairview Road, talking to anyone he met.

He shot at passing cars, killing George White from Newbury who happened to be driving through Hungerford. Ian Playle, the thirty-four-year-old chief clerk of West Berkshire Magistrates' Court, was driving down the A338 through the village with his wife Elizabeth, his six-year-old son Mark and their eighteen-month-old baby daughter Elizabeth when Ryan sprayed their car. Mr Playle was hit several times and died later at the John Radcliffe Hospital in Oxford.

As Ryan roamed the village where he had lived his entire life the death toll mounted. Ken Clements was killed as he walked down a footpath at the end of South View. Douglas Wainwright was shot in his car on Priory Avenue. Cab driver Marcus Barnard was on his way home to his wife and month-old baby when he was shot. Eric Vardy was also found dead in his car in Priory Road.

Ryan's last victim was Sandra Hill. She too was shot in her car on Priory Road. She was rushed to the local doctor's surgery, but it was too late. She died shortly after arrival.

In less than an hour and a half, Ryan's murderous rampage left fourteen dead and fifteen wounded. But there was nowhere to run to – and the police would soon be closing in on the quiet Berkshire village whose name would soon be synonymous with mindless murder.

At 12.40 p.m. Mrs Kabaub Dean, the cashier at the Golden Arrow service station, called the police. But she thought the shooting incident was just a robbery until much later when she heard about the bloodletting in Hungerford on the radio. Five minutes after her call the Wiltshire police alerted the neighbouring Thames Valley force, assuming that Ryan would have moved into their jurisdiction.

At 12.47 p.m. the Thames Valley police got their first 999 call from Hungerford. The caller reported a shooting in South View, the street where Ryan lived with his mother. Shortly after 1 p.m. Police Constable Roger Brereton arrived in South View. At 1.05 p.m. he radioed the message: '18. 10-9. 10-9.' It was the code for 'urgent assistance required, I have been shot.' No more was heard from him. His body was later recovered from his police car near Ryan's house. He had been shot in the back. He left a wife and two teenage sons.

By 2 p.m. the killing had stopped. Then the caretaker at John O'Gaunt Secondary School reported seeing a man enter the school building at around 1.52 p.m.

Michael Ryan had attended the school ten years before. It had made little academic impression on him. He had been in the C-stream for pupils of below average achievement. The headmaster David Lee could not recall him. Lyn Rowlands, who had been class-mates with Ryan at Hungerford County Primary School and John O'Gaunt Secondary School, said that he never seemed a very happy child. He was always on his own, always on the sidelines. Other children would try to include him in their games but he would be moody and sulky. Eventually people left him to his own devices. But she did not remember him ever being nasty in any way. He was not the kind of boy who got involved in fights. He was very introverted and 'a bit of a mystery'.

Another of his school-mates, Andy Purfitt, tells much the same story – that Ryan was a loner. He never mixed with anyone and did not play football with the other boys. But Purfitt remembers that Ryan was picked on by the other children a lot.

As if to compensate for this bullying, Ryan

developed an interest in guns. Even at the age of twelve, he used to fire a .177 air gun at the cows in the fields behind the house, a neighbour recalled. Later he went out at nights shooting rabbits. One night he met a man who was much bigger than him. The man got a bit stroppy, so Michael pulled a gun out of his pocket and pointed it at the man. The man turned on his heels and ran.

'That just goes to prove the power of the gun,' Ryan used to boast.

He collected ceremonial swords, military badges and medals, and military magazines. School friends say he preferred guns to girls. When he left school, one of the first things he did was get a small-arms licence.

During his last year at school, Ryan hardly ever turned up for classes. He left with no qualifications and drifted through a number of labouring jobs. He worked at a local nursery and Peter de Savary's theme park at Littlecote. Ryan lived for guns and seemed to disappear into a fantasy existence. He often boasted to neighbours of the latest gun he had purchased and the sound of him firing nearby was quite common.

Now, after his murderous rampage through his home town, Hungerford, Michael Ryan was back at school and – as ever – alone. The Chief Constable of the Thames Valley police, Colin Smith, claimed that prompt action by armed police officers prevented Ryan from killing more people than he did. But it was not until 5 p.m. that the police confirmed that Ryan was in the school. They surrounded it.

The local police admitted that they did know Ryan, but only in the way that most of the inhabitants of a quiet friendly market town knew each other. He had no criminal record. A local constable had visited Ryan's home in South View in June, just two months before the massacre, when Ryan had applied to have his firearms licence extended to cover the 7.62 calibre automatic rifle. Ryan already had a firearms licence and, when he registered his new Kalashnikov, the police had checked on the house to make sure that the gun was stored securely. The officer they sent was Police Constable Trevor Wainwright, the son of Douglas Wainwright who was later to become one of Ryan's victims. His sixty-three-year-old mother was also injured when Ryan opened fire on their car. They were on their way to visit their son.

Wainwright said of Ryan: 'From local knowledge I knew he was not a yob or mixed with yobs. He was not a villain and I knew he did not have a criminal record. He was a loner but you could not hold that against him. The checks were very thorough.'

The young police officer had checked that the cabinet where Ryan kept the weapons was secure, then approved the extension of his licence and forwarded it to the headquarters of Thames Valley Police. In doing so, he had sealed the fate of his own parents.

While Michael Ryan was holed up in his old school, the children of his first victim, James and Hannah Godfrey, had been found. Apparently, despite witnessing the horrific murder of their mother, they had been tired and had had a little sleep. When they awoke, they had gone to look for help.

They met Mrs Myra Rose, herself a grandmother, who was taking a stroll in the forest. She saw the two children coming down a hill towards her. The little boy was wearing a Thomas-the-Tank-Engine T-shirt and his sister had her hair tied back with a pink headband.

Two-year-old James grabbed Mrs Rose's hand and refused to let go. Hannah, who was four, acted as spokesman.

'A man in black shot my mummy,' she said. 'He has taken the car keys. James and me cannot drive a car and we are going home. We are tired.'

Seventy-five-year-old Mrs Rose lived in Bournemouth and was visiting friends in nearby Marlborough when she decided to go for a walk alone in the Savernake Forest. She found what the children were telling her hard to believe.

'It was such a horrific story for a little girl to tell,' Mrs Rose said, 'I did not know whether to believe it. The children were not crying.'

She was confused about what to do, but then she bumped into another family in the forest and told them what the children had said. One of them went to call the police and Mrs Rose sat down with the children to tell them stories.

'I don't think the youngsters really understood what had happened to their mother,' she told the newspapers later. 'James would not leave my side and I wanted to stay with the children.'

When the police came, they quickly found the bullet-riddled body of Susan Godfrey. Soon they were mounting a huge search of the 4,500-acre forest with teams of tracker dogs in case its glades contained the bodies of any further victims of Michael Ryan.

Talking to the police at John O'Gaunt School, Ryan appeared lucid and reasonable. He expressed no regret for killing Mrs Godfrey, nor any other of his victims. Only the murder of his mother seemed to trouble him.

Michael Ryan was thought of as a mummy's boy. Born when his mother Dorothy, a canteen lady, was thirty-three, he received the usual over-attention of a single child. He spent most of his time with his mother and was jealously guarded by his father. A friend of the family described Ryan as a 'spoilt little wimp'. It was said: 'He got everything he wanted from his mother.' She would buy him a new car every year.

Ryan's father, Alfred, was a council building inspector. Michael was devoted to him. When he died in 1985, two years before his son made the name Ryan notorious, Michael seemed to go to pieces. 'He was his life, you see,' said Michael's uncle Leslie Ryan. 'When he went, Michael seemed to go.'

He became violent and unpredictable, and he focused more of his attention on his collection of guns. The family were relieved when they heard that Michael was about to get married. The date was set, then the wedding was called off.

'He doesn't know whether he wants to be married or not,' his mother told relatives. 'First of all it's on and then it's off.'

Many doubt that there was a girl at all. He had certainly never been seen with one. Next-door neighbour Linda Lepetit said that Ryan and his mother had been close.

'It's unbelievable that he shot her,' she said. 'They got on so well. We could often hear them laughing and joking together. He had a natter to me and my children several times, but he was a bit of a loner.'

But others report a different story. Dennis Morley, a friend of the family, claims that Ryan used to beat his mother up.

'He used to hit his mother a lot,' said Morley. 'But he would not pick on a man.'

During his long conversations with the police from John O'Gaunt school, Ryan claimed to have been a member of the Parachute Regiment. He was not. But he was an avid reader of military and survivalist magazines, and he had fantasies about being a paratrooper. Along with his usual attire of a brown jacket and slacks, he wore a pair of Dutch parachuting boots. He also wore sunglasses in all weather and was self-conscious about going prematurely bald. Even his only drinking buddy described Ryan as 'extremely quiet, he never gave anything away about himself'.

Apart from walking his labrador, Ryan's only recreation had been shooting. He belonged to two shooting clubs where he spent an hour twice a week. Andrew White, partner in the Wiltshire Shooting Centre in Devizes, said: 'He'd come in for a chat, pick up his targets, go down to the range for an hour's shooting, come back, have another chat, and then go.'

But White did notice that, unlike some of the other riflemen at the 600-member club, Ryan would not use targets that showed a human figure or a soldier's head. He would insist on the standard circular accuracy targets.

During his negotiations with the police, he confessed to the murders he had committed. Although he could shoot other people, he could not kill himself, he mused. But at about 6.30 p.m. a muffled shot was heard from inside the school. Ryan did not answer any more. He had killed himself.

The armed police still held back though. There were fears that Ryan had been holding hostages and they could not be sure what had happened inside the school. It was only at 8.10 p.m. that armed officers finally burst into the classroom to find Ryan shot with his own gun – and the Hungerford massacre was over.

Britain was so shocked by Michael Ryan's murderous outburst that the BBC quickly dropped several films they had scheduled which depicted undue violence or gun play. The first casualty was an American movie called *Black Christmas* which was due to go out on BBC 1 at 11.50 on the night of the massacre. It depicted a psychopth killing college girls and was replaced with the Dick Emery comedy *Oh You Are Awful!*.

The BBC's own film *Body Contact*, described as a 'stylish pastiche with echoes of *Bonnie and Clyde*', was also dropped. The ITV company Anglia dropped the western *Nevada Smith* and switched an episode of *The Professionals* for a less violent one.

The day after the Hungerford massacre a fund was set up to provide support to the injured and the families of the dead.

Local millionaire Peter de Savary gave £10,000. He had employed Ryan as a labourer when he was building his medieval theme park at nearby Littlecote House and about eighty per cent of the people who worked at his theme park lived in Hungerford. Another anonymous doner gave £10,000 and Newbury District Council gave £5,000. Local radio stations GWR Radio and Radio 210 launched appeals. Soon smaller donations poured in and within a couple of days, the fund topped £50,000. Ryan's victims would also be eligible for compensation from the Criminal Injuries Compensation Board. Murder victims' spouses and children under eighteen would also be eligible for a bereavement award of £3,500 and a 'dependency' award.

Hardly a single person in Hungerford's 5,000 population was unaffected. In a community of that size everyone knew someone who had been killed. Quickly the Hungerford Family Unit was set up, giving ninety-minute grief therapy sessions. It was staffed by social workers who had counselled victims' families from the Zeebrugge ferry disaster and the Bradford tragedy where football fans had been burnt to death in a football stand.

The local church also played a role, offering prayers for the victims and flying its flag at half-mast. They also offered prayers for the soul of Michael Ryan. However, the church soon found itself in an awkward position. While Michael Ryan's mother Dorothy had asked to be buried at Coine in Wiltshire, close to the village of Cherhill where she was born, Ryan himself was to be buried in Hungerford alongside his victims. Some residents of Hungerford muttered darkly that, if he was buried there, his body would be dug up and thrown out.

The Prime Minister Margaret Thatcher was on

the streets of Hungerford two days after Michael Ryan. She visited the area where fourteen people had been gunned down and the four houses that had been gutted when Ryan set his mothers' house on fire. At the local vicarage she met some of the relatives of Ryan's victims and was soon close to tears. After visiting the wounded in the Princess Margaret Hospital in Swindon, Mrs Thatcher described the incident as 'not an accident in which we get a terrible tragedy, it is a crime, an evil crime'.

She pledged to tighten up the gun laws so that such a thing could never happen again. But it did. In April 1989, twenty-two-year-old Robert Sartin committed a 'copycat shooting' similar to Ryan's at Monkseaton, near Newcastle on Tyne, killing one and injuring fourteen.

In the 1980s, in fact, the whole of Europe was experiencing a spate of spree killings. In April 1983, twenty-seven-year-old Sevdet Yilmaz shot and killed six people and wounded another five in Delft, Holland. In June that year, thirty-four-year-old Karel Charva shot dead five people and wounded fourteen others in Eppstein, near Frankfurt. In November, thirty-four-year-old Miloud Amrani shot and killed five people, wounding three others, in Lyon. In January 1984, Russian teenager Anatoly Markov went on a drunken spree with his father's rifle. He shot at anything he could see – birds, squirrels, the tops of trees. When a helicopter flew over he shot at that too, fatally wounding the flight mechanic. Markov was jailed and his father was punished for buying the rifle illegally and failing to keep it in a secure place. In June 1985, Guy Martell rampaged through a series of towns in Brittany, killing seven and wounding five. In 1987, Belgian gunman shot and killed seven. In 1988, an army corporal shot and killed four people, wounding twelve others, and a military policeman in Italy killed four. Then in July 1989, thirty-one-year-old Christian Dornier committed the worst spree killing on mainland Europe – killing fourteen and wounding nine others. After a few *Pastis*, he shot his sister, mother, father and a guest at the lunch table. Then he got in his car and drove around the small village of Luxiol, shooting anyone he could find – including children, one as young as five, and a brother and sister in their eighties. He shot the first *gendarme* who came to their rescue. The rampage ended when he drove into an ambush set up by *gendarmes* on the road to the next village. No one knew what set off the rampage, but his brother said that Christian had never been the same since his military service eight years before.

Australia already had some experience of spree killing. In 1963, on a summer Saturday night in a comfortable Perth suburb, a gunman started picking off people, seemingly at random. Nicholas August, a poultry dealer and a married man, was out with Ocean Beach barmaid Rowena Reeves. They were sharing a drink in the car around 2 a.m. on 27 Januay 1963 when Rowena saw a man. Thinking he was a peeping Tom, August told him to 'bugger off'. The silent figure did not move, so August threw the empty bottle at him.

'Look out,' screamed Rowena to her companion. 'He's got a gun.'

The man raised a rifle and took careful aim at

August's head. At the last moment, Rowena pushed August's head down and the bullet nicked his neck. It bled profusely. Rowena yelled at him to start the car and run the gunman down. August sped off, with bullets singing past them. By the time he reached the hospital, Rowena was unconscious. The bullet emerging from his neck had lodged in Rowena's forearm. Both August and Rowena survived the incident.

Just over an hour later and a couple of miles away, fifty-four-year-old George Walmsley answered the door bell. He was shot immediately he opened the front door. The bullet hit him in the forehead and he was dead by the time his wife and daughter, woken by the shot, got downstairs.

Around the corner at Mrs Allen's boarding house, nineteen-year-old agricultural student from the University of Western Australia John Sturkey was sleeping on the verandah. At around 4 a.m. fellow student Scott McWilliam was awoken by Mrs Allen's niece Pauline. 'There's something wrong with John,' she said. McWilliam went out onto the verandah. A strange noise was coming from Sturkey's throat. McWilliam raised Sturkey's head. There was a bullet hole between his eyes.

Next morning Brian Weir, who lived nearby in Broome Street, did not show up for training at the Surf Lifesaving Club. One of the crew went round to get him out of bed. Brian was found with a bullet wound in his forehead and serious brain damage. He died from his wounds three years later.

The police had little to go on and the press offered a £1,000 reward for the capture of the 'Maniac Slayer'. Local homeowners slept with loaded guns next to their beds. Nothing happened for three weeks. Then the killer struck again.

Joy Noble was up early making breakfast one Saturday morning when she glanced out of the kitchen window of her West Perth home. Outside she saw the naked body of a young woman spread-eagled on the back lawn. At first she thought it was her daughter and she ran through the house shouting: 'Carline.' In fact, it was the body of Constance Lucy Madrill, a twenty-four-year-old social worker who lived in nearby Thomas Street. She had been raped, strangled and dumped on the Nobles' lawn. The attack had taken place in the girl's own apartment, while her flatmate, Jennifer Hurse, slept. No one could explain why the attacker had dragged her all the way to the Nobles' lawn, then abandoned her. An Aborigine had probably done it, the police concluded – even though there were no records of Aborigines in Western Australia attacking white girls. And it certainly had nothing to do with the shootings three weeks before.

Six months passed uneventfully. Then on the thundery night of 10 August, Shirley McLeod, an eighteen-year-old science student at the University of Western Australia, was babysitting Carl and Wendy Dowds' eight-month-old son, Mitchell. When the Dowdses returned from their party they found Shirley slumped on the sofa with a peaceful look on her face like she had just fallen asleep. She had been shot by a .22 rifle and was quite dead. Baby Mitchell was unharmed. There could be no doubt that this killing was linked with the murders in January.

Perth experienced mass panic. The *West Austra-*

lian advised people to lock their doors at night – unheard of in Perth before that time. Babysitters were warned not to sit near windows, and there were proposals to close the old alleyways that ran down the back of people's houses. The police began to fingerprint every male over twelve in the city, at a rate of 8,000 a week.

Then on Saturday 17 August an elderly couple were out picking flowers in Mount Pleasant when they spotted a rifle hidden in some bushes. It was a Winchester .22. The police believed that it had not been discarded but hidden there so it could be used again. They staked out the area for two weeks before a truck driver named Eric Edgar Cooke turned up, looking for the gun.

Cooke had been born in Perth in 1931 with a hare lip and a cleft palate. Early operations improved his condition, but his speech remained blurred and indistinct and his appearance was mocked by others. From an early age he suffered severe headaches and black-outs. These were aggravated by a fall from a bicycle and a dive into shallow water at fourteen. Doctors suspected brain damage, but X-rays and an exploratory operation revealed nothing.

At home, his father beat him regularly. At sixteen he spent three weeks in hospital after trying to protect his mother from one of his father's onslaughts. He told the doctors he had been fighting with other boys.

Expelled from several schools, Cooke quit completely at the age of fourteen. He took a series of manual jobs, none of which lasted long, before being called up for National Service. In the army, he was taught how to handle a rifle.

In November 1953 he married an eighteen-year-old immigrant from England called Sally. The couple had seven children – four boys and three girls. Their first child was born mentally handicapped and their eldest daughter, one of twins, was born without a right arm. Nevertheless it was a happy household. Cooke was a faithful husband and a loving father. Other children from all over the neighbourhood came to play in the Cookes' house.

However, behind it all was what Sally Cooke described as her husband's 'restlessness'. She could not keep him at home. He constantly went out on sprees of petty thieving. He had burgled some 250 houses and spent three short terms in prison before the police picked him up as a murder suspect.

At the police station Cooke claimed to have been home on the night Shirley McLeod was killed. His wife said he was not. Then Cooke confessed.

On the way home from bowling that day, he had started looking for somewhere to burgle. He found a house in Pearse Street with its back door open and went in. There was a couple sitting in the lounge, so Cooke crept through into the bedroom to look for money. Instead he found a Winchester .22. He took it, and some cartridges, thinking he could probably sell it later.

He said he remembered parking his car again on the way home, then – later – finding the rifle in his hand with a spent cartridge in the breach. It was only the next day, when he saw a report about the babysitter's murder on the television, that he realised what he had done.

The next day he was taken to the scene of Lucy Madrill's murder and confessed to that killing as well. He said he had been robbing the girls' flat when he had knocked over a framed photograph. Lucy had woken up and he had hit her. She tried to scream but he throttled her. He dragged her through into the next bedroom, strangled her with a lamp flex, then raped her. He had intended to hide the body. He dragged it outside and left it on the Nobles' lawn while he looked for a car to steal. But he could not find one, stole a bicycle instead and rode home.

Later he confessed to the spree on 26 January. He had shot five people that night because he 'wanted to hurt somebody,' he said. Out on his usual Saturday night prowl, he had stolen a Lithgow single-shot .22 and a tan-coloured Holden sedan.

He had been driving aimlessly when he saw a man and a woman in a parked car. The interior light went out, so Cooke thought he would stop and spy on the couple. He took the rifle with him. And when they spotted him and threw a bottle at him, he shot back.

In Broome Street he stopped again, intent on doing a bit more burglary. He clambered over some railings and climbed up on to a balcony. Inside some French windows a man lay sleeping. The bed barred Cooke's way into the room, so he shot from the hip at the sleeping body. The result was Brian Weir's irreversible brain damage.

Prowling around the block, Cooke saw a man sleeping on the verandah. Another shot from the hip ended John Sturkey's young life. The next killing was even more deliberate. He leant the rifle against the garage of a house he had picked randomly in Louise Street and went to ring the front door bell. Then he ran back to the gun and aimed at the doorway. When a man answered the door, Cooke shot him. Then he threw the rifle off the Narrows Bridge into the Swan River and returned the Holden to the house where he had stolen it. In the morning the owner noticed that the bulb of the interior light had been removed, but the matter was too petty to report to the police.

Only the death of John Sturkey upset Cooke. 'He was so young,' he told the police. 'He never had a chance. I will never meet him because he is up there and I'll be down there. I'm just a cold-blooded killer.'

With that last sentence, Cooke ruled out the possibility of being found not guilty by reason of insanity.

Cooke also confessed to the murder of thirty-three-year-old divorcee Patricia Vinico Berkman in 1959. Her lover, local radio personality Fotis Hountas, found her body in bed in her flat in South Perth. She had been stabbed repeatedly in the head and chest. She left a nine-year-old son. And Cooke said that he had killed wealthy society beauty Jillian Brewer later that year. Aged twenty-two, she had been viciously murdered in her own flat. The killer had used a hatchet and a pair of scissors. There were no fingerprints. The doors were locked from the inside and there was no sign of any windows being forced. The police were mystified.

Four months later, twenty-year-old deaf-mute

Darryl Beamish, arrested for molesting four little girls, confessed to the Brewer murder through a sign-language interpreter. At his trial, Beamish claimed the confession had been forced out of him. The prosecutor produced no other evidence. Nevertheless, Beamish was found guilty and sentenced to death.

Cooke's confession was extraordinarily detailed. His description of the flat on the night of the murder fitted exactly with the photographs taken by the scene-of-crime photographer. He even explained the locked doors – he had stolen the key to the flat on a previous raid.

On 17 March 1964, Beamish appeared before the appeal court with Cooke's statement. However, the three appeal court judges – one was the original trial judge, the other two had dismissed Beamish's appeals on two previous occasions – did not believe Cooke's confession. But they did commute Bemish's sentence from death to life imprisonment. Cooke was hanged in Fremantle Prison on 26 October 1964.

Cooke's January night rampage is peculiar, but he otherwise exhibited the profile of a serial, rather than a spree, killer. But in 1987 a lone gunman loosed off a hail of bullets in a more typical, random, mindless spree killing.

At 9.30 p.m. on Sunday, 9 August 1987, young Alan Jury was driving along Hoddle Street near the suburb of Clifton Hill, Melbourne, when he heard a noise like a firecracker. His windscreen shattered. Quickly realising that somene was shooting at him, he stamped down on the accelerator and roared away from the danger. At the next service station he reported that a gunman was firing at passing cars.

In the car behind him, Rita Vitcos also heard a bang and saw sparks fly off the surface of the road. She too accelerated away. Later, when she got out of the car, she found two bullet-holes in the driver's door and realised how lucky she had been.

Twenty-three-year-old Vesna Markonsky's windscreen exploded as she drove down Hoddle Street. She jammed on the brakes. When the car came to a halt she discovered that a bullet had hit her in the left arm. She got out and a second bullet hit her, then a third. Her boyfriend Zoran, who was following her, stopped too. So did a young doctor. More bullets filled the air as the two men ran towards the wounded girl. The doctor collapsed, hit.

Another driver pulled up behind Zoran's car. A bullet hit him in the right temple. He died instantly. A girl student stopped to help. She too was gunned down. When Zoran reached Vesna, he cradled her in his arms. She spoke a few words, then lost consciousness.

Constable Belinda Bourchier arrived in a police car shortly afterwards. Zoran ran to her and tried to pull her revolver out of its holster. Covered in blood and in a state of shock, he wanted to kill the bastard who had just murdered his girlfriend, he yelled. More shots screamed past them. 'Let's get out of here,' said Constable Bourchier, and they ran for cover behind some trees at the edge of the road.

The gunman continued firing with deadly accuracy. More windscreens shattered and cars careered across the road. A motorcyclist swerved and crashed. He lay in the road trapped under his bike and two more bullets slammed into his body.

After ten minutes of shooting the police turned up in force. The shots were coming from the 'nature strip', a grass verge alongside Clifton Hill railway station. The police set up road-blocks and closed off the area.

A police helicopter was called in. It flew in low over the nature strip. Its search light swept the ground. But the gunman had vanished.

A few minutes later a police car, turning into Hoddle Street from the north, came under fire. A policeman on a road-block there was also winged by a bullet. Another shot struck the helicopter flying overhead, but bounced off its armoured underside.

Seeing the gunman near the track, a signalman managed to stop an oncoming train. He ran up the line, expecting to be shot in the back. But the gunman now seemed to be firing into the ground. The signalman reached the train and told the driver to reverse. When he looked back, the gunman had disappeared.

In a street close by, two constables in a police car spotted a man with a rifle running along the road. They pursued him. The gunman turned in to a lane and they stopped the car, closing off the end. Out of the darkness of the lane came a hail of bullets. One shot hit Constable John Delahunty in the head. He flung himself to the ground and managed to crawl towards the gunman. His partner, Constable Lockman, crawled after him. They got within a few yards of the gunman when the wounded Delahunty saw his head rise above some bushes. Delahunty leapt to his feet and fired his revolver.

The gunman ducked back down behind the bushes. A moment later a voice called out: 'Don't shoot me, don't shoot me.'

'Put your gun down and come out with your arms up,' Delahunty shouted back.

A dark silhouette rose from behind the bushes. 'Don't shoot me,' said the gunman again as he walked forward with his arms high above his head. He had a small moustache, a military haircut and identified himself as nineteen-year-old Julian Knight.

Knight was an illegitimate child who had been adopted when he was a baby. His adoptive father was a career army officer, whom he greatly admired, and it was an emotional shock when his parents divorced when he was twelve.

Although he was generally regarded as bright, his schoolwork soon began to deteriorate. His reports said he was lazy, too easily distracted and too complacent about his abilities. He always had difficulty accepting authority. Unlike other spree killers, Knight was not shy. He had girlfriends and something of a reputation as the 'class clown' at Fitzroy High School. But from an early age he was preoccupied with Charles Whitman and other lone snipers. Eventually he was expelled from school for his violent outbursts. Then he was accepted by the royal Military College at Duntroon. He was almost nineteen when he went to the Military College in January 1987. An army assessor described him as immature, over-confident and stubborn. He could not knuckle down to army discipline. In May he was charged with eight offences, including four counts of being absent without leave. Then, on 31 May, after a weekend confined to barracks, he slipped out and got drunk in a night-club near Duntroon. A sergeant counted him and ordered him out. Knight stabbed him twice in the face with a penknife. He was charged with assault and discharged from Duntroon in July 1987, after only seven months.

Back at the police station, Knight seemed calm and subdued. He described how he had started the evening by drinking twelve glasses of beer in a local pub to alleviate a terrible feeling of depression. Since his discharge, his whole life had been turned upside-down. His mother had changed his bedroom into a sitting-room, so he was forced to camp in his own home. It was just a few yards from Hoddle Street, on the other side of the railway tracks. His girlfriend had thrown him over. He owed the bank thousands of dollars. A car he had hoped to sell had broken down that afternoon, and something had snapped.

He had decided it was time to die – but to commit suicide offended his sense of military honour. Since his schooldays, he had fantasised about wars, particularly heroic 'last stands'. He decided to go down fighting.

He left home that evening at 9.25 p.m., carrying a shotgun and two rifles. He crossed the railway line to the nature strip. He knelt down, took careful aim and started to shoot at the cars coming down Hoddle Street.

He kept on shooting until he had used up all his ammunition. He claimed to have hoped that a 'battle' might develop, but no one shot at him until Constable Delahunty fired his revolver. However, by then Knight had no ammunition let. He groped in his pocket for the last bullet he said he had saved for himself. It had gone. So he surrendered, like a soldier who was surrounded and had run out of ammunition.

In the space of forty-five minutes Knight had fired at more than fifty cars, hitting twenty-six people. Seven of his victims were dead, or dying in the nearest hospital. Two days later, when what he had done had sunk in, Julian Knight had a nervous breakdown and had to be confined to a padded cell. In November 1988 he was sentenced to life imprisonment. Julian Knight will not be eligible for parole until the year 2013.

Melbourne had scarcely recovered from the shock of the Hoddle Street rampage when four months later another mad gunman claimed a further eight victims.

On 8 December 1987, twenty-two-year-old Frank Vitkovic went to the post office, ostensibly to kill an old schoolfriend against whom he harboured a grudge. He was suffering from depression and severe headaches. But the gun misfired and his friend escaped. Vitkovic then began to shoot at random.

Twenty-year-old Judy Morris photographed the last sunset of her life on Monday from the roof of her father's funeral parlour.

'It's beautiful,' said Judy, a Telecom Credit Union teller, as she pointed her camera at the horizon. 'I want it on film so I can always remember.'

She was speaking to her fiancé, nineteen-year-old Jason Miles, an apprentice chef she had met just a year before. According to Judy's father, funeral director Ken Morris, it was Jason who had coaxed his shy daughter out of her shell.

Shortly before sunset that night Judy told her fiancé that something was worrying her. Her workmates at the Credit Union on the fifth floor of the Australia Post building, at 191 Queen Street, had met about security that morning. The tellers had complained that the bullet-proof screens they had asked for a year before had still not been installed.

'She was horrified at not having any security at work,' Jason said. 'Not for herself, but for everyone else.'

As Jason moved to go that night, Judy said: 'Don't go.' They lay in each other's arms for a long time. It was as if she knew her time was up, Miles said.

Next morning Judy Morris waved to her mother, Nola, as she walked to the train stop and called out that she would see her that night. Six-and-a-half hours later Frank Vitkovic caught another train to Queen Street and entered the blue-tiled foyer of the Australia Post building.

As Judy and Jason had the previous evening contemplated the happy course of their own lines it is likely that Vitkovic had already decided the course of his. Vitkovic came from the West Preston area of North Melbourne, home to many European immigrants of the late 1950s and 1960s. Yugoslav house painter Drago Vitkovic and his wife lived in a small white-painted weatherboard house on May Street, the very picture of respectability. The front lawn had been covered with concrete to give more off-street space for Mr Vitkovic's brown Valiant station wagon and the family's two other small vehicles.

In these affluent surroundings, their son Frank grew into a good-looking, big framed youth who was over six feet tall. At high school he was placed in the top five per cent of students. Vitkovic also had a passion for playing tennis, becoming something of a legend on the twin clay courts of St Raphael's tennis club. A strong backhand drive floored many opponents and scared others. Margaret O'Leary, a former club secretary, recalled that Vitkovic sometimes aimed his returns at an opponent's body. It was enough to help him win the club championship in 1983.

The young sons of immigrant families in the club quickly identified with Vitkovic. They became known in the clubhouse as 'the ethnics'. Mrs O'Cleary recalled that some of the young men idolised Vitkovic and his confidence blossomed.

'The topic of conversation was always Frank Vitkovic' she said. 'He found it very hard to lose.'

Everyone agreed that Vitkovic was destined for bigger things. Nobody was surprised when, in 1984, he won a place at Melbourne University's Law School. To start with everything went fine. Vitkovic told tennis-club friends he was 'breezing through'. But in early 1986 things began to go wrong. Midway through his last year, Vitkovic abandoned his studies and helped his father paint houses.

Those who knew him still detected no hint that Vitkovic was having problems. His family were good people. Nobody ever expected anything bad to happen to Frank.

Vitkovic returned to Law School at the beginning of 1987, but it was a brief and unhappy experience. He left his studies again soon after because of 'unsatisfactory progress'. He also sought help from Melbourne University's Counselling Service during this period. He did not work after leaving university.

Vitkovic kept a file of Melbourne newspaper clippings of Julian Knight's massacre on Hoddle Street. Vitkovic underlined sections of the clippings in red. He also kept Rambo videos in his bedroom.

In mid-September he had obtained a gun permit from the Central Firearms Registry in Melbourne after failing just one of fourteen questions. It was: 'Should firearms be unloaded before you enter a house or building.' He had answered: 'No.'

In mid-September, a salesman from Precision Guns and Ammo in Victoria Street, West Melbourne, sold Vitkovic an M-1 semi-automatic rifle for £275, on a two-week lay-by. Vitkovic sawed the stock and barrel off the seventy-five centimetre weapon to make it easy to conceal.

The night before he went into the Australia Post building, he wrote in his diary: 'The anger in my head has got too much for me. I've got to get rid of my violent impulses. The time has come to die. There is no other way out.'

Judy Morris returned to her office from her 1 p.m. lunch-break on top of the world. Not only had she had the spectacular picture of the sunset developed, but she had bought a new outfit – white slacks with braces and a matching pink blouse.

She showed them to her closest friend, a young supervisor who also worked behind the credit union counter.

Judy also passed the pictures of the sunset around her friends in the credit union. Twenty-two-year-old Con Margellis, one of the regular staff, may have seen them.

Margellis is the only apparent link between Vitkovic and the 1,000 people working that day in the Queen Street offices. He lived just a few streets from the Vitkovics in West Preston. He and Vitkovic had been at school together and had been friends for a number of years.

At 4.10 p.m. that Tuesday Vitkovic emerged from the lift and greeted Mr Margellis inside the fifth-floor credit union office with the word 'G'day'.

Vitkovic brought out the carbine from under his green top. He began firing shots in the direction of his friend. Police ruled out any homosexual relationship between them. Nor was there any dispute over a woman. Nevertheless Vitkovic was now shooting with murderous intent at his former classmate.

The Telecom credit union staff scattered in fear. Someone pressed the alarm button. Judy Morris and her best friend ran towards the glass exit doors. A shot rang out. Both women fell. They lay on the ground until Vitkovic finished shooting and disappeared out of the exit to the lift wells. Margellis was safe. He had hidden in the women's toilets. But Judy Morris was dead.

The security doors shut tight behind Vitkovic, trapping him outside. He kicked the doors, trying to get back in. He went to the elevators and waited until one of the pink arrows flashed up. Then he rode to the twelfth floor.

The Philatelic Bureau was quiet when Vitkovic burst in. In the customer sales section he let rip with automatic rifle-fire. The bureau's twenty-nine-year-old supervisor Warren Spencer was killed while trying to take cover behind the office photocopier. His twenty-four-year-old wife, Susan, mother of their two children, who also worked at the bureau, watched in horror as her husband died. Twenty-year-old Julie McBean and eighteen-year-old Nancy Avigone were shot dead at their desks.

Below, Melbourne became aware of the shootings. As crowds began to stare from the street, Vitkovic took a sniper's perch from a broken twelfth-floor window. He fired several bullets at the first motorcycle police officers who arrived at 4.15 p.m.

Vitkovic ran down the stairs to the eleventh floor, which housed the *Australian Post* accounts department. In the stairwell Vitkovic fired one volley that blew a fist-sized hole in the office window to his right. Turning left he confronted Michael McGuire in the data-processing room, where McGuire trained staff and fixed machines. Vitkovic fired at point-blank range into the young father of three. One bullet passed through the partition McGuire sheltered against and punched a crater in the corridor wall. McGuire had been hoping to be home early that night. His youngest daughter was celebrating her fifth birthday.

The staff in the accounts department now found their escape path blocked by the killer. The shots rang out as Vitkovic entered the room, his fire concentrated to the far corners of desks. Thrity-two-year-old Rodney Brown was shot beside the desk he had worked at for seven years. He died in the arms of an ambulanceman. Thirty-eight-year-old Marianne van Ewyk and Catherine Dowling, twenty-eight, died as they cowered under their desks.

Van Ewyk, who had emigrated from Holland as a child, had worked with the *Post* since she was a teenager. Next to her desk was a school-term calendar to keep track of holidays she could spend with her only son. At 4.30 p.m. Marianne's husband, Bernie Sharp, rang her to warn her of a rail strike. At the same time Frank Vitkovic was downstairs, waiting for the elevator.

The accounts department assistant manager Tony Gloria then put an end to the massacre. A quiet man who was never known to lose his temper, he tackled the gunman.

A head shorter than Vitkovic, he grabbed the killer around the waist. Another of the office workers, who had been shot in the shoulder, helped to drag Vitkovic down. A third man grabbed the rifle and hid it in the fridge.

Vitkovic, who was now bent on taking his own life, struggled to make his way through to the broken window. Gloria fought to save him. Office workers in nearby buildings saw the struggle and the shower of glass that preceded the killer as he fell to the pavement sixty metres below, where he died.

12

The Body Count Climbs

It was just another McDonald's along a busy highway in southern California, and a day like any other day. Kids showed up for free ice cream, a Wednesday special. Mexicans stopped by for fast food American-style on their way to or from Tijuana, just over the border. Mario Yepez Lopez and his wife, April, finished eating and took their two-year-old daughter Griselda out to romp in the McDonald's playground. Her father heard a popping noise – and then another pop, like 'a soda can exploding,' he said. He turned to see a man inside put a pistol on the counter, then a rifle – a semi-automatic Uzi. Then the man took a shotgun and fired into the body of a woman who already lay sprawled on the floor.

Lopez pushed his family behind the playground's brick wall. As they huddled there in the 96°F heat, the shooting went on quite methodically. Eventually the screams, and the cries of the children, died away.

The bullets kept flying – smashing through plate glass, burrowing into cars, ricocheting off the pavement, plunking into homes. The heavy shooting was over in five minutes. But the pops and staccato

305

bursts continued sporadically for more than an hour, and, Lopez recalled: 'It seemed like it would never end.' When silence finally fell and it was safe to stand up, Lopez said, he felt as if he had been given a new life.

The Lopez family had escaped what was then the worst mass murder by one gunman in one day in US history. Twenty-one were killed in all. Rescue workers found the bodies of twenty victims and one of nineteen wounded people died a day later. Five were teenagers and five were even younger. One baby was carried from the carnage still alive, but critically wounded in the abdomen and pancreas. Other victims were slumped, dead, over their food. One still clutched his baseball cap. Others were prostrate on the floor. Sprawled in their midst was their killer, forty-one-year-old James Oliver Huberty. He had been dropped by a SWAT-team marksman seventy-five minutes after the shooting started. Now he was in no position to tell anybody why.

Huberty launched his attack on McDonald's from his apartment just 200 yards away in a shabby area of San Ysidro, a dusty San Diego suburb about a mile north of the Mexican border. He was from Ohio. His parents divorced when he was at grade school. He graduated with a degree in sociology from Malone College, a Quaker institution, in Canton, Ohio. Then he worked as an apprentice embalmer, dropped that, and became a welder.

Although Huberty pulled the trigger in San Ysidro on 25 July 1984, the hammer was cocked more than a year before, when he lost his welder's job and subsequently his home in Massillon, a northern Ohio industrial town. His wife recalled that he had put a gun to his head. Later he said: 'You should have let me kill myself.' After the massacre, she wished she had. Long before he lost his job, his neighbours had come to know him as a man to avoid. He was sullen, full of unfocused anger, a gun-nut always ready to get even with someone. Huberty had left with his wife, Etna, and his two daughters, fourteen and ten, to build a new life in California seven months before the massacre. Then just two weeks before his rampage, Huberty lost his job as a condominium security guard.

The day before the massacre, at Etna's urging, Huberty called a mental-health clinic to seek counselling, but his call was not returned. The clinic said later that there was no record of such a call. Huberty began his last morning at 9 a.m. in court for a minor traffic violation. He behaved reasonably enough and was pleased when the judge sent him away without a fine. After he left court, at about noon, he took Etna and his teenage daughter, Zelia, to lunch across the street at another McDonald's. Then the family spent the afternoon at the San Diego Zoo. As Huberty looked at the animals, his widow said later that he had seemed to reach his terrible decision. He had turned to Etna and said: 'Society had their chance.'

Back home, Etna washed dishes and lay down in the bedroom for a nap. Her husband came in, wearing a dark maroon shirt and camouflage trousers, for a kiss goodbye. Did he need money? she asked. He said no. Then he muttered: 'I'm going hunting – hunting for humans.'

Huberty's wife dismissed this. Her husband had

been saying wild things for a long time. Huberty climbed into his battered black Mercury Marquis. Its bumper sticker read 'I'm Not Deaf, I'm Just Ignoring You.' And he drove the half block to McDonald's.

At about 4 p.m. the diners looked up from their Big Macs as the tall, bespectacled man strode in. He had a 9-mm Browning automatic pistol in his belt, a 12-bore pump-action shotgun in his hand and a 9-mm Uzi semi-automatic rifle slung over one shoulder. 'Everybody get down on the floor or I'll kill somebody,' he shouted. The forty-five customers complied immediately. Then he killed them anyway.

In the first ten minutes, while Huberty sprayed the inside of the restaurant with bullets, twenty people died, including four who had tried to run out of the building when the shooting started. One of them, eleven-year-old Omar Hernandez, made it as far as the bike rack before he was shot in the back. Another eleven-year-old, David Flores, was also killed. Joshua Coleman fell to the ground wounded. He lay still, singing quietly to himself, and survived.

In panic, Maria Diaz fled with her daughter out of a side door when the shooting started, then realised that she had left her two-year-old son inside. She crept back to the window and saw him sitting obediently in a booth. She motioned him towards the door, nudged it open, and the boy toddled to safety.

The miracle was that anybody escaped at all – and that ten people came out of the restaurant alive. Five had hidden in a storage area. One woman played dead beside her murdered husband. A mexican couple hid behind chair backs while Huberty made his first killing circuit, then slipped out of the door.

Huberty also fired into the first patrol car arriving at the McDonald's. Officers cordoned off San Ysidro Boulevard and Interstate 5, and quickly issued a Code 10 call for a SWAT team. The gunfire was so heavy that the police thought there was more than one gunman inside. One fireman was hit, but the bullet had passed through his fire truck and, slowed, hitting him softly on the head.

The police marksmen held their fire for more than an hour, worried that the gunman had hostages. They did not attempt to contact Huberty himself by telephone, bullhorn or any other means.

'Our interest in negotiation was gone,' said Police Commander Larry Gore. 'We wanted to take him out as soon as we could.'

At 5 p.m. the gunfire slackened. A McDonald's employee crept from the basement with vital information. Huberty held no hostages. The SWAT team got a green light. 'Fix him in your sights and take him out,' they were ordered.

Officer Chuck Foster took aim with his .308 calibre rifle from the roof of the post office next door. Two other officers fired four rounds, but only Foster's single bullet struck Huberty, in the chest, killing him instantly.

'He dropped like a stone,' one cop recalled.

In the aftermath, the few people who had been close to Huberty over the years could only understand his last assault as the explosion at the end of a long, sputtering fuse. 'He had a gripe against society,' said a friend from Ohio. 'Something's been building up inside of Jim for years. I just don't know what set it off.'

Why had Huberty chosen a McDonald's for his massacre? Neighbours suggested that his dislike of Mexicans and children – the restaurant's regular customers – might have had something to do with it.

The McDonald's Corporation contributed $1 million to a welfare fund for the massacre's survivors. Within two days of the carnage, workmen had replaced windows and scrubbed the blood from the interior. And they had cleaned the pavement outside where the young boys had fallen. The golden arches were shining again on San Ysidro Boulevard, ready to reopen for business – and hopefully to become once more, for all the world, just another McDonald's. It failed. The McDonald's restaurant in San Ysidro, where James Huberty massacred twenty-one people, was razed to the ground on 28 July 1984. The site is now a memorial to his victims.

Edward Mann had a grudge against IBM, where he worked for more than thirteen years. Then one day in 1982 he drove his car through the glass door of the lobby of the IBM building at Bethesda, Maryland. With his face concealed by a mask, he went on a shooting spree which left two IBM employees dead and wounded another eight as they cowered in office cubicles and corridors. Seven hours later he quietly surrendered.

Former history teacher Carl Brown, fifty-one, rode his bike into a welding shop in Miami after buying two shotguns, an automatic rifle and some ammunition from a gun shop. He killed eight and wounded three, before himself being killed by a passing motorist. After the massacre, Miami thought it might be wise to introduce a 'cooling off' period, rather than let people buy guns over the counter with no delay.

Wayne Lee Crossley, a thirty-one-year-old unemployed carpenter from Hot Springs, Arkansas, boasted during his regular drinking binges: 'I'm going to die in a gun battle with the police.' He was nearly right.

Crossley was a Rambo-style survivalist who rambled on about 'living wild with nature'. He had a skull tattooed on his arms, loved guns and camouflage clothing, allegedly pistol-whipped his elderly parents, and twice pulled guns on bar-owners who had tried to eject him for rowdiness.

Crossley's last rampage began when a police officer stopped his car near the Hot Springs city hall. Crossley shot him three times with a .45 calibre pistol, wounding him seriously. The officer shot back with his .357 Magnum, hitting Crossley and a passenger in his car. But Crossley, bleeding profusely, drove the car to the Grand Central Motor Lodge. He had been thrown out of the motel a few weeks earlier. Now he had vengeance on his mind. He wounded a bartender with his pistol, then, grabbing a shotgun from his car, he fatally wounded Helen Frazee, the bar's owner. He went on to kill two customers and a truck driver who had stopped to make a phone call. When the police closed in, they found Crossley's body in the lobby. He had shot himself in the head.

Patrick Henry Sherrill was a postman. He was known as 'Fat Pat', 'Crazy Pat' – but never, ever, 'Postman Pat'. He just wasn't that nice, or that efficient. After sixteen months as a part-time postman in Edmond, Oklahoma, Sherrill was still receiving complaints over slow performance and misdirected mail.

The summer sun was just over the horizon on 20 August 1986 when Sherrill reported for work as usual. He was wearing his blue US Mail uniform, with his mailbag slung over his shoulder. But instead of carrying letters, it contained instruments of death: three pistols and several boxes of ammunition. One survivor described what followed this way: 'Imagine your worst nightmare; then scream as loud as you can.'

Without a word, Sherrill gunned down Richard Esser, one of the supervisors who had criticised his work record, and fellow postman Mike Rockne at point-blank range. The gunman then chased a group of fleeing employees through a side exit, shooting one man who died later in the parking lot.

Sherrill pursued his quarry through the labyrinthine corridors of the sorting office. He bolted several doors to prevent their escape, then he sought out co-workers who were hiding under tables and in cubicles. Three were shot at one work station, five at another.

Debbie Smith was sorting letters when the shooting started. 'I froze, I couldn't run,' she said. 'He came to shoot clerks in the box section next to mine.'

She hid. And Sherrill passed her by and opened

fire in the next section. As she ran for the door, she said she could hear all the clerks screaming as they were shot. Two employees escaped by hiding in broom cupboards. Another survivor locked herself in a vault where the stamps were kept.

The police arrived just minutes after the shooting had started. For forty-five minutes they tried to communicate with Sherrill by telephone and bullhorn. There was no reply. A SWAT team went in. They found Sherrill's body among the carnage. After killing fourteen people and wounding another six, he had put a bullet into his own head.

Sherrill's motive was thought to have been revenge. The day before, he had been reprimanded by supervisor Bill Bland with Esser present. Bland had threatened to fire him. But, on the morning of the massacre, Bland had overslept. So Esser was both Sherrill's first victim and final companion. Their bodies were found less than eighteen inches apart.

Forty-four-year-old Sherrill had lived on the same street in Oklahoma City for twenty years. He was notorious in the area for mowing his lawn at midnight, tying up dogs with baling wire or cycling alone on a bicycle made for two. He could often be seen staring blankly out of his window wearing combat fatigues. He was also an avid reader of *Soldier of Fortune* and *Soviet Life* magazines. An ex-Marine sharpshooter, he often talked about his time in Vietnam. He in fact never got further than Camp LeJeune, North Carolina, before he was discharged in 1966.

After his mother, who shared the house, died, most of Sherrill's social contact was via his ham radio set. He remained a reservist though, and in 1984 he joined the Oklahoma National Guard's marksmanship team. This allowed him to sign out of the armoury his two deadly accurate .45s, as well as a supply of 'woodcutters' – flat-nosed bullets that mushroom out inside their victims. These were used against his co-workers.

One of Sherrill's neighbours pointed out that whoever Crazy Pat was, he was no Rambo, but a shy, gentle little man who said 'please' and 'thank you'. However, in his room, the police found ten sets of camouflage fatigues, limbless human silhouettes and dozens of bull's-eye targets nailed to boxes and walls.

Like Alvin Lee King, retired Air Force Sergeant Ronald Gene Simmons had been accused of incest with his daughter. Unlike King, Simmons was not an upstanding citizen. His daughter Loretta's classmates remember him always with a beer in his hand. They also remember that he stayed in one room all the time – it was dark, spooky and it stank.

In 1981, his sixteen-year-old daughter Sheila's teachers suspected Simmons was carrying on an incestuous affair with her. They were seen kissing at the school gates in a suggestive manner. Then Sheila became pregnant with her father's child. Charges were brought by his wife, forty-six-year-old Rebecca, who described Simmons as a violent and abusive father. But the charges were dropped because the Simmons family had moved from New Mexico to Russell, Arkansas. Left behind in a New Mexico safety deposit box was a long letter addressed to Sheila. In it Simmons accused her of abusing his trust and threatened to see her 'in hell'.

In Simmons' 'fortress-like' house he ruled his fourteen-member family with an iron fist. His wife long considered divorcing him, but never had the courage. Whatever his family did was not good enough – and he decided to kill them all.

At Walmart he bought a .22-calibre handgun and, on 23 December 1987, he shot his wife, seven children, four grandchildren, and a son-in-law and a daughter-in-law. He also strangled another grandchild with fishing line and put the body in the boot of his car. He buried his family in a mass grave, having soaked them in kerosene. He covered the grave with coils of barbed wire – to keep animals and people away, he said.

Five days later Simmons drove to Russellville where he shot and killed James Chaffin, a thirty-three-year-old employee of an oil company where Simmons had worked, and twenty-four-year-old Kathy Kendrick, who had not responded to his amorous advances. He also shot Joyce Butts, who had worked with him in a car salesroom, and Roberta Woodley. Both survived and testified against him at his trial for the murder of Chaffin and Kendrick. He was found guilty and sentenced to death – 'anything short of death would be cruel and unusual punishment,' Simmons said.

Next, he was tried for the mass murder of his family. While the jury were out, Simmons attacked the prosecutor and tried to grab a deputy's pistol. After four hours, the jury returned and found him guilty. Again he was sentenced to death.

In a copy-cat killing on New Year's Day 1988,

forty-year-old Robert Dreesman, who had a history of mental illness, shot and killed six of his family before taking his own life. As the family sat around his parents' dining table, Dreesman came in and shot his seventy-nine-year-old father John Dreesman, his seventy-four-year-old mother Agnes, his forty-eight-year-old sister Marilyn who was visiting from Hawaii and her three children, eight-year-old Joshua, eleven-year-old Jennifer and twelve-year-old Jason. Each was shot in the head and chest. Then Dreesman blew his own brains out. Friends speculated that Dreesman was jealous of the attention his parents lavished on his niece and nephews.

But the worst mass shooting in America's history was perpetrated by thirty-five-year-old George Hennard. On 16 October 1991 Hennard drove his truck through the plate-glas window of Luby's restaurant in Killeen, Texas, and began a ten-minute orgy of killing that left twenty-three people dead – the worst mass shooting in America's history.

It was lunchtime in Killeen and the diner was crowded. 'Texas, this is what you have done for me,' Hennard shouted as he opened fire with two semi-automatic pistols.

The first victim was a man who had been hit by Hennard's truck as it ploughed through the window. He was trying to get up when Hennard advanced on him.

'Today is pay-day,' said Hennard as he shot him, point-blank. A child cried: 'He's just shot Daddy.'

Then Hennard turned on the lunch queue and started picking off the customers one by one. In his blue T-shirt and dark glasses, Hennard had the blank look of the robot from *The Terminator*, one witness said. It was plain that his intention was to kill everyone.

When his guns were empty, he coolly changed the magazines and continued the slaughter. 'Was it worth it, people?' he taunted. More than a hundred spent cartridges were found among the wreckage of the restaurant.

The killings may have been motivated by a pathological hatred of women. George Hennard's mother was highly strung and domineering. He had often talked about killing her. According to a friend, he compared her to a snake, picturing her head on a rattlesnake's body. After the carnage and Hennard's death, all she was concerned about was her own tragedy – the death of her beautiful son. In a letter to Jill Fritz and Jana Jernignan – two sisters with whom Hennard was obsessed – he referred to 'the abundance of evil women' and 'female vipers' in Killeen and his home-town of nearby Belton. Of the twenty-two victims, fourteen were women.

Hennard was heard shouting 'You bitch' at one woman before pumping bullets into her defenceless body.

But he showed mercy to another woman. He told Anica McNeil, who was with her four-year-old daughter Lakeshia, to 'get your baby and get out of here'.

'Tell everybody, Bell County was bad today,' he shouted after them as they scuttled to safety. It was the only time he showed compassion. Anica's own mother, Olga Taylor, who was lunching with her daughter and granddaughter, was then coldly gunned down by the killer.

As the massacre continued, seventy-one-year-old retired builder Al Gratia, cowering behind a table, decided that someone had to do something. He got up and walked towards the crazed gunman. A bullet smashed into his chest. Gratia's daughter, Susanna, took the opportunity to escape. But his wife, sixty-seven-year-old Ursula, could not leave her dying husband. She too was killed.

Distraught women were hiding under the tables, screaming and crying. Another, hiding in the toilets with her daughter, dodged bullets ricocheting off the walls.

Some managd to escape, thanks to twenty-three-stone car mechanic Tommy Vaughn. He smashed through a back window and let fifteen people scramble to safety as the gunman bore down on them. But those who stayed behind in Luby's were tracked down and murdered by Hennard, who showed all the coolness of a professional executioner.

Fifty-six-year-old Aden McElveen had found himself trapped under Hennard's jeep as the gunman advanced on him. He was convinced he was going to be next. Then, ten minutes after the shooting had started, he heard sirens wailing outside. The police ordered Hennard to drop his gun. He refused. The police opened fire. In the ensuing gun battle, Hennard was hit twice. He staggered into the back of the restaurant and turned his gun on himself.

Rescuers found a scene of appalling horror. Bodies lay scattered among a battlefield of upturned tables. The wounded were helicoptered out to an army hospital at nearby Fort Hood.

'It was worse than anything I saw in Vietnam,' said one medic.

Twelve hours later one of the restaurants employees, Mark Mathews, was found alive, hiding in a dishwasher.

And so the killing continues. In March 1993, forty-one-year-old Leonard Leabeater held forty policemen at bay during a siege at Hanging Rock. He was one of three men who confessed to five murders. The killings started when twenty-two-year-old Robert Steele cut the throat of his fourteen-year-old girlfriend after she told him she was pregnant. He shot her, then incinerated her body. Steele, Leabeater and twenty-five-year-old Raymond Bassett, who was mentally retarded, then shot three men in the face at point-blank range and pushed a fourth, alive, off a cliff. Steele and Bassett gave themselves up. Leabeater shot himself rather than be taken alive.

The next day an Adelaide schoolboy wounded two school-mates and three passersby with a semi-automatic rifle. He surrendered to the police after barricading himself in his school.

On 5 April 1993 a factory worker in the city of Chongqing, southwest China, shot three workmates with a hunting rifle after a row over time-keeping. Then he scaled the factory wall and began firing randomly at traffic and passing pedestrians, killing five others, including three members of a family of four. After killing the driver, the gunman stole a taxi and drove it off a cliff, killing himself.

You can never tell who might go berserk. Sixty-
one-year-old retired librarian William Cruse snapped one day, killing six – including two policemen
– and attempting to kill another twenty-four in
a shopping centre in Palm Bay, Florida. The jury
recommended death. A farmer in Iowa, $800,000 in
debt, shot his bank manager, his wife and another
farmer, before turning the gun on himself. The manager of a nursing home in Maine that had recently
lost its licence killed one person, wounded another
three, then committed suicide. Michael Hayes of
Winston-Salem, North Carolina shot nine people,
killing four of them, because he wanted to be
famous. And California winery worker Ramon Sal-
cido killed seven people with knives and bullets,
and slashed the throats of his three little daughters.
One, two-year-old Carmina, survived. She identified her father as the killer.

In 1987, twenty-six-year-old Josef Schwab
slaughtered five people in the remote 'Top End'
region of New South Wales and an unknown
intruder killed four teenage girls who were
watching TV in a plush Sydney suburb. Joseph
Wesbecker, forty-seven, blamed the drug Prozac for
the spree in which he killed eight fellow workers
at the printing plant he worked at and wounded
nineteen others. In 1990 three Red Army soldiers
went on a shooting spree, killing eight of their comrades, including a lieutenant colonel, at a military
depot in the Ukraine. After sprayng the depot with
machine-gun-fire, they escaped on a truck but were
captured when it broke down.

That same year, a gunman with a high-powered
rifle went on a shooting spree in New Zealand,

killing eight people including a toddler and a policeman. The bodies were strewn on the street of Aramoana, a seaside village with a population of only about fifty. The community there will never recover.

MICHAEL WINNER'S TRUE CRIMES

Working closely with police all over the country, the makers of LWT's highly acclaimed TV series, *Michael Winner's True Crimes*, have reconstructed some of the most compelling crime stories to have hit the headlines in recent years.

Based on the series, this collection of true stories highlights the inspirational work of the police in solving such complex crimes as the babyfood blackmail of 1989 and the Knightsbridge safe deposit robbery.

Michael Winner, director of the *Death Wish* films and founder and Chairman of the Police Memorial Trust, introduces this extraordinary record of brilliant police methods, containing many of the official photographs of the time.

Price £4.99
ISBN 1–85283–752–7

IN SUSPICIOUS CIRCUMSTANCES

Based on the successful TV series

Who poisoned three members of the Lord
Mayor of London's family?

The strange case of Mollie Mozelle, the
vanishing showgirl

Scandal at Number 10 – did corruption in high
places lead to the perfect murder?

Here are eleven true cases of infamous and
grisly crimes from the 1870s to the 1980s – all
of them unresolved. In each instance the
murderer was never caught or it is likely
the wrong person was convicted.

Recent extensive research has now thrown new
light on these investigations and you are
invited to make up your own mind as to what
really happened . . .

Based on the Granada television series of the
same name, IN SUSPICIOUS
CIRCUMSTANCES offers rare insight into
some of the most compelling crime stories in
recent British history.

Price £4.99
ISBN 1–85283–413–7

BOXTREE'S
TRUE CRIME SERIES

MURDER IN MIND

Mindhunting the Serial Killers

By Mike Morley & Steve Clark
Published in association with Central
Television

Cannibalism, necrophilia, torture and
sadism are the hallmarks of the world's most
notorious serial killers. Multiple murderers
such as Jeffrey Dahmer, Arthur Shawcross,
Robert Berdella and Dennis Nilsen all
turned their darkest fantasies into
horrifying reality.

Murder In Mind explores what makes
people kill and how detectives are
developing special psychological skills to
trap the rising number of serial killers
around the world. The book includes
interviews with the killers and probes the
secret world of the FBI 'mindhunters'.

Price £4.99
ISBN 1–85283–408–0

CONTRACT KILLERS

They are shadowy figures who murder for money. Anonymous assassins who ruthlessly carry out the evil desires of others. They slip in and out of people's lives without fear or feeling. They are the contract killers.

A hitman can be a professional assassin or merely a casual acquaintance picked up in a bar. Some command thousands of pounds for a job well done, while others have been promised nothing more than a second-hand car, a radio and sex. Many are employed to eliminate unwanted spouses or business partners, sought out by seemingly respectable public figures who wish to distance themselves from the brutality of the murder and resulting scandal. Judges, policemen, lawyers, union leaders – even men of the cloth: all have hired the services of the contract killer.

Some plots succeed. Others fail dramatically. Their stories, collected from around the world, are told here.

B⬛XTREE

Coming in March 1994 . . .
THE FLESH EATERS

When Man eats Man . . .

Cannibalism holds a macabre fascination over most people and it is usually associated with the lonely islands of the Pacific and the impenetrable jungles of Africa. For centuries explorers have brought back tales of tribes who delighted in eating human flesh. They also told horrifying stories about men and women being roasted alive, and of witnessing human limbs cut off and cooked and eaten in front of suffering victims.

In fact such practises are also far from being unusual in the 'civilized' areas of the world: in Britain and Europe, North and South America, Australasia, China and Japan. In this gruesome and enthralling book the facts about cannibalism and blood drinking in these areas are explored, from historical times to the present day. Subjects range from the grisly Monster of East Lothian to the Vampire Killer of Dusseldorf, from the Cannibals of Peak County to the human flesh shops of Brazil, and from Aboriginal sacrificial customs to the extraordinary story of the Japanese student accused of eating his girlfriend.

This fascinating book also contains accounts of cannibalism at sea, of the eating of human flesh by witches and warlocks, and the obsession for blood by real life vampires . . .

BOXTREE